Percy Dearmer

About the author

DONALD GRAY was a Canon of Westminster and Chaplain to the Speaker of the House of Commons from 1987 to 1998. Previously Rector of Liverpool, he served on the Liturgical Commission as a member and consultant for over twenty-five years, and as a member (chairman 1989–94) of the Joint Liturgical Group from 1969–1996.

A former President of Societas Liturgica, he is currently Chairman of the Alcuin Club and President of the Society for Liturgical Study.

Dr Gray was involved in the establishment of the International Anglican Liturgical Consultation, and was its first Chairman; and of the English Language Liturgical Consultation, through which he worked on the Revised Common Lectionary and other ecumenical liturgical texts.

He was appointed CBE in 1998.

His other writings include *Earth and Altar* (Canterbury Press 1986); *Chaplain to Mr Speaker* (HMSO 1991); *Ronald Jasper, His Life, His Work and the ASB* (SPCK 1997) and compiled *All Majesty and Power, A Book of Royal Prayers* (Hodder & Stoughton 2000). A Festschrift (*Like a two-edged sword*, ed. Martin Dudley, Canterbury Press) was published in 1995.

Percy Dearmer

A Parson's Pilgrimage

Donald Gray

CANTERBURY PRESS
Norwich

© Donald Gray 2000

First published in 2000 by The Canterbury Press Norwich
(a publishing imprint of Hymns Ancient & Modern Limited
a registered charity)
St Mary's Works, St Mary's Plain
Norwich, Norfolk, NR3 3BH

All rights reserved. No part of this publication which is copyright may be reproduced, stored in a retrieval system, or transmitted, in any form or by any means, electronic, mechanical, photocopying, recording or otherwise, without the prior permission of the publisher.

A catalogue record of this book is available
from the British Library

ISBN 1-85311-335-2

Typeset by Regent Typesetting, London
and printed in Great Britain by
Biddles Ltd, Guildford and King's Lynn

In piam memoriam
HHG
1902–1959
CMG
1906–1999

In piam memoriam
JHE
1904–1959
CMC
1906–1969

Contents

Preface ix
Acknowledgements xi

Introduction 1
1. Childhood, School and Oxford 6
2. Ordination, Marriage and First Parishes 26
3. *The Parson's Handbook*, the Alcuin Club and the English Use 36
4. Primrose Hill 57
5. Home and Family in Hampstead 82
6. The War and the Leaving of Primrose Hill 93
7. Aftermath 110
8. The Wandering Scholar 123
9. The Church and Art 131
10. Down Among the Liberals 144
11. Worship: Conformity or Change? 155
12. At the Abbey 169
13. The Man and His Message 189

Appendix: Bibliographical Note on Sources Used 198
Index 207

Preface

The resolve to write a biography of Percy Dearmer has been with me for a number of years; meeting Gillian Warr and Imogen Nichols, his daughters, and discovering their willingness to allow me access to family papers and memories, gave it an invaluable boost. I apologize to them that I have allowed other writing to delay completion of the task. A further early bonus was the pleasure of meeting Geoffrey Dearmer and to stay with him. The kind co-operation of the Dearmer family throughout has been of the greatest possible encouragement and assistance.

Along the way I have been grateful for many other kindnesses. Vicars of St Mary's Primrose Hill, past and present, have been generous in their enthusiasm. The Ven. George Timms, whom I succeeded as Chairman of the Alcuin Club, was pleased to know that I had decided to tackle the project. The Revd Howard Hollis has written letters from Australia, Canon John Ovenden first opened the files at Primrose Hill to me, and the Revd Robert Atwell, the present incumbent, has continued his predecessors' interest.

The willingness of the Revd Canon Professor Paul Bradshaw to read and comment on the whole of the work is most gratefully acknowledged; as is the kindness of the Revd Michael Thompson in devoting many hours in England and Burgundy to preparing a text worthy of presentation to the publisher. My daughter Alison once again gave invaluable help in compiling the index. Because of the delays, already mentioned, this book has proved to be the major preoccupation of my first two years of retirement. Consequently, it has claimed a large proportion of my wife Joyce's time, as I have no computer skills. She knows, I trust, how most grateful I am.

The book is dedicated to my parents who, at Christmas 1951 bought me, at my request, my first copy of *The Parson's Handbook*. This was not just youthful ecclesiological precocity – I was hoping to start my ordination training the following autumn at King's College London. That book immediately inspired me; and I trust that I have done justice to the author of that inspiration.

Donald Gray

Stamford, Lincolnshire
Pentecost 2000

Acknowledgements

Permission to include extracts from Nan Dearmer's *The Life of Percy Dearmer* has kindly been given by Mrs Gillian Warr, and to include Geoffrey Dearmer's poem 'To Christopher' by the Revd Juliet Woollcombe. Photograph of St Mary's Primrose Hill, 1903, copyright London Metropolitan Archives; all other photographs are the property of Mrs Gillian Warr, Mrs Imogen Nichols and the Revd Juliet Woollcombe and are used with their consent.

Introduction

A certain extravagance of dress never completely deserted Percy Dearmer. In an Oxford barely ten years devoid of Wilde and his aesthetic coterie, Dearmer was known and recognized around the University for his bright blue shirts worn with loud checks and flowing Liberty ties. He was strikingly handsome and the extravagance of his clothes added to the distinctiveness of his appearance. Sartorial splendour was to continue to be amongst his stock in trade, even after ordination.

G. K. Chesterton, one of Dearmer's religious protégés, and himself no anonymous or shrinking violet, tells an engaging story about the style in which the young priest sallied forth upon his pastoral duties. It was Dearmer's custom to walk about in a cassock topped by a priest's gown. There were those who, to his disgust, called this a 'Geneva Gown'. Not so, he said; such a gown was an integral part of clerical dress dating from before the Reformation. 'The Gown comes to us from the Middle Ages; and the Priest's Gown – so far from having anything to do with Geneva – was as bitterly opposed by the Puritans as the cope or surplice.' So it was, thus garbed, with an ample tippet or scarf around his neck and clutching his square cap (in velvet for a doctor, he insisted), that he accompanied Chesterton on their walks and talks together. However, the strictly traditional and national character of his dress was completely misunderstood by the little boys in the street, Chesterton reported. 'Somebody would call out, "No Popery", or "To Hell with the Pope" or some other sentiment of a larger or more liberal religion.' Dearmer's response to those calumnies, Chesterton recalls, was sternly to confront his mockers and scoffers with a concise item of historical and ecclesiological information: 'Are you aware,' he would say, 'that this is the precise costume in which Latimer went to the stake?'

So to introduce the subject of this biography in this way is not to belittle him or poke fun at him; rather the opposite. It is to confront head-on the accusations (which, surprisingly, linger on from a past generation) of Dearmer's addiction to 'British Museum Religion', while introducing a man of great character and good humour to a generation which has probably never heard of him. I have little doubt that in the presence of such a cultivated humorist as Chesterton, Dearmer was attempting to keep his end up, with what was surely a carefully calculated and premeditated squib.

On being told that I was undertaking a biography of Percy Dearmer, a large proportion of those who recognized the name (sadly, too many did not) said something like, 'I remember him – he was the hymn-writer.' Of course, it is true that Dearmer did write hymns. Seventeen of his contributions, some of which are translations or adaptations, survive in *The New English Hymnal* of 1986 – only one less than in his own *The English Hymnal*, published eighty years earlier. But to reduce his contribution to hymnology to that level alone – that of a writer of hymns – is completely to misunderstand and undervalue the extent of the revolution that his brainchild *The English Hymnal* brought about. Further, it is grossly to underestimate the breadth of his many accomplishments.

We need to look afresh at the 'British Museum Religion' jibe. This was a phrase coined, with the best possible intentions, by his friend Fr James Adderley. Its continuing careless use represents a failure to appreciate the amazing influence, particularly between the two World Wars, of *The Parson's Handbook*. If, as I believe, this book has informed the instinctive tastes of the average English Anglican for a standard of dignity in worship which is 'not too high, not too low', then that much-abused term 'seminal' here truly finds a use.

In the 1920s and 1930s 'Prayer Book Catholic' was a much-valued designation for a style of worship, doctrine and pastoral practice. It was not just a convenient term for use in locum-duty and curacy advertisements in *The Church Times*, but was descriptive of a broad and impressive swathe of Anglican tradition which was attracted neither to Geneva nor to Rome. To these parishes, and to their parish priests, the dignified ordering of both sanctuary and ceremonial in accordance with the direction of *The Parson's Handbook* did not seem to be excessively antiquarian, and certainly was to be preferred to those who, through the Baroque spectacles of the Society of SS. Peter and Paul, read Adrian Fortescue and other Roman Catholic luminaries for guidance and direction. If such things as the Liturgical Movement and Vatican II have brought about a narrowing of the gap between the ways of worship of both Rome and Canterbury, that must be a considerable cause for joy, even if it does create problems when attempting to define the essential ethos and character of Anglicanism and Anglican worship.

Dearmer and his followers would be mortified to discover that these days their delightful 'English Altars', complete with riddel posts and all necessary curtains and dorsals, are completely obsolete and redundant in the flood of western-facing celebrations. Does this mean that the standards and principles that Dearmer and his followers embraced have no contemporary relevance? I dare to think that we are fast approaching the time when, to use the current jargon, we need to 'revisit' these principles. Having tasted the heady fruits of liturgical freedom and spontaneity, there are those who would now wish to return to some ordered forms of rite and ceremony. Not the military precision which was once the style, but certainly a less casual and more dignified ordering of things than has often obtained in more recent times. These are more relaxed and informal days, but our worship should still have dignity and display a reasonable modicum of planning and preparation, which give confidence to the participants as well as relieving the anxieties of a congregation too often unnecessarily disturbed by *ad hoc* decisions in the sanctuary.

If all this suggests that a study of the life and work of Dearmer might be no more than harking back to the past, a nostalgic stirring of memories of an age now completely dead and gone, there are three immediate correctives. First, Dearmer was one of the earliest advocates of the ministry of women in the Church. He befriended, supported and eventually worked in harness with Maude Royden who, more than seventy years ago, confronted the Church of England with her claim that women should be admitted to the Anglican priesthood. Coupled with that must go his deep interest in the Ministry of Healing, being the first Chairman of the Guild of Health, which predates by ten years the Church of England's own Guild of St Raphael, founded with the aim of restoring the Ministry of Healing as part of the normal pastoral practice of the Church.

Thirdly, there is Dearmer's 'Christian Socialism'. Here we find another tradition brought strongly back into fashion after the General Election of 1997. Indeed, we now have seen a Prime Minister able to commend this tradition to the extent of contributing a foreword to Alan Wilkinson's *Christian Socialism: Scott Holland to Tony Blair*. However, we have to be cautious with our terminology here, and we must not be too quick to transfer the ideals of those pioneers who were 'socializing Christianity and Christianizing Socialism' in the nineteenth century, into the polemics of contemporary parliamentary politics.

Liturgical reform (for that is what it was) using art and artists to bring colour and inspiration into the Church; finding strong and suitable songs for the people of God to sing; affirming the unity of the ministry of both men and women in the priesthood; ministering to bodies as well as minds and spirits; confronting those who saw Christian faith and belief as only to do with personal morality and nothing to do with the needs of society as a whole: this sounds like a challenging programme for the Church in a new millennium. Yet these were the aims and concerns of this Church of England priest at the turn of the previous century.

Introduction

It has been said that Dearmer had a rare talent, but not the kind of talent that would ever make him a Bishop. W. R. Matthews, himself a distinguished Dean of St Paul's, even believed that Dearmer's own ambition to be Dean of one of our Cathedrals was misplaced. He thought a man of such original and active intelligence would have been stifled as he attempted to make his way against the statutes and precedents of an English Cathedral. It is perhaps true that no other church in Christendom could have produced such a man, and having produced him, kept him in her fold. Nonetheless many, with Matthews, will recognize the failure of the Church of England to make anything like the best use of Dearmer's talents.

So, we have in Percy Dearmer not simply a man for antiquarian study or nostalgic remembrance, but a hero of the faith for our inspiration – and our thanksgiving.

I

Childhood, School and Oxford

Neither family records nor recollections supply more than the factual bare bones about Percy Dearmer's childhood. He was the second child of Thomas and Caroline Miriam Dearmer, who had married late in life; Thomas was forty-five and his bride thirty-seven on the day of their wedding. They had met at the school which belonged to Percy's mother – then Miss Turner.

Miss Turner had built up a flourishing establishment at Somerset House in Maida Vale, considered to be the best school for 'young ladies' in that part of London. It had a considerable reputation, much of which derived directly from the ability, energy and enthusiasm of its Head. It was select, with no more than thirty in the school. In those days it stood amidst fields, but it attracted pupils from the nearby new and growing residential district. It was to Somerset House that Thomas Dearmer came to teach drawing.

Photographs of Thomas reveal him as a smartly dressed, bewhiskered, greying, but lively looking man. He had commenced a career as a bank clerk with Bouverie's Bank in the City, but that way of life was never going to be congenial to a man of artistic and musical talents. There is a family tradition that the Dearmers were of French, possibly Huguenot, origin and that Thomas seemed both in appearance and manner a Frenchman. What is certainly true is that he was a friendly and sociable person, having a large number of friends – many, like himself, keen to make music. He played the flute and they formed themselves into small orchestral group.

It was this sophisticated and talented man who attracted the

Childhood, School and Oxford

more serious and practical Caroline Miriam. Their marriage, it is said, was a surprise to her neighbours and acquaintances and, we can well imagine, was of the greatest possible excitement to the young ladies at her school.

The Dearmers' first child was born on 21 October 1863. Although named after his father, he was always known by his second name, Edgar. In a sepia print, at about the age of nine, clad in a velvet suit with knickerbockers, he appears to regard the world with rather more good humour than his five-year-old brother. As his brother and his nephews were to do later, Thomas Edgar Dearmer entered Westminster School in September 1876, but left before his fifteenth birthday at Whitsuntide 1878. None of the Dearmers made any particular impression during their time at Westminster. In Edgar's school days Westminster had hardly begun to emerge from a period during which it had been severely starved of funds by the Dean and Chapter, and the proposals of the reforming Public School Act of 1868 had barely begun to take effect. Attempts to modernize the curriculum under Charles Broderick Scott had failed, but he managed to preserve the structure and Westminster location of the school. Among others, the Dean of Westminster was of the opinion that the unhealthiness of central London argued for the total removal of the school to the countryside. Whether any early exposure to these perceived dangers damaged Edgar's health is not known, but he died at the age of 29 in 1892.

There were three and a half years between the Dearmer brothers. Percy was born on 27 February 1867. Of his childhood he left no written record, nor is there any autobiographical material amongst his papers, apart from two diaries dating from two widely separated periods of his life. Any details of his youngest days must come from the memoir that his second wife, Nan, wrote soon after his death.

For a biographer of Dearmer this book must, of necessity, be a constant source of reference, while keeping in mind the partiality of a loving and admiring wife. She admits that he was not always an easy man to understand: 'He did not show the whole of himself, even to those he loved: he was at times as elusive as a dragon-fly; one vivid flash and he was gone.' Additionally, it was impossible for her at such an early date to assess the influence of Dearmer on the many aspects of Church life in which he was engaged during his sixty-nine years. Nan Dearmer had no illusions about this and admits in 1941: 'It is still too early to estimate Percy's influence on the Church and on the world, and I am not the right person to do it, even if I could.' It is the task that this book has undertaken.

Nan Dearmer remembers that Percy told her of memories of long walks with his father and elder brother into the countryside, which then lay so close to Kilburn. He recalled sailing boats on the pond and a particular occasion when he was taken to visit the house of some of his father's friends in Hampstead, where he was given cake and, to his immense delight, sips of wine in the middle of the morning. His earliest 'religious' memories centred around the power of intercession. Taught (unwisely, as it turned out) to pray for whatever he wanted, since God answered prayers, for a week before Christmas he prayed for a bicycle. His belief in the power of prayer was rudely shaken when Christmas morning revealed not a bicycle but a tricycle. His faith in God, he said, was temporarily shattered.

Early schooling was given in his mother's school by one of the pupil teachers, but later he attended a small 'prep' in the neighbourhood. From the first he was an imaginative child who was frightened by Grimm's *Fairy Tales*, and he hated the Cruickshank drawings that he discovered in his father's volume of Dickens (a personal friend of Thomas Dearmer). A lingering, unpleasant memory was of a nursemaid who told him of the policeman who would come and take away naughty boys. The sensitive character of his father is demonstrated in that not only did he show his anger and displeasure to the nursemaid, but he took Percy out, introduced him to a policeman and had them shake hands.

Sadly, Thomas Dearmer, artist and musician, died in 1877, when Percy was only ten years old, thus removing a tender and understanding parent who would have carefully nurtured his son's own developing artistic interests. In her memoir Nan begins by saying, 'It is remarkable how many men of outstanding originality seem to owe little to their heredity.' Some characteristics, she suggests, can be traced to parents or grandparents, 'but the particular genius of the man has often little to account for it.' Then she surprisingly declares, 'Percy Dearmer was such a man.' We know little of Thomas Dearmer, but what we do know of this man, who was brave enough to forgo a commercial career in order to concentrate on his drawing and painting, surely suggests that shared genes must account for his son's constant concern throughout his life for art and beauty. Percy was convinced about the high seriousness of art. 'We are tempted to regard the arts because of their delightfulness as a mere pastime; we are discovering that in them we touch the eternal world – that art is in fact religious.' Surely thus speaks the son of Thomas Dearmer who, in the records of Westminster School, on entering his son, describes his occupation as no more and no less than 'artist'. And that is without calling to account other inherited skills passed down from the flautist to a son who made a singular contribution to the history of church music.

Edgar and Percy were now the sole concern of the widowed Caroline Miriam. About her we can only accept the judgement of her younger, and allegedly less favourite son, as recorded by Nan. It is said that Percy retained no gentle memories of his mother, only harsh ones, and that as a wife and mother she was lacking in charm 'and indeed in all the more endearing qualities'. Such an assessment, recalled by a thoughtful and sensitive person, sets bells ringing in our post-Jungian minds. It is no wonder that his wife, looking back over twenty years of marriage, did not always find him an easy man to understand. Nan was of the opinion that this failure of affection on his mother's part left an indelible mark on Percy. By nature he was affectionate, peace-loving and courteous, but his mother turned his natural affection for her into a cold dislike which, even in after years, he was never able to overcome. This was, Nan Dearmer believed, the reason for the reserve and shyness which was otherwise unnatural for so warm-hearted a person. A mother, thus described by her child, must have cast a cloud across his otherwise sunny personality.

Caroline Miriam was, it cannot be denied, an able and, indeed, financially successful school-mistress, whose pupils spoke highly of her. However, shortly after her husband's death she decided to give up the school and initially spent some months in Germany at Wiesbaden – it would seem primarily in order to take Edgar away from Westminster, as his health was already a cause for concern. On her return to England she took a house on the north side of Streatham Common and Percy was sent to Streatham School. These were unhappy days for him. He was at the mercy of his mother's emotional and difficult temperament and he was constantly oppressed by her lack of kindness towards him and her obvious favouring of his sickly brother Edgar. It was a school friendship which brought some relief from his mother's ungraciousness. He befriended Cyril Crofton Adams, later to become a distinguished general, and found, in the Adamses' home, a joy and happiness which contrasted vividly with the atmosphere in the Dearmer household across the Common. Mrs Crofton Adams was a young, pretty woman of great charm who welcomed Percy, and consequently he spent many hours of his holidays in the company of Cyril and his brothers and sisters.

Despite its continuing reputation for toughness, and his brother's breakdown of health while there, Percy was himself sent to Westminster in January 1880. He was, in Westminster terminology, 'Up Grant's' – that is, a resident of the school's oldest boarding-house. Although belonging entirely to the school, Grant's was then still run primarily as a private business venture, with the Housemaster standing the financial risks involved. In Dearmer's day the Housemaster was the Revd Charles Alfred 'Soapy' Jones. As we have noted, it was a time of change and development at the school. More changes

Childhood, School and Oxford

were soon to be implemented after Dearmer had left. Like his brother, he was only there briefly – a mere sixteen months.

One of his school memories was of a fight he provoked. Westminster had a reputation for hardness and fighting; Wellington reckoned that because of this the school provided his best officers. The tradition of 'the mill' on College Garth – open-ended bouts of single combat on the Green in the middle of the Cloisters – had officially ended in 1875, but the fighting culture lived on. (Those who to this day witness the violence of the pancake 'greaze' each Shrove Tuesday, all for the reward of the Dean's Guinea for the retrieval of the largest fragment of a high-tossed pancake, may well wonder if this is a tradition entirely forsaken.) Percy fought his fight, after a number of attempts to make someone angry enough to take him on, in Little Cloister. It was within that Cloister that he was to make his last and final home. Just then, Dearmer said, it never occurred to him or his companions that there were people living behind those doors. Later he reminisced, 'We little boys did not realise what it meant to be brought up under the shadow of the Abbey, though we were a little awed by it.'

A fascinating snippet of Percy's school days came to light in 1940 when, out of the blue, Arthur Jay wrote to Percy's son Geoffrey. Jay told how he had travelled daily to Victoria on the same 8.14 a.m. train as the young Westminster schoolboy. Jay was an apprentice in the upholstery trade. 'I was impressed by the quiet, studious little fellow, as he was then, who used to, so apparently shyly, take the farthest corner of the compartment, and pore over his books so closely all the journey, his lips moving, apparently committing [to memory] some rather tough passage of Greek or Latin and too interested to notice other passengers.' Years later, on seeing Percy mentioned in a newspaper, Jay recognized him and wrote to his former travelling companion. Percy kindly acknowledged the letter but told Jay that he had 'no very great remembrance of what, it seemed, was not a very happy time in his life – he gave no sort of particulars.'

These Westminster days were of only a short duration, since

Caroline Miriam decided that Percy should continue his education in Switzerland. The school she chose was at Vevey, on Lake Geneva. This was a Lutheran school, which appealed to his mother, who was a staunch Evangelical. While running the school in Maida Vale she had avoided the parish church of St Augustine Kilburn because of its High Church tradition and had taken her pupils to the mission church of St John's. Had she detected an interest in 'popish ways' in her younger son, which she thought a spell in Calvin's Geneva would snuff out?

Whatever else it did, Vevey gave the young man fluency in French and a life-long pleasure in French literature. The Swiss school provided a rounded education considerably less violent than his recent English Public School experience. It equipped him so well that when he returned to England in 1884 he passed the Oxford Local Examination with ease, gaining credit level in most subjects. This stage of his education completed, his mother, who had now moved to Putney Hill, seemed to lose all interest in his studies, being more and more absorbed with worries about the health of her elder and delicate son, Edgar. Paradoxically, her apparent indifference seems to have proved a spur to Percy; he determined to embark upon a scheme of private study which was to equip, and indeed inspire, him for the greater part of his life's work.

So it was that rather than idling, as he might well have done without parental guidance, he discovered and was enthralled by the museums of London. Of these the one which especially attracted his interest was the Victoria and Albert Museum. The 'V & A' had moved to South Kensington in 1857 and, with the help of funds voted by Parliament and with the active encouragement of Prince Albert, the Royal Commission of the 1851 Great Exhibition had bought over eighty acres of land to further the aims of the Exhibition and to extend 'the influence of Science and Art upon Productive Industry' by building various museums, concert halls, colleges, schools and premises for learned societies. Its first director, Sir Henry Cole, declared that its policy was 'to assemble a splendid collection of objects representing the application of Fine Art to manufacturers'. So he assembled glass, plate and china, enamels, armour, medals, jewellery, ivories and furniture. Sir Roy Strong has said, 'for over a century the Museum has proved an extremely capacious handbag.' Already, by the time when Percy was visiting it, that 'handbag' was rapidly filling with fascinating and intriguing *objets d'art*. Dearmer's methods were thorough and systematic, a precursor of the technique he applied to many subsequent avenues of study. He was training the artistic eye, inherited from his father, to appreciate lovely things. He borrowed textbooks to inform his observations and help him date and categorize what he was seeing. Unfortunately, this crucial period of private study was brought to an end by his mother's impetuosity. She decided to move house yet again, this time out of London, in order to live in Eastbourne. Now the young student had nothing to do. He went on long solitary walks, and although given a bicycle, he was not allowed any pocket money, so he was unable to pay for repairs, and consequently the bicycle eventually remained unusable in an outhouse.

By now Mrs Dearmer had cut herself off from all of her and Thomas's friends. The sole solitary exception was their physician, Dr Davson. Fortunately for Percy, Davson came to visit their Eastbourne home. Shocked at finding Percy doing nothing, he strongly advised that the young man should be sent to Oxford. It was decided that Percy should go off to a tutor for coaching straight away. The result was that he matriculated in June 1886, and then went up to Christ Church for the Michaelmas Term of that year.

At the University to read History, Dearmer immediately came under the influence of a unique Welshman, York Powell. In appearance and dress Powell resembled a sea captain, betraying his long love of the sea. He was broad, burly and bearded, brusque in manner, with dark hair and eyes, and a deep, rich laugh. Dearmer and he quickly took to each other. A contemporary said the Oxford of that period 'was a place of curiously incongruous manners and enthusiasms', and York Powell was very much part of that life and style. Although a scholar of great attainments, he was also generous with his time. Alongside that generosity was a complete lack of ambition. His time was his friends' time, and the hours that might have been spent on his own work were freely lavished upon the assistance of others. His love of learning was excitingly coupled with a love of life. His interests ranged from boxing and fencing to the latest Portuguese novel, with a staggering range of subsidiary subjects in between. To have Powell as a mentor, as Percy Dearmer did, was to enjoy the friendship of a polymath who had humour, sensitivity and a wide aesthetic appreciation. It was a most fortunate convergence of personalities which was to have a lasting influence on the nineteen-year-old undergraduate.

One important thing they did not share, or see eye to eye on, was religion. Powell had long ago rejected Christianity and in religion described himself as a 'decent heathen Aryan'. It was another form of 'faith' to which he 'converted' Dearmer, who had arrived in Oxford, as his friend Harold Anson described it, 'an ardent conservative and a member of the Primrose League'. Powell introduced him to Socialism. The change was fairly rapid. Percy became very much involved in the political life of the University, but not in the conservative interest. Quickly making friends and contacts, he became widely known about the University. All this would influence another aspect of his future work.

The Oxford in which Percy and his fellow undergraduates arrived in 1886 was a place already much changed from the first half of the nineteenth century. There had occurred a great revolution in Oxford life as a result of the virtual disestablishment of the Church as the controlling force in the University. The Church was not hated, as it was on the Continent; and there was no movement to execute bishops and clerical dignitaries (in fact they were on the whole liked and respected). What had happened was that there had developed a strong revulsion against clerical dominance and a corresponding desire for lay government in the University. The changes were nowhere more obvious than at Dearmer's

Childhood, School and Oxford

college, Christ Church. The Chapter had to cope with the fact that a leading advocate of change – in fact the Chairman of the Parliamentary Commission appointed to deal with the matter of University reform – was their own Chairman and Dean, Henry George Liddell. The Chapter, including the great Dr Pusey, violently objected to the new statutes. But, having made their protest, it must be said that they subsequently did their best to make the new dispensation work satisfactorily, and a new Governing Body was appointed. In 1882, just before Dearmer arrived, these new statutes had come into force at Christ Church. By the nature of things, not least because the College Chapel was also a cathedral, the College (known as 'The House') was still a considerable clerical stronghold, but the clergy no longer held a stranglehold. Even so, some of the old and bold found it difficult to accept the changed situation. Dr Liddon, Pusey's biographer (who held a Studentship at Christ Church, together with his Canonry of St Paul's), in speaking with his younger colleagues, used to shake his head sadly and say, 'Dear friend, you are doing nothing else but combing the hair of a corpse.'

Taking a far more positive line was another of the dons, who gathered around him a group of young men with whom he enjoyed talking theology on a Sunday evening. Thomas Banks Strong, who later became Dean of Christ Church and subsequently Bishop of Ripon and then of Oxford, was of somewhat eccentric appearance with peculiar mannerisms, which to the conventional mind might appear to be not a little undignified. Harold Anson tells how he would talk with his pupils with his legs on the fireplace or waving them over the window ledge. Along with Harold Anson (to be Master of the Temple and Strong's biographer), Strong befriended Ronald Burrows (later Dean of King's College London), F. W. Douglass (of the Oxford Mission to Calcutta), J. B. Seaton (a future Bishop of Wakefield) – and Percy Dearmer.

This was all a heady brew for a still rather immature Percy. In her biography his wife Nan speculated that his previous somewhat unsystematic education was a drawback, and apparently there were those who did not think him particularly clever. Whether true or not, Dearmer had a great zest for life and a considerable enthusiasm for many things, so that in addition to those scholastic and intellectual challenges from York Powell, T. B. Strong and others, he found time to row, play football and join the Oxford University Dramatic Society. He was also fond of debating, being a member of both the Twenty Club and the most prestigious Palmerston Club. It is said he spoke at debates in measured and felicitous phrases with easy, natural gestures.

Yet it must be to the influence of Powell and Strong on the impressionable undergraduate that we must trace so much of Dearmer's future life, work and indeed achievements. Powell drew him away from his conservative politics and Strong introduced him to a style of churchmanship which would certainly not have been approved by his Evangelical mother. From these two strands came a synthesis which found its practical outworking in a movement which at that time was gaining strength in the Church of England – Christian Socialism.

'Christian Socialism' is an uneasy designation. The Movement's latest historian, Alan Wilkinson, has described it as 'a portmanteau term which covers a wide range from those who were (in Edwardian days) New Liberals to those in our own day who advocate a Marxist liberation theology.' Dearmer and his circle were far from any advocacy of Marxism. We know that Percy decorated his somewhat dark rooms in Peckwater Quad in Christ Church with Morris Tapestries, perhaps even before York Powell had introduced him to such writings as Morris's *News from Nowhere* or *John Ball*. Morris, was to be a continuing inspiration. In one of his books (*Art and Religion*) Dearmer said that Morris had shown that 'what we call by the light name of ugliness is a moral as well as an aesthetic evil – corrupt, sinister, and polluting.' At Oxford the artist's son began to realise that there were social, political and religious implications behind his natural instinct to celebrate beauty. Powell emphasized the social and political, Strong taught him about the religious. When William Morris died in 1896 Dearmer was among the many disciples and admirers who assembled on a cold and wet October morning at Paddington Station to see the body of the one who had been the source of their inspiration carried to the train which was to bear it to Kelmscott for his burial.

Christian Socialism in England had its origins in the writings of Frederick Denison Maurice in the 1850s and 1860s. By calling himself a Socialist, Maurice wanted to signify that he agreed with the Socialists in their view that fellowship and co-operation represented the true order of society, whereas competition, selfishness and rivalry were expressions of what he called, in the first of his 'Tracts on Christian Socialism', 'a dividing, destructive principle'. At the same time, Socialists were not fighting for a new system of their own devising but for God's established order against the new competitive world which man's selfishness had created. Maurice said, 'A brotherhood to be real demands a Father; therefore it is that we speak of Christian Socialism.' He went so far as to assert that he seriously believed that 'Christianity is the only foundation of Socialism, and that a true Socialism is the necessity of a sound Christianity.' For Maurice and his friends Socialism was a co-operative order of society wherein all laboured for the common good rather than private gain. To bring this about, co-operative societies for the production of goods were to be set up. The success of all this was only limited in Maurice's own lifetime: the arrival of the Co-operative Movement, the establishment of the Working Men's College, the promoting of Provident Societies, leaving the next generation, many of whom had read and been inspired by Maurice's writings, to provide more practical and 'hands-on' Christian Socialism in the parishes of the Church of England.

It was out of the squalor of the Victorian slums that the second, and more militant, stage of the Christian Socialist Movement arose: the Ritualists. They were themselves a second stage of the Oxford Movement, abandoning some of the more hesitant Tractarians who, although 'High Church', were not attracted (indeed, were repelled) by Ritualist 'Romanism', as they believed it to be. This new breed of Anglo-Catholics realised that those who were seen as illiterate social outcasts could be taught more effectively by eye (or even nose) than solely by ear.

One place where this policy was adopted was Bethnal Green, in the parish of St Matthew, where Stewart Headlam was a curate. Although personally given to High Church worship, Headlam believed that it was not sufficient to provide opportunities for the parishioners to give glory to God in ways of splendour and beauty which contrasted starkly with the hideousness and degradation of their background. They (and, perhaps more importantly, others in the Church of England) had to be led on to realise that the Ritual Movement meant more than this. The vision displayed in the full ceremonial richness of Catholic worship should be allowed to deepen the mystery of the word made flesh – that which was incarnate at Bethlehem and now present in the faithful through Communion. This presence in the Sacrament of the altar was to be found throughout the East End, throughout Britain and, indeed, throughout the world, in conditions and surroundings every bit as hostile as those of the Nativity. This was an activity full of profound significance – political significance. The Sacrament of the altar, and the Church which celebrated that Sacrament, were 'extending the Incarnation', and that fact should dignify, inform and necessitate political and social action by Christians. With this principle as his stimulus, Headlam founded the Guild of St Matthew (the GSM) in 1877. The Guild possessed three objectives:

1. To get rid, by every possible means, of the existing prejudices, especially on the part of secularists, against the Church, her Sacraments and doctrines, and to endeavour to justify God to the people.
2. To promote frequent and reverent worship in the Holy Communion and a better observance of the teaching of the

Church of England, as set forth in the Book of Common Prayer.

3. To promote the study of social and political questions in the light of the Incarnation.

In order to carry out these objectives, the Guild also had three rules. The first was to propagandize both collectively and by personal influence; the second, to communicate as a body on all great festivals and to celebrate the Holy Communion regularly on Sundays and Saints' Days; and the third was that they should meet annually in united worship and for business on the Feast of St Matthew (21 September). These objectives and rules fully justify Professor Peter Jones' description of the Guild as the first example of 'Sacramental Socialism'.

Such an emphasis on the importance of political and social action did not appeal to all High Churchmen, including Headlam's Vicar at Bethnal Green, and he was dismissed from his curacy the following year. The Guild now moved out from its local beginnings to become a nationally organized propagandist society. One of the places where a branch of the Guild had been established was Oxford University, and Percy Dearmer joined. The founder of the Oxford branch was Lewis Donaldson who, while Vicar of Leicester, led the first march to London of the unemployed in 1905 and, coincidentally, was years later to be a fellow Canon with Dearmer at Westminster Abbey. Dearmer's membership of the GSM was not nominal. In 1889 he became the Oxford Secretary and began writing in its journal, *Church Reformer*. The historian Jo Clayton, one of York Powell's favourite pupils, was a firm and convinced Socialist who wrote widely on the subject. In a definitive study of the early years, in which Clayton was very much involved (*The Rise and Decline of Socialism in Great Britain 1884-1924*), he says that if Headlam and the Anglican Christian Socialists had not persistently declared that the economics of Socialism were not contrary to the principles of the New Testament, the success that Socialists won when they formed the Labour Party at the turn of the century would not have been achieved. They successfully formed a party, in contrast to other such parties in Europe, which has never been anti-clerical or anti-Christian.

In that same book Clayton also observed that for Dearmer the gospel of Christian Socialism meant more than economic change. It meant opening the kingdom of art and beauty to all. He reckoned that Percy was never a whole-hearted Anglo-Catholic theologically; his views were broader than that. A Christian Socialism which could open windows revealing beauty in art and music to all was bound to have his enthusiastic support. For this reason, perhaps above all else, Dearmer's mind began to change concerning the future. Originally he had intended to pursue architecture; now his thoughts turned towards ordination. His mother was furious, and threatened to cut off his money. Luckily, by visiting Somerset House in the Strand and examining his father's will, Dearmer discovered that he had been entitled to a small income from his father's estate on becoming twenty-one. Now twenty-three, he was able to collect some 'back pay'. Even this was not enough to supply all his needs, and at this point Charles Gore came to the rescue. Gore offered Dearmer a job as his secretary at Pusey House.

Pusey House had been founded in 1884 through the energies of Dr Liddon as a memorial to Dr Pusey in an attempt to counteract the changing nature of the University – reforms which Liddon and others of his ilk saw as an increasing secularization. Pusey's own library was purchased as a nucleus and an endowment was raised for a Principal and one or more resident priests who were to be known as Librarians. The aim of the House was to combine study with pastoral work in the University. At the beginning there was a distinct hope that in time the community would tend towards the religious life. Indeed, with Gore as one of the original trio of priest-Librarians, the aspirations which resulted in the Community of the Resurrection and the founding of Mirfield can be seen taking shape at Pusey House. The other two Librarians were Canon V. S. S. Coles and F. E. Brightman.

Childhood, School and Oxford

Stuckey Coles was a large man who was remarkable for his enormous capacity for friendship; he was an amusing talker with an ability to burst the balloon of pompousness with mild ridicule. The possessor of ample private means, he distributed them lavishly, while living himself in severe simplicity.

In the future Dearmer's and Frank Edward Brightman's paths would inevitably cross. Brightman was already gaining an immense reputation as a liturgical scholar when he and Dearmer lived at Pusey House. Theirs was a friendship which survived many years, even when their liturgical tastes began to diverge. Brightman and Coles had very different personalities. Brightman was a delightful companion in small gatherings, but he could not abide humanity in the mass. G. L. Prestige called Brightman 'a scholarly recluse'.

It was the third and most senior member of the Pusey House Librarians for whom Percy was to work. Gore was another of that brilliant band of young Dons who had arrived on the Oxford scene having been brought up under Anglo-Catholic influences more modern than those of the original Tractarians. He combined a devout and passionate belief in Catholic tradition with a frank acceptance of modern methods of criticism as applied to the Bible and, within certain limits, to Catholic dogma. He had wide knowledge not only of theology, but of poetry, painting and modern literature. Over tea in Pusey House, Gore would often be found sitting on the floor or tied up in knots in a chair. He would speak of Ruskin, of Matthew Arnold, of Browning, of Kipling; or he would discourse on Socialism, before he and his young companions passed from tea to chapel. Dearmer's friend and Oxford companion, Harold Anson, remembering the occasions when they were in Gore's company, said:

> It was a complete revelation to find one who cared so intensely for the modern outlook, for beauty of form, colour and speech, accepting joyfully the new revelations of science and yet so utterly convinced of the living truth of Christianity and the reality of the Church as the Body of Christ.

Gore realised that some guidelines were necessary for Percy. He had worked long and hard on many causes and interests during his time as an undergraduate – sadly, to the detriment of his studies. The result of this was that at his final examinations in June 1890 he gained no more than a third-class degree in Modern History. His future work in Church history and liturgiology was to belie so undistinguished a result, but at the time it was a disappointment. He was capable of better, his use of time had been very often ill-disciplined and his interests were too diverse, however high-minded and worthy the causes he had embraced. With this in mind and in order to focus the ordinand, Gore proposed a few conditions. He laid down that Dearmer went to Pusey House

> (a) nominally as my secretary. This is to guard myself: it will not involve more than a couple of hours' work a week.
>
> (b) really to do your own work and use the house as best you can to prepare for orders. There are no specified rules you will be under, but we breakfast early at 8.00 and expect the household to be in at Compline (9.45), except when there is a special reason (such as a Club or meeting) to the contrary. As to Office, Communion, reading etc., every resident in the house is expected to aim at some definitive rule, though the rule will be very various according to people's needs, and instincts. I hope you will come.

Dearmer took part in an important early ecumenical venture in 1890 which was to make a considerable impact on University life. It was the second gathering, at the home of Robert and Hugh Barbour at Bonskeid in Perthshire, of students and others concerned with the religious life in the University. The inspiration came from the two brothers and Henry Drummond, a well-known figure in the world of science and religion. Significantly, J. B. Reynolds was also present. Reynolds, an American, had already been the catalyst in the formation of the first student Christian fellowships in Europe. This quiet New Englander had brought together Christian students in Germany and Scandinavia.

Attending the two-week-long conference were students from Oxford, Cambridge, the Scottish universities and Trinity College Dublin. Ruth Rouse in *The World's Student Christian Federation* (1948) complained that Britain had forgotten this meeting at Bonskeid, which was, in effect, the beginning of the Student Christian Movement (SCM) in these islands. It was Percy's first venture into the world of conferences, which he was happily to visit for many years thereafter. There were also great benefits in the setting for the conference. In a letter to a Christ Church friend, Stuart Johnson, he wrote:

> It is the most perfect country, covered with silver birch which is infinitely more effective in masses than fir; we went up a mountain yesterday, and had a most wonderful view, right across Scotland, the Firth of Forth, Dundee, Skye etc. Everything is most jolly and the Barbours are ideal.

In December 1890 to early January 1891 Dearmer accompanied Gore and two other Pusey House men to Florence. Percy kept a detailed and meticulous diary which survives. In minuscule handwriting (contrasting very much with his later more florid hand) he describes all the art and architecture that he saw with an already developed critical eye – a result of those long hours of study in the V & A.

Yet it is a young man's diary, and his fellow guests in the hotel are also objects of study. They include 'the Dragon or old Crossbones, Pink Shawl (his companion), the Bride and Bridegroom (who sit at a side table and giggle), the irascible German, the sad Lady, the White Queen (her hair pins are always coming out)'. They are looked after by 'the jolly *femme de chambre* and *L'Adorable*, the perfect German waiter. A very good cast, don't you think?'

High Mass in the Cathedral on Christmas Day included 'an enormous amount of censing and various dressings and undressings' but 'no impressions, no enthusiasm, the music rotten. The service must have had an enormous amount of time and money spent on it; but it might as well have been at the bottom of the sea, and the people were right to flock to the side altars.'

The time together with Charles Gore at Pusey House was the beginning of a friendship which lasted for many years. While at Pusey House Dearmer continued to work for the Christian Socialist cause, but he and others had come to realise that the Guild of St Matthew was the purveyor of a meat too strong for the digestion of many Anglicans. It was necessary, as Fr James Adderley said (using a much-mixed metaphor), that, 'If the Church is not to be starved from its inability to retain its food it is necessary in the company of Heaven for the more moderate physicians of the Christian Social Union to provide a diet.'

The Christian Social Union was formed as a consequence of a series of lectures on 'Economic Morals' given by Wilfrid Richmond at Sion College, London in 1889 under the auspices of B. F. Westcott, Henry Scott Holland and John Carter. It was formally inaugurated at meetings held in Pusey House and in the Chapter House at St Paul's in November of that year. Gore wrote in later years:

> Its motive was the sense that Christianity, and especially the Church of England, had lamentably failed to bear its social witness – its witness to the principles of divine justice and human brotherhood which lie at its heart. It had left the economic and industrial world to build itself up on quite fundamentally un-Christian premises, as if Christianity had got nothing to do with the matter.

Unlike the Guild of St Matthew, the CSU did not draw its members from any one political party. They might hold any political and economic theories they liked – as long as they allowed the Christian law to govern their social practice.

Dearmer was present at the Oxford meeting and later wrote the definitive account of the Union's formation. He was appointed a member of the executive committee. The president of the Oxford branch, with whom he had to work closely, was Henry Scott Holland. A preacher of great power and clear orthodoxy, it is sad that he is now mainly remembered for a bowdlerized extract ('Death is nothing at all . . .') from one of his sermons on St Paul's epistles. If one reads the sermon in its entirety, one sees that Scott Holland avoids the sleight of hand on the fact of death that is so commonly read into this extract. One admirer graphically said that to hear Scott Holland preach was like looking at some mountain torrent in spate, rushing down in sparkling foam, leaping from rock to rock, carrying down every kind of debris which it gathered in its passage, with a fire and vividness which seems tireless and yet never aimless or dull. In more measured tones the then Dean of Winchester said that, at the end of the nineteenth century, there was probably no clergyman whose influence was felt in so many and such various quarters. He was a boyhood friend of Gore's and the time came when, at St Paul's and Westminster Abbey, both were the popular preachers to whom people crowded. They were known as 'the "and" and the "but" Canons' because of the words that each pronounced with such thrilling emphasis. So Scott Holland was another 'giant in the land' who helped to develop and mould the character of Dearmer.

Unfortunately Dearmer's work for Gore at Pusey House and for Scott Holland in the CSU provided him with neither a living salary nor a title for ordination. That had to be sought elsewhere, ideally not too far from these stimulating activities. The solution though was to be a curacy at St Anne's South Lambeth.

2

Ordination, Marriage and First Parishes

The Feast of St Thomas had long been the traditional date for Advent ordinations in the Church of England, and it was on the eve of that day (20 December 1891) that Percy Dearmer was made Deacon by Randall Davidson in Rochester Cathedral. Although Davidson had been consecrated Bishop the previous April, he had hardly performed any duties in his diocese, having been struck down with a stomach ulcer a mere eleven days after the consecration service in Westminster Abbey.

Despite the fact that Dearmer was one of Davidson's own ordinands, the future Archbishop never took to him. It was not on account of his politics, as might be assumed. Rather surprisingly, all his life Davidson had admired Stewart Headlam and counted him as a friend. In Headlam's last illness Davidson (by then Archbishop of Canterbury) wrote him a warm and friendly letter recalling their common London experiences. It does not seem, then, that it was Dearmer's work for the Guild of St Matthew or the CSU that alienated the Primate. Harold Anson believed that, for Davidson, Percy could never be a model parish priest because the Archbishop could not begin to understand a priest who quite seriously thought that colour, ceremony and good poetry were dear to the heart of God. Anson said, 'I tried more than once to interpret Dearmer to the great Archbishop but I am sure he always thought of him as a rather effeminate man, who was more interested in colours than in commentaries, and preferred writing to house to house visiting.' As we shall see, this was an assessment that Davidson took with him to Lambeth. Particularly it was to dog Percy's career after the First World War while Davidson was still Primate. However, the Archbishop's judgement was not entirely coloured by his suspicion of Percy's aesthetic interests.

Percy's Vicar at St Anne's South Lambeth was W. A. Morris, known affectionately as 'Brother Bob' to the London gas workers. Conrad Noel described him as 'a vigorous Socialist with a tremendous voice, a bushy black beard, and remarkable eyes.' Noel also says Morris had a rough tongue. He had previously been a curate of St Peter's Vauxhall. Dearmer wrote that his influence over the gas workers, always strong, 'was increased ten-fold by his action during the gas strike of 1890 when he stood forth as the courageous, enthusiastic champion of men – a kind of priest of the barricades.' In 1891 Archbishop Benson, to the surprise, if not horror, of many, appointed Morris to the vacancy at St Anne's. His Grace's diary reveals clearly the political motive of the appointment. The entry for 6 March 1891 reads:

> Gave Morris, the instigator of the men in the gas strike, the living of St Anne's in the middle of them . . . It is far better that such a man should work out and help them to work out just solutions than to remove their leader and send someone else who could not sympathize with them. He is a fine romantic, large-eyed, Chartist-looking fellow, and I think he will make something of his life.

Dearmer reckoned the task killed Morris. 'Utterly unselfish, quite humble, brave, simple and strenuous . . . he was loved, trusted and understood.' Percy recalls that the local people said Morris was so unlike a Parson. With such an examplar, it was always going to be difficult for their new curate. Dearmer found the work difficult and at times disheartening. His shyness prevented him from getting alongside the people in the way Morris was able to do, however sensitive he was to their sufferings and however anxious to serve their needs.

Nonetheless, the experience only served to deepen his conviction of the injustice of the prevailing social system. Even death did not provide an escape; he wrote of the 'dreadful poverty pressing at the gates of death . . . how relentless poverty is, when the poor are ill or dying: how lonely, how wearisome, how harassing'. South Lambeth left an indelible mark on the whole of his future ministry, even if Archbishop Davidson was unable to discern it in Dearmer's life-long concern for the poor and oppressed.

Percy Dearmer's diaconate year included another event which was profoundly to shape his future – his marriage to Mabel Jessie Pritchard White. Although, like the best marriages, it might be said to have been made in heaven, the manner of its earthly accomplishment was far from ideal. The match was energetically opposed by both families. Mabel and Percy had known each other for a number of years. For a while they had been what Percy described as 'good friends', but suddenly in November 1891, he reports, 'all that is gone, utterly gone. This is so different. You do not seek, it comes, sweeps down on you and changes you, and fills you with love.'

Mabel White was nineteen, Percy twenty-four. Mabel had been born in Caernarvon and her childhood had been a lonely one. Her father, Surgeon-Major William White, had died and her mother, Selina, had remarried. It was from her stepfather, Mr Beamish, a solicitor by profession, that the main opposition came. Beamish was pushing against an open door when persuading Percy's mother of the foolishness of the proposed marriage. Caroline Miriam had no intention of offering any financial assistance to the couple and set her face against the marriage. No doubt Caroline objected because she believed that Mabel would only encourage Percy in what she conceived as his foolishness – his political and aesthetic enthusiasms. In this she was absolutely correct.

Mabel's literary executor, Stephen Gwynn (an author, journalist, MP and Irish Patriot who admitted having been, at one time, in love with her), wrote a short memoir in which he tells of her early enthusiasm for acting. She put it aside because 'They thought I was not pretty enough.' Gwynn comments that although she could not be called beautiful, in a conventional way, no photograph could ever capture 'the poise of her figure, crowned with its mass of brilliant (red-gold) hair, the living quality of her voice, all the radiation of her personality.' She was tall and slender, but, he says, in those days 'also wild with the sheer desire of living – grasping at life with both hands.' This was not a girl who would appeal to the strict and formal former school-mistress! Her vitality did not attract her prospective mother-in-law, and her extreme Socialist views had already antagonized her stepfather.

Independent life started for Mabel when she commenced her art studies at Hubert Herkomer's school at Bushey. She had already identified in her art a ready way to escape the oppression of the Beamish home life. Marriage would complete that separation and so, faced with parental opposition, she applied to be made a Ward in Chancery. The immediate effect of this was that she and Percy were bound over neither to see nor to communicate with each other while an assessment was made of the desirability of their marriage. It was now that Charles Gore took a hand in the affair and, in February 1898, he accompanied Percy on a visit to his mother. It was a hot-blooded confrontation during which Percy lost his temper, but Caroline was impressed by Gore and he convinced her to withdraw her objections. At a further court hearing, at which representations were made by not only Charles Gore and Harold Anson, but now also by his mother, the marriage was allowed, with Mr Justice North commenting to Percy, 'You seem a sensible young man so I shall allow you to marry.' But turning to Mabel, he told her to 'remember there will be no money for fal-lals.'

The wedding took place in St John's Richmond on 26 May 1892 with the Vicar of St Anne's South Lambeth (Fr Morris) conducting the service. The newly married couple made their home at 59 South Lambeth Road, nearly opposite St Anne's Church. The Socialist couple furnished their house with Morris chintzes and wallpapers, while Morris tapestries covered the doors and Burne-Jones engravings adorned the walls. P. E. T. Widdrington, the leading theologian of the sacramental Socialist movement in the 1920s, recollected that although the Dearmers had 'spent a prodigal sum on decoration there was a striking absence of furniture.' He also notes what was a continuing dichotomy in Percy's dress – rather than either a white collar or a clerical collar he was wearing 'a blue shirt and a wonderful tie'. It was obviously not a day for the pious and sartorial commemoration of Latimer and Ridley.

For Mabel these early days were far from easy. Later she turned aside from her drawing and painting and found that she had a talent for writing. Her words, in contrast to her visual images, had some success. She found that both writing and producing drama was more artistically satisfying and began to concentrate in that direction. In one of her early novels, *The Difficult Way* (1905), which she later transferred to the stage, she draws freely on her memories of those days as a curate's wife in South Lambeth. She had struggled with butchers' bills and had felt the strain of poverty, like her fictional heroine Nan Pilgrim:

> The Pilgrims thought their home perfection. Bare, austere, the plain walls of the little sitting room were lit up by one spark of colour – a sketch of Landsbury that brought with it a breath of hot cornfields and flaming poppies ... There was, of course, a kitchen and a bedroom furnished in the bare waste of that rambling house; but in these rooms packing cases took the place of most of the articles of furniture considered indispensable to the existence of the newly married.

For Mabel and Percy pretty things were important and necessities often so dull. In those early days, in order to relieve their poverty, Percy worked on his journalism, producing articles and reviews for *The Daily Chronicle*, *The Commonwealth* and other periodicals while Mabel worked, as she always did, slowly and painstakingly on her drawings.

The possibility of adding to the family's coffers by her

artistic work was seriously curtailed by the arrival of their first son, Geoffrey, on 21 March 1893, and by the birth, exactly one year later (21 March 1894), of a second boy, whom they named Christopher. Geoffrey was a sturdy baby, who proved this by living to the age of 103; Christopher was always more delicate and often ill.

Just before Christopher's birth the tensions between Dearmer and his Vicar became acute. It was not a wholesale falling out; there was no sudden and bitter disagreement about parochial policy or mission strategy. As far as one can see, from the limited evidence available, they remained on reasonable terms. The developing problem can be sensed in Nan Dearmer's memoir, even though she nowhere alludes to it. It may be that she did not know the full facts of the matter. The seeds of the problem, obvious to those who know anything about parish life, are to be found in the twenty-four pages devoted to 'St Anne's South Lambeth', together with the beginning of the chapter on 'Early Married Life'. Already, at his ordination to the diaconate, Percy was Secretary of the London CSU and was still involved in the Guild of St Matthew. Additionally, as we have seen, he was very busy with his journalism and other writings. He was regularly to be seen on platforms at political meetings and speaking at CSU or GSM gatherings. There were also lectures on Socialism in north-country villages, work for the Fabian Society, and time spent organizing midday sermons in the City at St Edmund's Lombard Street. All these things were being done by an assistant curate in his mid-twenties, who had only been ordained for a couple of years. He was meant to be assisting Fr Morris, who was labouring with a population of 10,000 in an incredibly rough and tough parish (one to which the Dearmers were unable to persuade a cabbie to take them after an evening with friends in another part of London).

It could not continue thus. At the end of 1893 Morris wrote to the Bishop of Rochester explaining that Dearmer must leave the parish. He was in a quandary: 'I do not want to do anything which would sacrifice Mr Dearmer, however much it be for the benefit of St Anne's.' Morris had obviously issued an ultimatum to Dearmer, and this he explained to the Bishop: 'He should give up his CSU secretaryship and literary work for two or three years and devote himself completely to parish work.' He needed, Morris believed, 'actual personal contact with the needs and thoughts of individuals'. He obviously thought that there was a practical need for less words and more deeds by the young curate. The other alternative he suggested was that he could 'go to a more well-heeled parish'. He told Bishop Davidson that his leaving would be 'a great wrench for both of us, as we love each other much.' His genuine affection for Dearmer no doubt emboldened him to speak the truth in love to his diocesan Bishop when he summed up the situation, saying that although Dearmer 'may make a Scott Holland he will never make a Charles Lowder.'

It must have been this evidence, and with the knowledge of a pastoral breakdown at the beginning of his ministry, which informed Davidson's judgement – an attitude which Anson accurately surmises while wrongly identifying its motivation. Dearmer never again worked in the diocese of Rochester nor was he ever offered a post in the Canterbury diocese.

With this information, his move to St John's, Great Marlborough Street in the diocese of London becomes plain. The idea was that Percy would work part time as a curate at St John's and would use the rest of his time in journalism and speaking, mainly on behalf of the CSU. This was an arrangement agreed from the outset by the parish. The Dearmers initially went to live in part of 28 Duke Street, Manchester Square, but later moved to 9 Devonport Street, to share a house with Miss Emily Mullholland, who was a great supporter of CSU.

One of Percy's new acquaintances was Gertrude Tuckwell, the formidable opposer of low wage-rates, poor sanitation and bad industrial conditions. She had grown up in an atmosphere of left-wing thought, and had come into contact with many of the progressive thinkers of her day, in and out of Parliament. Gertrude combined a love of the arts with a

Ordination, Marriage and First Parishes 33

fervour for the welfare of the poor. In this she was a natural soul-mate for Mabel and Percy.

Gertrude is a good example of the friends and acquaintances, colleagues and companions with whom the young couple began to mix in London. It is not easy to find a category into which to place the varying styles, enthusiasms, passions and preoccupations of these folk. 'Progressive', 'bohemian' and 'radical' fail to fit all these people. 'Interesting', 'exciting' and 'challenging' would be indisputable; with them life would seldom be dull or pedestrian. Among those with whom the Dearmers came into contact were a number of Mabel's new-found literary and artistic colleagues. Through book illustration she came to know those involved in *The Yellow Book*, a handsome but short-lived publication. Startling in its time, it gained an immediate notoriety. The flavour of its style can be deduced from the fact that Aubrey Beardsley was its first Art Editor and that the first issue contained a Max Beerbohm essay entitled 'A Defence of Cosmetics'. Another figure on the scene just then was Laurence Housman, brother of the poet, who trained as an artist but is now chiefly remembered as a writer and dramatist, concentrating on Socialist and pacifist themes. Evelyn Sharp was another writer for *The Yellow Book* and was a campaigner for women's suffrage and for peace. Also among the contributors were Netta Syrett; the American author Harry Harland, who wrote about Jewish immigrant life under the pseudonym of Sydney Luska and was the literary editor of *The Yellow Book*; and Richard le Gallienne, one of the original members of the Rhymers Club with W. B. Yeats and Oscar Wilde.

Meanwhile Percy was becoming acquainted with a wider circle of churchmen, particularly through his friend and supporter in time of need, Charles Gore. The Community of the Resurrection had been formed and Gore was living with some members of the Community in the precincts of Westminster Abbey. Gore had been appointed a Canon of Westminster in 1894, as already noted, joining in London his friend and compatriot Scott Holland, who had been made a Canon of

St Paul's ten years earlier. So it was that Dearmer had counsellors at both the West and the East Minsters of the capital.

An International Socialist Congress was held in London in 1896 which two Church of England priests attended as delegates – Percy Dearmer and Conrad Noel. The latter had come to know Percy in South Lambeth. In 1893 Noel had been refused ordination by the Bishop of Exeter on the morning of the ordination service. Frederick Temple, who was to become Archbishop of Canterbury (1896–1902), told him that he had been wrestling with the Lord all night in prayer and had come to the conclusion that it would be 'dangerous' to ordain Noel. This disgraceful incident is omitted from even the latest biography of Temple. Conrad Noel took time to recover from this rebuff, and for a while lived in a doss-house – Rowton House, off South Lambeth Road. One evening he decided to call on the local curate, whom he knew by reputation. In his autobiography Noel tells of their first meeting:

> It was from Rowton House that I called on Percy Dearmer, and he was surprised when he opened the door to see a tramp with a red handkerchief knotted round his throat. We talked of the Guild of St Matthew and of our common enthusiasm for Christian Socialism. I became fast friends with W. A. Morris and Percy Dearmer ... these friendships and my stay at Rowton House proved to be a worthy conclusion to my theological training.

In the Church of England there still exist, to this day, a few rare examples of an extraordinary ecclesiastical arrangement known as a Proprietary Chapel. These are chapels built by subscription and maintained by private individuals, without any official ecclesiastical constitutional existence or any parochial rights. They were usually found in London or fashionable watering places. Often they were centres of extreme Evangelical or, occasionally, High Church doctrine. Although many of them had disappeared by the 1890s, one still existed in Mayfair – the Berkeley Chapel. It had a dignified tradition, the future King George V attended children's services there and the music for many years was in the hands of the plainsong expert Henry Briggs. In 1897 the Hon. James Adderley accepted the post of priest-in-charge of the Chapel and offered Percy Dearmer a position as his assistant. It was a mission to the rich, but Fr Adderley, a Christ Church man like Dearmer, had previously been the first head of Oxford House, founded by Scott Holland, Edward Talbot and others as a place where University men 'might study the poor and render some service to struggling humanity'. Later Adderley helped found the Franciscan Community of the Divine Compassion, but discovered that he had no real vocation to the life of a friar. Percy had known Fr Adderley when he and Mabel had gone in 1889 to help him in his previous work at the Christ Church Mission in Poplar during the Dock Strike. Indeed, there had been a real possibility that Percy might have served his first curacy in Poplar with him. Would this have been as traumatic as his South Lambeth experience? It was at the Berkeley Chapel that Percy first experimented with the idea of Catechism teaching for children. Describing the work, Adderley's biographer, T. P. Stevens, said, 'The Revd Percy Dearmer undertook work among children, for which he showed positive genius.'

The time at the Berkeley Chapel was only short. At the end of the year they moved again, when Percy became curate at St Mark's Marylebone Road, where the Vicar was Morris Fuller. It had been described as a parish of 'shabby gentility', with many flats and some drab back streets. The Dearmers lived in 5 Hyde Park Mansions where, according to Stephen Gwynn, they crowded into a little flat in which the growing family lacked space. Morris Fuller was not at all well and was often away from his duties. Fuller, a committed High Churchman, had instituted an elaborate ceremonial at St Mark's based on the Roman Rite. This did not appeal to Percy at all, and Fr Fuller's absences gave him the opportunity to shape things his own way. This was particularly important because, in 1899, he nailed his liturgical and ceremonial colours firmly to the mast for all to see and read in the publication of his best-known book *The Parson's Handbook*.

3

The Parson's Handbook, the Alcuin Club and the English Use

In Davidson's estimation, Dearmer stood condemned because the Archbishop believed that he preferred writing to house-to-house visitation. It is certainly true that, in the psalmist's words, Percy had 'the pen of a ready writer'. He wrote quickly and fluently. The British Library catalogue contains nearly a hundred items under Dearmer's name, including twenty-six books (with another eleven to which he made major contributions), twenty booklets and pamphlets of various lengths, and fifteen books of hymns and carols of which he was either the editor or the compiler.

We have noted his journalism, so crucial to the family finances, which he commenced at Pusey House and continued at South Lambeth. In addition, in the 1890s he began to attempt more substantial work. The first was a polemical political pamphlet entitled *Christian Socialism, Practical Christianity* which came out in 1897. In May of the same year Dearmer produced the first of what was to become a famous and long-running series called 'Bell's Cathedral Guides'. His subject for the initial volume was one he knew well – Oxford Cathedral. Uniquely, the chapel at the Oxford college of Christ Church doubles as the Cathedral Church of the Diocese of Oxford. Christ Church, of course, had been Dearmer's college. The publishers must have been pleased with the result, as he was immediately commissioned to write on Wells Cathedral for the same series. Concurrently Percy was selecting and arranging a 300-page collection of religious pamphlets for Kegan Paul, to which he contributed an introduction and some notes. With all this in hand, we must wonder with amazement how he was able, in addition to his parochial duties at St Mark's, to produce the immense amount of detail included in *The Parson's Handbook*, which was published by Grant Richards in the Spring of 1899.

Why was the *Handbook* published by this now largely forgotten publishing house? Richards had only commenced business in 1897, but he had contacts and acquaintances in the circle in which Dearmer moved. He became the publisher of a journal called *The Savoy* – the successor, in many ways, of *The Yellow Book*. The original prospectus of *The Savoy* promised contributions from Bernard Shaw, Havelock Ellis, W. B. Yeats and Aubrey Beardsley. Additionally, Richards was G. K. Chesterton's first publisher and published many of Shaw's plays, the poems of Elizabeth Meynall, A. E. Housman and later Robert Tressell's notorious 'Socialist' novel *The Ragged Trousered Philanthropists*.

Richards, who described himself as 'An old Literary Sportsman engaged in author hunting', was a fashionable and left-inclining publisher. It no doubt gave him and Dearmer a certain amount of amusement to be involved in the production of such an outspoken book. From 1907 onwards publication of the *Handbook* was in the hands of Humphrey Milford and the Oxford University Press.

The book was an instant best-seller. Published in March, it was reprinted four months later with an additional preface in which Dearmer was able to pick up some of the points of criticism which had been made against the book on publication.

What was Dearmer's aim in *The Parson's Handbook*? In the first place, a remedying of what he saw as the 'lamentable confusion, lawlessness and vulgarity which are conspicuous in the Church at the present time.'

Looking back on liturgical and ceremonial developments in the Church of England during the nineteenth century, it is crucial to keep in mind the way in which the Oxford

Movement progressed – by division and sub-division. There was not always the easy, unbroken, clear line of succession that many assume. The Tractarians, although reluctant to admit it, were building on an existing High Church movement within the Church of England which can be traced back to the eighteenth century and earlier through such groups as the Hackney Phalanx, 'the Orthodox' and 'Nobody's Friends' to Laudianism, Andrewes, Bancroft and the like. The Tractarians and especially their immediate followers were too quick to forget or neglect the extent of this heritage. 'The victors write the history', it is said, and the influence of the Anglo-Catholic historians of the nineteenth century, until quite recently, has held sway. An impression has been given that it was the Tractarians' influence alone which rescued the Church of England from deep sloth, slovenly worship and indifference. Two of Dearmer's particular friends and associates drew attention to the historical inaccuracy of such contentions. Wickham Legg, in his splendidly titled *English Church Life from the Restoration to the Tractarian Movement considered in some of its neglected or forgotten features*, made the point in 1914, but the untruth surrounding the allegations of eighteenth-century and early nineteenth-century ceremonial neglect had been unmasked by Francis Eeles in 1910. In an Alcuin publication (which he was encouraged by Dearmer to write), *Traditional Ceremonial and Customs connected with The Scottish Liturgy*, Eeles said:

> Nothing is more common at the present day than to be told that the interest in the details of liturgical practice consequent on the Oxford Movement has been without precedent in the churches of the Anglican Communion since the Reformation. Certain controversialists are never tired of insisting that any sort of regard for the externals of worship – let alone the use of what is commonly called ceremonial – is an innovation upon the post-Reformation usage of the Church. They interpret the Prayer Book in the light of the slovenly neglect prevalent in England in the early part of

the nineteenth century. Plausible though this theory may seem at first sight, it turns out to be untenable when the light of history is thrown upon it. The slovenliness of the late eighteenth and early nineteenth centuries was itself of the nature of an innovation; it was not merely contrary to the letter and spirit of the Prayer Book, but it was in marked contrast to the practice of the better appointed churches in the seventeenth century and in the earlier part of the eighteenth.

Through the writings of Peter Nockles and others, we now know that Eeles was right. It is clear that some old-fashioned High Churchmen did not go the full way with the Tractarians, and certainly there were those who drew back after the 1840s desertions to Rome of Newman, Ward, Manning and others. There was a major division in the ranks in the 1860s. The movement split yet again when the influence of the more extreme Ritualists began to be felt – usually very visually and flamboyantly.

It is quite clear that in the first place, the 'Cambridge Movement' of J. M. Neale and his fellow Ecclesiologists was more crucial in bringing about change in the appearance of English churches and in the conduct of worship than were the Oxford-based writings and teachings of Keble or Pusey. The original Tractarians were heirs of a tradition supporting a loyalty to the Prayer Book, but these later Ritualist followers created a situation in which the tensions involved in using the Prayer Book for High Church worship were laid bare for all to see. Their practices were far beyond anything the Ecclesiologists had imagined. It has been said that a Church of England worshipper of the 1660s would have noticed few liturgical changes in his parish church if he had returned there in the 1840s, whereas sixty years later, in many places he would have found it hard to believe that the services had any relationship whatever with those authorized by the Book of Common Prayer. The result of these more extensive variations in the liturgy was that the history of the Church of England in the second half of the nineteenth century was besmirched by ritual riots, ritual trials, imprisonments and considerable liturgical anarchy. The situation was hardly helped by the government's attempt in 1874 to crush Ritualism by passing the Public Worship Regulation Act. As a result of this Act, no fewer than five Church of England priests were sent to jail for the 'crime' of ritual offences.

Around this time there were moves by a few Catholic-minded Anglicans to restore the 1549 Prayer Book, but if its contents cropped up in discussions, it was most likely to be in the context of church furnishings, especially in regard to the question: 'What is allowed by the Ornaments Rubric?' The great liturgical word among many High Churchmen was 'interpolation'. The 'interpolation' of what they believed was 'missing' from the 1662 rite was of more interest to the Anglo-Catholics than most other things, and it was the Roman Use to which they went to provide what they perceived to be the Prayer Book's deficiencies.

This is where Dearmer came in. Temperamentally a High Churchman, with a high doctrine of the Church and its sacraments, he was never attracted to the extremes of Anglo-Catholicism; least of all the imitation of continental ultramontanism. The problem was that his researches into Anglican liturgical history led him to advocate both vestments and ceremonial which the man (or woman) in the street would confidently dub 'High Church', whereas Dearmer could unerringly quote chapter and verse, and all the authorities, for the legality of those so-called 'High Church' items. He wanted to prove that they were strictly in accordance with the formularies of the Church of England. Dearmer insisted that at the Reformation it was not ritual, nor beauty, nor symbolism that had been abolished, but only certain ceremonies. Some of these ceremonies had originally been of 'godly intent' but 'had at length turned to vanity and superstition'. He pointed out that the Church, down the ages, had often provided indiscreet devotions, but that was not in any way to suggest that all ceremonies needed to be expunged.

In *The Parson's Handbook*, he explained, he was including the greatest elaboration of ceremonial which was, in his opinion (and he granted that in this area much must be a matter of opinion), compatible with loyalty to the Church of England. The Church of England, Dearmer argued, was a comprehensive church. For his book to be at all useful in such a church, it needed to provide for the more elaborate type of service. To do otherwise would leave the more extreme church to 'the too tender mercies of the fancy ritualists'. At one and the same time he pleaded with those who might think the provisions of the book too elaborate to ask themselves whether or not it might be of some little use to them. Percy knew that some portions of his book advocated the restoration of matters which had fallen into disuse, yet were actually necessary provisions contained in the Prayer Book. The only way that 'the credit and peace of the Church' would be advanced, he believed, would be if all tried to conform to the directions of the Prayer Book.

It seemed obvious to Dearmer that the lawlessness which was abroad in the Church of England was not only confined, as was popularly supposed, to the 'advanced' clergy. In the original introduction of the 1899 first edition of the *Handbook* Dearmer boldly suggested that lawlessness was even greater among those who claimed to dislike ceremonial. 'The lawlessness is due to a conservatism which prefers late Hanoverian tradition to the plain words of the Prayer Book.' It was impossible, he maintained, to read the Prayer Book aright through Hanoverian spectacles. Wesley and the Methodists, however, were excluded from his criticisms. Dearmer explained that the very name 'Methodist' is what 'Ritualist' meant in those days: that is, those taking care to properly follow the feasts and other observances in the Church.

Dearmer was considerably less charitable about Ritualists. 'Would that they always deserved the name', he said sadly. He granted that some started from a position of carefully observing the rites and ceremonies of the Church of England, and were subsequently driven into their position by 'prelatical ignorance of liturgical matters'. Then some of the alleged miscreants were prosecuted by unconstitutional courts, as Dearmer judged them, for activities which were in fact loyal to the Prayer Book – as a result of which they moved unconsciously (he generously adjudged it) into 'a spirit of confirmed lawlessness'. Many of those who had begun by taking their stand on the Ornaments Rubric ended by denying it in favour of 'the customs of a very hostile foreign church'. By now having lost all patience with them, Dearmer said in a trenchant condemnation:

> They seemed almost to agree with their former opponents that such ornaments as were in this Church of England in the second year of Edward VI, should not be in use today; and some of them seemed to prefer to the liturgical forms 'in the said Book prescribed' those forms which the Book had rather proscribed.

Dearmer believed that by loyal observance of the formularies of the Church of England it was possible to have a form of worship which was properly Catholic and had firm roots in the tradition of Christian worship from the earliest days. He would have nothing to do with rites and ceremonies which were not allowed by the Church of England, but would challenge those who alleged, from historical ignorance, that certain practices were not within the Anglican tradition. One of his favourite examples of an attitude based on crude prejudice rather than a study of the historical facts was the subject of the use of incense in Church of England worship. He would begin by alluding in the first place to the references to incense in the New Testament: at the announcement of the birth of John the Baptist; as one of the gifts presented to the infant Jesus. However, when it came to references to incense in the last book in the Bible, he indulged himself in hyperbole as he described the twenty-eight bowls of incense used in the ideal worship of the redeemed, and concluded by observing that 'the Sarum Missal itself hardly gives a more complicated description of the use of incense.'

What we would now call 'media interest' in the ritualistic controversies of the Church of England centred around such matters as incense, vestments and various articles of church furnishings. The *Handbook* gives clear guidance as to the use and deployment of these, but Dearmer was an artist, and it was matters of taste which concerned him more than the mere use and provision of dalmatics and tunicles, altar linen, basons, cruets, processional torches and such like. 'Vulgarity' was a favourite word, and he condemned the low standards applied to the design of most ecclesiastical articles.

Dearmer described himself as having spent much of his life among those who earn their living by writing and drawing, and therefore claimed that he was acutely conscious of the alienation of those 'most influential classes in modern society'. The clergy worked on purely commercial lines, he said, and were mostly content with decoration that was the ridicule of competent artists. Did Mabel stand at his elbow as he added, 'or is ignored by them as not being even amusing'? Whereas in the past, he said, the Church had called into her service great artists and craftsmen, her place as patroness of art had been taken by the Merchants of Birmingham, Manchester and Liverpool. There was also another alienated class – the working class. For vulgarity, Dearmer explained, in the long run always means cheapness, 'and cheapness means the tyranny of the sweaters.' He expounded in his *Parson's Handbook*, so often mistakenly mocked for its ecclesiastical dilettantism, one of the favourite lines of argument of the Christian Socialist:

> A modern preacher often stands in a sweated pulpit, wearing a sweated surplice over a suit of clothes that were not produced under fair conditions, and, holding a sweated book in one hand, with the other he points to the machine-made cross at the jerry-built altar, and appeals to the sacred principles of mutual sacrifice and love.

Dearmer wrote, 'I make no apology for freely recommending the shops which in my opinion it is best for the parson to go for certain things . . . without some guide of this kind it is impossible for any of us to furnish our churches aright.' Here, then, is a book of great practicality. Clear ceremonial directions for the performance of the liturgy: 'All should bow sensibly, and neither ostentatiously nor familiarly.' Advice on clerical dress inside and outside church: 'Nowadays cassocks with buttons down the front are often worn, but neither beauty nor convenience is gained by the excessive number of buttons'; and then practicality creeps in – 'the buttons are apt to stick in the knees.' Artistic wisdom about furnishings: 'Care should be taken that there is really a place for everything. A cupboard should be painted a pleasant colour. Varnished pitch pine and imitation wood grains, are almost as destructive of warmth and beauty as is oak graining.'

This practicality in the *Handbook* does not entirely obscure the scholarship. It remains a matter of amazement that what would have been the result of a lifetime of diligent study for many was achieved by Dearmer in the midst of two demanding curacies, however sympathetic his incumbent might be. He had immersed himself in all he could discover about the ancient Sarum Use, which was the most widely used version of the Roman rite in England at the time of the Reformation, but he was not an antiquarian. His proposal for what became known as the English Use (and was so described on the title page of *The Parson's Handbook*) was for a suitably modified and adapted form of rites and ceremonies which would fit the Book of Common Prayer. We now know that the Sarum Rite was not radically different to the way in which the Liturgy was celebrated in France, the Low Countries and Germany at the comparable time. The Sarum Rite represented the trend of liturgical practice throughout northern Europe in the late Middle Ages. As Cyril Pocknee commented in his 1965 extensive revision and rewriting of *The Parson's Handbook*, 'Thus apparelled amices and full surplices were in use everywhere', and there was nothing insular about an altar surrounded by four posts and enshrined by curtains in the fifteenth and early sixteenth centuries.

Dearmer wanted the English Use to provide a kind of liturgical *zone sanitaire* against the advancing hordes of the advocates of the rococo, which he believed to be entirely 'un-English' – a term he would have applied, with equal relish, to the Tridentine ceremonial directions for the ordering of worship. He was utterly convinced that the English Use could provide all the beauty and dignity that ought to accompany the celebration of the Holy Eucharist, and he was sure of its complete Catholicity. Further, this was a Catholicity guaranteed by the authority of the Church of England, which is indisputably part of the One, Holy, Catholic and Apostolic Church, ordering its affairs according to the traditions handed down from the past to the present day. This was, for Dearmer, without question the source of liturgical authority. In *The Parson's Handbook* he did not advocate anything that could not be supported by ecclesiastical law. In the recent past some points had been hard won, he knew, but that did not affect their legality. The important principle was: 'whether the ceremonial is used little or much, the services of our Church should at least be conducted on the legitimate lines, if only that they may be freed from what is anomalous, irreverent, tawdry or grotesque.'

As we have seen, the book was a huge publishing success. Dom Anselm Hughes of Nashdom Abbey, who wrote his own 'personal account of the Catholic Movement in the twentieth century' entitled *The Rivers of the Flood*, believed it to be altogether a 'strong' book. 'For that very reason it was acceptable and refreshing after the hum-and-haw of the pietistic or amateurish or tentatively-exploring-avenue flavour of so much that had gone before.' *The Church Times* thought it was the most sensible of all the numerous clerical guides that had appeared. The newspaper appealed to its readers to 'help Mr Dearmer on in the good work and not be too proud to acknowledge that we have made mistakes in the past.' Prophetically, *The Church Times* stated that when there had dawned a full realisation of what was possible by following the English tradition and customs, and when 'the spirit of contempt' had been altogether banished from English churchmen, then 'Mr Dearmer will have a full share of the credit that will fall to those who have helped to bring it about.' Meanwhile the High Church newspaper *The Guardian* was of the opinion that such a handbook could only be produced by someone who had 'an unusual combination of qualifications' – first, antiquarian, historical, liturgical and practical knowledge; secondly, considerable taste; and thirdly, 'a great need of practical sense'. *The Guardian* recorded that it was 'a welcome fact that Mr Dearmer has these three qualifications in no common degree.'

Already by November 1899 the *Handbook*'s fame had crossed the Atlantic. The review in the American *Churchman* thought that the book would add not mere conformity 'but worshipful dignity and spiritual suggestiveness, to the Church services'. Even secular journals praised Dearmer as 'a competent ecclesiologist, whose literary skill is as conspicuous as his absence of fanaticism.' There were those who chose to mock the 'British Museum Religion' that the book was supposed to advocate, and so Percy added an extra preface in the reprinting which was necessary by July. In this he was at his waspish best when he took on some of his critics who saw no point in some of his 'very practical and humdrum directions' (Percy's own phrase), especially in the chapter on vestries:

> I do not think the clergy will complain of them; for they know too well what it is to be called upon to write a certificate on the back of an old envelope, with a crossed nib and a dry inkpot. But the criticisms on this point afford a curious illustration of the strength with which generations of careless slovenlihood have impressed us. If I had written a Cricketer's Handbook, no one would have complained of *minutiae*; if a Cookery Book, every one would have been up in arms against me for the superficial treatment of a great

and serious subject. Yet I cannot help thinking that the worship of God calls for as careful treatment as the playing of games, and that an orderly complement of accessories is as necessary in the church as in the scullery.

The publication history of *The Parson's Handbook* is complicated by the fact that the original publisher, Grant Richards, did not distinguish, as we might well do today, between 'editions' and 'impressions'. After the first edition in March 1899, a second edition appeared in July of that same year; it included an additional preface, but otherwise it was what had been published four months earlier. What is called the 'third edition' (but is unchanged from the July printing) was produced in November 1899. Then, in 1902, came the fourth edition and with it many changes, not least a considerable expansion of material. The first three editions had comprised 223 pages, but there were 471 in the fourth edition. The number of chapters had also increased from eight to eighteen. Dearmer said, 'The original *Parson's Handbook* aimed at providing notes and suggestions only, the new *Parson's Handbook* attempts to supply complete directions for the conduct of all services and more elaborate forms of these services.' By 1907 there was a sixth edition and the size had increased again to 562 pages. The publisher had also changed, production being then in the hands of Henry Frowde at the Oxford University Press. In 1932 the OUP published the twelfth edition. By now it had a completely rewritten introduction and 'English Use' had become 'Anglican Use' on the title page. The twelfth edition continued to remain in print for a further twenty-five years. An eighth impression of that edition was published by Oxford University Press in 1962 with this significant publisher's note: 'The present impression, like the previous ones, is not a new edition but a reprint. While certain details are clearly out of date it is believed that Dr Dearmer's work retains its essential value.'

Dearmer never claimed to be an original scholar, but it is apparent from his writings, even when they became a little ephemeral later in his life, that he had a good historical sense and, if necessary, could see his way precisely through obscuring undergrowth. In the first edition of *The Parson's Handbook* he provided just enough footnotes and references, together with a short bibliography, to encourage the reader to pursue further any point of interest. An examination of these notes reveals a reliance on a number of recently published works of the Alcuin Club. Dearmer and the Alcuin Club are so often linked in the minds of those who know something of this period of English Church history that it is important to look at the founding of the Club and Percy Dearmer's contribution to its early life.

Perhaps the most interesting fact about the Alcuin Club is that its founders were all laymen. On 12 January 1897 Dr John Wickham Legg, Mr H. B. Briggs, Mr William St John Hope and Mr J. T. Micklethwaite met at 15 Dean's Yard in Westminster Abbey, Micklethwaite's office as Surveyor of the Fabric at the Abbey. The record of the meeting says that they decided to form a club with the object of 'promoting the study of the history and use of the Book of Common Prayer'. The Prayer Book was, for many years, to be central in all the Club's activities and the touch-stone and guiding principle of its publications. The Anglican ethos of the Club was further emphasized by restricting membership to those in communion with the Church of England. The four laymen also resolved that 'The work of the Club [will] be the publication of Tracts dealing with the Object of the Club, and such other works as may seem desirable, with reproductions of miniatures from MSS and photographs of Church Furniture, Ornaments and Vestments.'

They were a remarkable group. Wickham Legg had been a highly talented and skilled physician who, ten years earlier, at the age of 43, resigned all his appointments, gave away his medical books and retired from practice. Already the study of liturgies was a strong interest in his life and he now had the leisure to bring to it, as Dr Ollard wrote, 'the accurate scientific training which, joined to his brilliance and eagerness for research, had made his reputation as a physician.' One of his earliest tasks was editing what is still the definitive edition of *The Westminster Missal*. His edition of the *Sarum Missal* similarly continues to be authoritative. Wickham Legg was no lover of the extravagance of later Anglo-Catholic liturgical fashions imported from the Continent. Nor was he in favour of Prayer Book reform, but, remarkably, he prefigured the present-day historiographical revisionism of the Oxford Movement. In his *English Life from the Restoration to the Tractarian Movement*, published in 1914, he, like F. C. Eeles, demonstrated the degree to which the Tractarians had exaggerated the state of affairs in the Church of England at the beginning of the nineteenth century.

> We are told that the eighteenth century was a time of 'general decay of religion', of 'poisoning of the blood', or 'a black spot on the shining history of England'. The least injurious reproaches are accusations of slovenliness, sloth, 'marasmus', and on the part of the clergy of attention only to fees and preferment. Some of these attacks have been made by men belonging to the Church of England, made, most likely, in good faith, but of late to be traced to a mere following of the multitude and of the prejudices and fashion of the day. Perhaps there was a leaning on the part of the writers of the nineteenth century and of the Victorian epoch to plume themselves on the supposed excellency of their own age, as an age of 'progress', 'enlightenment', etc. The lustre of the age in which they wrote could be heightened by darkening the age which went immediately before.

Among his many academic correspondents and acquaintances Wickham Legg particularly valued the friendship of Monsignor Ratti, prefect of the Vatican Library and author of the 1913 critical edition of the Ambrosian Missal. In 1922 he became Pope Pius XI.

William Henry St John Hope was the son of a clergyman and his mother was the daughter of a priest. His taste for ecclesiology, inherited from his father, was nurtured at the

Woodard School at Hurstpierpoint. He became a close friend of Henry Bradshaw, in whose memory the eponymous society for editing rare liturgical texts was founded. After a short period of teaching, he became Assistant Secretary to the Society of Antiquaries and remained there for twenty-five years. His chief interest was in ecclesiastical architecture. Retiring at fifty-six he undertook (by Royal command) the writing of a two-volume monograph on Windsor Castle, for which he was rewarded with a knighthood. Hope produced the very first Alcuin Club Collection ('Collections' is the name given to the Club's main series of publications), entitled *English Altars: from Illuminated Manuscripts with descriptive notes* (published in 1899).

John Thomas Micklethwaite was a Yorkshire-born architect. His father came from Mirfield and his mother from Manchester. He was a graduate of King's College London, and became a pupil of George Gilbert Scott. His entry in *The Dictionary of National Biography* says, 'he formed a lifelong friendship with a fellow pupil, Mr Somers Clarke.' Micklethwaite was a convinced Tractarian. It is said of his designs that, though not strikingly original, they were 'invariably scholarly and correct'. In 1898 he was appointed to succeed J. L. Pearson as Surveyor of the Fabric at the Abbey. As well as being a founder of the Alcuin Club he was also in at the beginning of the Henry Bradshaw Society and the St Paul's Ecclesiological Society.

The fourth of the founding fathers of the Alcuin Club was the plainsong enthusiast and expert H. B. Briggs. He founded the Plainsong and Medieval Music Society in 1888, to which he recruited Micklethwaite, Wickham Legg and St John Hope. He was able to devote a considerable amount of time to the Society because, as Dom Anselm Hughes avows in *Septuagesima*, his account of its first seventy years, Briggs belonged to 'that almost extinct species of Civil Servant with a quasi-sinecure post in the Indian Office'. No doubt Briggs would have applied his energies as diligently to the Alcuin Club, had not the fates decreed otherwise: 'a cold, a prescription from the doctor, a slip by the chemist who compounded the medicine, and sudden death in early middle age.' This occurred in 1901, so that the work which probably best preserves his name, the *Manual of Plainsong* (commonly referred to as 'Briggs and Frere'), was published posthumously in 1902.

The choice of Alcuin as the Club patron was dictated by the desire to use the name of a famous English liturgist. Alcuin (735–804), educated at the Minster School of York, went to France at the invitation of Charlemagne to help him in his educational reforms. Although called a 'Club', the Alcuin Club has never had any premises and its main activity to the present day is the publication of books on liturgical subjects. After the initial meeting at the beginning of the month, the four founders met again on 28 January, when they elected Wickham Legg as chairman and six priests (including the liturgists F. E. Brightman and W. H. Frere) and four further laymen (including the architect Ninian Comper) into membership. We do not know when Dearmer became a member. The only evidence is the fact, already mentioned, that he knew and quoted from the Club publications by early 1899, within two years of its foundation, and that in 1901 he was mentioned in a Club publication as a member of the Committee. He remained on the Committee for thirty years.

The names of these liturgical pioneers have mainly faded from the memory, yet we ought not to forget that there were many distinguished scholars at work at that time. Dearmer was always anxious to acknowledge his own indebtedness to those scholars who, in the late nineteenth and early twentieth centuries, had made the study of liturgy not only respectable, but of importance in the Church. As late as the twelfth edition of *The Parson's Handbook* in 1932, Dearmer was paying tribute to the work of 'certain remarkable scholars, among the chief being Dr Wickham Legg and Sir W. St John Hope', by whose labours the correction of liturgical confusion had been made possible and who had challenged churchmen to 'set themselves in order'.

But let us return to the early days of the Alcuin Club. Their first publication was a tract by the architect J. T. Micklethwaite, *The Ornaments of the Rubric*, to which Dearmer refers with approval in *The Parson's Handbook*. However, the Alcuin Club Committee minutely scrutinized the manuscript and eventually only agreed to it being published with a disclaimer that, although the tract was being issued under the authority of the Alcuin Club Committee, the author was responsible for its details. For many years the Committee exercised tight control over its publications, with the result that there is evidence in the minutes of many rows and fallings out. Resignations were far from uncommon, and it would seem that liturgical scholarship was well capable of producing bitchiness and jealous rivalry. There is no particular evidence that this spirit of antagonism motivated Dearmer, but we have noted his long service on the Committee, so he must have been involved in some of the Club's disagreements.

His membership of the Club seems to have survived an early snub. The records of the Club are spasmodic and have intriguing (and, for the historian, annoying) lacunae. In the surviving Minute Books the evidence that Dr Peter Jagger unearthed in 1975, for his history of the Club, that the Alcuin Club turned down the opportunity to publish *The Parson's Handbook* in 1899, is now missing. Jagger says, 'Dearmer's *Parson's Handbook* was turned down as unsuitable, but when commercially published was so successful that it went into many editions and sold several thousand copies.' If there were any hard feelings, they seem to have disappeared by 1903, when the Alcuin Club published, as Collection V (that is, in its main publication series), an edition by Percy of *Dat Boexken Vander Missen (The Booklet of the Mass)* by Brother Gherit Vander Goude. These were thirty-four sixteenth-century woodcuts illustrating the celebration of the Mass, taken from the only complete edition, printed in Antwerp in 1507. The pictures are a valuable visible commentary on the ceremonial used at a High Mass of the period because, as Dearmer explains in his preface, the rubrics of the continental secular (that is, non-monastic) Missals of the time of *Dat Boexken* are even more scanty than those of the Book of Common Prayer. He maintains that it would be impossible to reconstruct a complete ceremonial from the liturgical books of this day, if one was barred from studying either the Sarum books or the monastic books. The conclusion to which Dearmer comes, on this evidence, is that the average sixteenth-century parish priest did not trouble himself about the details in matters of ceremonial, but was content to follow broadly the tradition of his diocese. Dearmer maintains from the woodcut that there is no sign of fussiness in the services and that they show that a service may be sober and simple, even to the verge of plainness, and yet at the same time be carried out with the proper ornaments of the Church and 'remain dignified, reverent and beautiful'.

The next piece of work which he undertook for the Alcuin Club was seven years later. The Club's Collection (no. X) for 1910 was *Fifty Pictures of Gothic Altars*, 'selected and described by Percy Dearmer', as the title page states. It was intended to complement the very first of the Club's Collections in which W. H. St John Hope had provided thirty-six pictures of English altars from the tenth to the sixteenth centuries. Dearmer's pictures include many from continental sources, in order to 'illustrate the whole subject of the Holy Table in Western Europe in the Gothic period.' Dearmer grants that it is unfortunately seldom that the best altars are represented. The artist often shows a very average altar because the subject matter of the miniature is intended to be other than a recording of ecclesiastical furniture. Furthermore, Dearmer's choice, he admits, has been influenced by his concern to produce a book intended to be of some practical use, which necessitated the use of 'good, bad and indifferent miniatures . . . so long as they could be said to illustrate the subject.' That Percy was proud of this publication, and that it had found a receptive readership is evidenced by the fact that in 1921 he approached his fellow members of the Alcuin Club Committee to ask permission to produce a new edition of *Fifty*

Pictures. It seems that, at first, although the Club had no intention of bringing out a new edition themselves, they were unwilling to allow Dearmer to do so. However, he pressed the point, querying the Alcuin Club's claim that they owned the copyright of the pictures. The matter rumbled on for a number of meetings until, after taking legal advice, an agreement was reached between Percy and the Committee. With admirable generosity, Dearmer suggested that the Club should have the whole of the royalties from sales; quite rightly, the Committee insisted that they should be divided, with the Alcuin Club retaining the copyright. Sadly, there is no evidence that this planned second edition ever appeared; there is no trace of it in the catalogue of the British Library.

It might be wondered, looking back over eighty years or more, why there should be detailed and intense interest in such an arcane subject as 'gothic altars'. The fact is that this was a hectic period of both church building and redecoration and refurbishing of churches. Many of the inhibitions about what was 'High' and what was 'Low' were beginning to disappear and a consensus was being reached which was able to accept an enhanced visual element in churches which only a few years earlier would have been quite unthinkable. In 1906 the Royal Commission on Ecclesiastical Discipline wisely said that modern thought and feelings were able to accommodate a care for ceremonial and also a sense of dignity in worship which had not been around in the nineteenth century. Public transport and a greater mobility of the population had opened the eyes of many and enabled them to appreciate new standards of beauty in architecture and furnishings, both in Britain and abroad. The Art and Crafts Movement, for instance, inspired those who wished to move away from Victorian gloom, not least in their churches, with a new excitement for colour and design. It was an atmosphere in which both Percy and Mabel revelled; Mabel in her designs, and later the theatre; Percy in his crusading zeal for the renewal of church interiors which would thus become 'sacramental' in their proclamation of a God of Truth and Beauty.

Symbolic of this new approach in church design was what became known as 'the English Altar'.

In 1912 Percy contributed 'notes descriptive and explanatory' and an introduction entitled 'The Present Opportunity' for that year's Alcuin Club Collection which was entitled *Illustrations of the Liturgy*. The book contained thirteen drawings of the celebration of the Holy Communion in a parish church by the artist Clement O. Skilbeck. The drawings comprise a clear and unfussy visual guide to the written ceremonial directions of *The Parson's Handbook*. Peter Anson, who wrote the comprehensive *Fashions in Church Furnishings 1840–1940*, was personally inspired by Dearmer's work and he wrote of the illustrations in that book:

> Every altar is provided with a dorsal and riddel curtains. Most of the chancels have screens. The clergy wear eucharistic vestment of the correct 1548 shape. The servers are vested in girded albs and amices, both adorned with apparels. The choir of men and boys are clothed in the long surplices. Here can be seen the intention of the Alcuin Club to refurnish every Anglican place of worship on 1548 lines. No deviations from this line were permitted.

In the lengthy introduction to the Skilbeck book, which Percy contributed, he used the recent coronation of King George V to argue for a restoration of beauty and dignity in worship. The Coronation had been performed in the Abbey 'with a ceremonial majestic, even gorgeous, and yet simple'. What, he asked, if the service had been spoilt by that 'traditional slovenliness and inadequacy which obscures the character of other collegiate or cathedral services', 'that drab formality and absence of prayers' which he believed characterized such services. He quotes with approval a writer who described the moment when a dignitary of an English cathedral opened his mouth either to read, sing or pray: 'the divine influence engendered by the architecture and the hallowed associations of the building and by the music of the choir are rather more than neutralized and sensitive worshippers of God through the medium of art go away shocked.'

How can change in these matters be brought about? By 'just what is done in literature, in art, in science and in politics, in every branch of human activity. You can educate, you can show man the beauty of the right way.' In this process of education Dearmer was anxious to include the Bishops, seeking to 'remove the autocratic ignorance which still unhappily lingers among some of our Bishops.' No wonder Davidson, if he read or was told about these sentiments, had no time for this misguided priest who advocated lessons in art appreciation for the episcopacy.

Dearmer continued: 'It is to foster such knowledge and such a spirit that the Alcuin Club exists, resting on no party, but appealing to the scientific spirit and the love of noble art and basing all its work upon "strict obedience" to the Prayer Book.'

It was a crusade that would absorb the best years of his life, and in its advocacy he could rely on the artistic encouragement of his wife. But was it practical pastoral politics? Could these principles be applied in an ordinary parish church? By the time *Illustrations of the Liturgy* appeared in 1912, Percy Dearmer had already twelve years of hands-on experience of applying them in the north London suburban parish which will always be connected with the name of Percy Dearmer – St Mary's Primrose Hill.

4

Primrose Hill

By what, or on whose, recommendation the Trustees of the Benefice of St Mary's Primrose Hill (which is in Belsize Park, Hampstead) chose for their third Vicar the Curate of St Mark's Marylebone we have no way of discovering at this distance. The parish, though, had decided 'Christian Socialist' links from its foundation, and it may well have seemed natural to continue that tradition by appointing the London Secretary of the Christian Social Union, who had impeccable Guild of St Matthew associations.

Around the 1850s two Hampstead businessmen, George William Bell and George Bell (they were not related), who were distressed at the number of ragged and destitute boys on the streets of London, decided that something must be done for them. They discussed the problem with two of their friends, F. D. Maurice and Thomas Hughes. The first of these we have already noted for the inspiration he gave to the Christian Socialist Movement. The contribution to Christian Socialism of the author of *Tom Brown's Schooldays* is less appreciated. Edward Norman, in *The Victorian Christian Socialists*, says, 'Hughes never lost his early faith in Christian Socialism and devoted a life-time to political activity to further the cause.' Encouraged by Hughes and Maurice, the Bells bought a house in Euston Road where the boys were taught a trade. In 1865 the work was transferred to Regent Park Road, Hampstead and 'The Boys' Home' ('The Home for Training and Maintaining of Destitute Boys not Convicted of Crime') became established there. By 1890 it was able to accommodate 150 boys. There was a chapel and regular services conducted by the Chaplain, Charles James Fuller. These services attracted local residents and eventually part of the parish of St Saviour's Eton Road was assigned to Fuller as a Mission District. Soon the chapel was not big enough for the increasing congregation drawn from the new houses being built locally, and a permanent church was planned. First, for five years, there was a corrugated-iron building. Then, on the Feast of the Visitation of Our Lady, 1872, the present church was opened for worship, with Fuller as priest-in-charge. Fuller was a Tractarian and his High Church services and Catholic teaching proved attractive to many, perhaps because of their novelty and daring, as much as anything else. However, there were many parishioners who were alienated by their style. Sadly, that included George Bell and most of the Boys' Home people, and there was an increasing reliance on the support of folk from outside the parish boundaries.

Fuller is described as 'a young clergyman inspired by the ideals of Keble and Pusey, and on fire with the Christian Socialism of Maurice.' Despite local opposition, St Mary's became alive with the conviction that the Catholic faith was something which must play its full part in every aspect of daily life, and not be limited to the narrow confines of Sunday worship only. Not only were the Sacraments duly administered, but also 'the wants of the needy [were] relieved, injustices righted and ignorance dispelled.'

St Mary's gained an early reputation for 'advanced worship'. By 1874 vestments and a full Choral Eucharist were in place. When the prosecutions under the Public Worship Regulation Act commenced, Fuller was threatened with legal action by the Bishop of London (John Jackson). Forced to comply with the Bishop's directions, he stripped the church of much of its Catholic impedimentation. It was only when Frederick Temple arrived as Diocesan Bishop in 1885 that things improved. Not only did Bishop Temple allow the services to resume as before, but he personally went to Primrose Hill to consecrate the church – the first church consecration of his episcopate. A good deal of the initial enthusiasm had been lost by the end of Fuller's ministry, but his successor, Albert Spencer, with great energy, virtually refounded St Mary's, with the result that Dearmer inherited at his induction in 1901 not only a flourishing and well-equipped church with good music but also an already well-established High Church tradition.

Dearmer's induction was, as such services usually were then, a quiet affair, not the ecclesiastical jamboree of today. It took place at Evensong on Friday 15 February 1901, and Percy was inducted into the rights, appurtenance and privileges of the living, witnessed by only a small congregation. St Mary's possesses a 'log book' in which a record of notable parochial events is supposed to be kept. It is a particular surprise to discover that some alleged incidents of note from the early part of Dearmer's incumbency are not there. As a result, we must rely upon that notoriously unreliable source, the 'collective memory'.

It is said that one of his first actions was to dispose of the six candlesticks on the high altar; 'burnt in the church furnace' is the rather unlikely accusation. Certainly, he wasted little time in adapting the interior of the church to the principles and standards he had proposed in *The Parson's Handbook*. He knew that a large number of clergy and laity were quietly waiting to see if he would put his preaching into practice. Percy did not intend to disappoint them. His convictions were heartfelt and based upon his careful and painstaking researches, not least in the British Museum. What he would do was entirely supported by his careful study of the Prayer Book rubrics. He would not go beyond those prescriptions, but equally, in most cases, he would insist on a full implementation of their directions.

St Mary's was a brick building with stone facings. Dearmer decided that the interior should be lime-washed throughout, but commenced by tackling the vault and the walls of the chancel and the side chapel. He took this bold step in order that the lime-wash could be a foil to the colour he intended to introduce by hangings and pictures, and equally to be a background to the vestments of clergy and servers. Dearmer's ambition was to lower the Bodley reredos. G. F. Bodley, the distinguished Tractarian architect, had designed a very fine and lofty triptych as the reredos behind the high altar. Dearmer was convinced that it was far too high for the proportions of St Mary's. First of all, he introduced side curtains and then, in 1915, he lowered the reredos and lengthened the altar. In after years, Dearmer was to confess that he probably made some of his first changes far too quickly, but it is a common mistake for priests in their first charge to throw themselves headlong into changes. Usually they decide to act differently in their second and subsequent parishes, and no doubt Percy would have done, if he had ever been given the chance of another living.

Nan Dearmer maintains that Percy's strategy for Primrose Hill was three-fold. In the first place, he introduced those structural and ceremonial changes, based upon *The Parson's Handbook*, which would produce worship which was both beautiful and dignified. Yet this was not an end in itself; it was motivated by the second and more important principle – the need to proclaim and advance the social witness of the Church. His wife writes about his disappointment, and later extreme frustration, at a Church, and its clergy, who could only focus on the external and ritual aspects of his work and witness. For Dearmer, she insists, 'beauty of worship and social teaching were bound closely together.' Even now the temptation is to emphasize, with or without approval, Percy Dearmer's liturgical interests and conveniently forget his lifelong commitment (which certainly took different forms over the years) to the importance of the Church's careful study of social questions. Though he never entirely deserted his liturgical studies, he devoted more and more time to the outworking of the Christian gospel in the world outside the confines of the church's walls – even if he did prefer them lime-washed!

The third part of his grand plan has not been forgotten subsequently; instead it has been misunderstood. Believing that only the best in art was fit to be employed in the worship of

God, Dearmer had become increasingly dissatisfied (to put it mildly) with the musical standards obtaining in the Church. At a time when more and more music was available – concerts and recitals were within range of a populace served by public transport; musical expertise and techniques were improving year by year; and new wealth was providing at least a piano in many homes – the level of the Church's music was pitifully inadequate for its divine task. There were those who failed to recognize the disgrace of the situation – but not Percy Dearmer. His particular *bête noire* was the state of the hymn.

> I will only say with all the solemnity of which I am capable that you will not with the hymn books at present in general use either hold the present generation or secure any influence with the next. While our hymns are what they are, the best and most intelligent people must go away from us. We could not respect them were it otherwise.
>
> The clergy are roundly accused of culpable negligence in this matter. 'Giving out a hymn' has always been one of their professional duties. They don't expect to take pleasure in the music; it is a noise to be made. They don't ask themselves whether the words are worthy, or are true, still less whether they can in any sense be called literature; because of course people only care for the tune, and the tune they leave to the organist.

In a series of lectures in then Philadelphia in 1919 he encouraged his hearers to burn the then current American Hymnal as being deficient in poetry, depraved in sentimentality and mawkish and provincial in its music.

Hymns had begun to appear in Anglican worship in the late eighteenth and early nineteenth centuries. Hymnody arrived in the first place with metrical Psalms, which were acceptable because they were the words of Scripture. Horton Davies says that while they did not break the laws of God, they played ducks and drakes with the laws of metre. 'The awkward inversions and plodding progressions of their sad doggerel were calculated to dampen the ardour of the most enthusiastic singers!'

At first Tractarians regarded hymns with the greatest suspicion, being reminiscent of Protestant Nonconformity. Through the work of such people as the Wesleys, hymns had become a staple of Nonconformist worship. Under the leadership of J. M. Neale that view changed with the appearance in 1851 of *Hymnal Noted*. This was a collection of translations of Latin hymns, together with their plainsong. About the same time less 'advanced' churchmen adopted other collections. These trends came together with the appearance in 1861 of *Hymns, Ancient and Modern*. This book, it has been said, was remarkable for its eclecticism, bringing together examples of plainsong, metrical psalmody, chorale and old church-tune. To this mixture was added new tunes of a distinctive type by such 'modern' composers as J. B. Dykes, F. A. Gore Ouseley and W. H. Monk.

It was this hymn book that attracted much of Dearmer's polemical fire. It was not only its musical and poetical deficiencies which he believed disqualified it for use in worship, but also the Christian Socialist detected the fact that it had all the defects of its age: 'An age with which we have little in common; the religious world was interested in its own salvation, but was much less interested in God, and not at all in its neighbour – except when he lived a long way off.'

Hymns, Ancient and Modern was first published in 1861, and it soon became something of a national institution. Even so the Proprietors, a group of Church of England clergymen, were engaged in the continual process of change and revision. First of all an appendix was added to the book in 1868, and then a completely revised edition appeared in 1875, to which a supplement was added fourteen years later. It was this edition that Dearmer and a group of friends found sufficiently unsatisfactory that they decided to get together to consider the possibility of producing their own supplement for that hymnbook. The group was an intriguing one. It was led by the Revd the Hon. A. F. A. Hanbury Tracy, the Vicar of St Barnabas

Pimlico, the church for which J. M. Neale had produced his *Hymnal Noted*, and which had a long tradition of experimenting in hymnody. Another member was George Ratcliffe Woodward, Hanbury Tracy's former curate and an early advocate of both plainsong and the English carol. Athelstan Riley, an uncompromising conservative High Church layman, once said of Woodward, 'I have never known a man with really liberal principles who was *thoroughly* sound on matters of faith.' Also in the group was D. C. Lathbury, a historian and a biographer of Dean Church.

They met frequently at first, but hearing that a completely new edition of *Ancient and Modern* was soon to appear, they decided to bide their time and await the publication of the new book. When it appeared in 1904 it proved a great disappointment all round. It never took off. Those who had used the old book much preferred what they had, with the result that the 1889 edition was republished in 1916 with a second supplement. For the High Church critics of *Ancient and Modern* there was now no excuse not to set to and produce a book containing the material they believed was needed for their style of worship. This would also be a collection able to uphold the artistic standards essential, in their opinion, in such a project. In order to accomplish the task the committee was enlarged by the inclusion of W. J. Birkbeck, an expert on the Orthodox Church, and Canon T. A. Lacey, an extremely gifted liturgist, the author of the Alcuin Club's best-selling *Liturgical Interpolations*.

The new volume was originally to be called *English Hymns* and was to contain words only, but within weeks of commencing the work it became obvious that they must abandon the idea of merely producing some kind of supplement and must undertake the much more demanding task of compiling a completely new hymn book. The next essential was a musical editor.

In order to find the right man, Percy consulted Cecil Sharp and Scott Holland, both of whom recommended Ralph Vaughan Williams. Why was there such unanimity between a

Canon of St Paul's and a collector of folk-songs and, furthermore, why should the proposal of the name of this thirty-two-year-old musician strike a chord with Dearmer? It was not because of any glowing evidence of Vaughan Williams's Christian faith. He had been born in his father's parsonage at Down Ampney in Gloucestershire into a family which consisted chiefly of lawyers and parsons, and had been confirmed at Charterhouse (he didn't follow his father to Westminster), but Vaughan Williams always maintained that his views were atheistic when he left school. His second wife, Ursula, says that although he later 'drifted into a cheerful agnosticism', he was never a professing Christian. This did not prevent him from becoming a church musician. He was organist for Hanbury Tracy at St Barnabas Pimlico from 1895 until 1899 where, at first, he made his Communion as 'part of the show', but eventually he desisted. This decision brought him into conflict with the Vicar, who made Communicating a condition of him remaining in the post – a condition that Vaughan Williams was unable to accept. This confrontation makes all the more remarkable Hanbury Tracy's agreement to his appointment as Musical Editor.

The St Barnabas connection does not end there. For many years Scott Holland had enjoyed worshipping at that church, encouraged by his aunt (Miss Jane Gifford). Presumably he first met Vaughan Williams at St Barnabas. Once again Christian Socialism binds these threads together. We have already encountered Scott Holland's views on this subject. Vaughan Williams, in his *Dictionary of National Biography* entry on Sharp, identified Cecil's interest in folk songs as a natural manifestation of his outlook: 'In politics he inclined to the Fabian socialist view.' Thus it was that both of Vaughan Williams's sponsors were Christian Socialists. While he appealed to these two men of decided views, he himself has been described as belonging to 'that small class of Englishmen who are by temperament and upbringing radical traditionalists or conservative liberals.' At that time, Dearmer would have put his own position further to the left, but he recognized that the musician whom his colleagues were recommending was 'rightly thinking'. Anyway, as he eventually explained to Vaughan Williams, they were not looking for a musical knight, but someone they knew about and could trust. Vaughan Williams described their first meeting like this:

> It must have been in 1904 that I was sitting in my study in Barton Street, Westminster, when a cab drove up to the door and 'Mr Dearmer' was announced. I just knew his name vaguely as a parson who invited tramps to sleep in his drawing room; but he had not come to me about tramps. He went straight to the point and asked me to edit the music of a hymn book. I protested that I knew very little about hymns but he explained to me that Cecil Sharp had suggested my name, and I found out afterwards that Canon Scott Holland had also suggested me as a possible editor, and the final clinch was given when I understood that if I did not do the job it would be offered to a well-known Church musician with whose musical ideas I was much out of sympathy. I thought it over for twenty-four hours and then decided to accept but I found the work occupied me two years and that my bill for clerical expenses alone came to two hundred and fifty pounds. The truth is I determined to do the work thoroughly, and that, besides being a compendium of all the tunes of worth that were already in use, the book should, in addition, be a thesaurus of all the finest hymn tunes in the world – at all events all such as were compatible with the metres of the words for which I had to find tunes. Sometimes I went further, and when I found a tune for which no English words were available I took it to Dearmer, as literary editor, and told him he must write or get somebody else to write suitable words.

This multi-talented group had long and frequent meetings, chiefly at the home of Athelstan Riley, but occasionally at Primrose Hill or in Pimlico. In 1956 Vaughan Williams was asked to contribute 'some reminiscences of the English Hymnal' to a booklet called *The First Fifty Years* published by the Oxford University Press. A comparison of Vaughan Williams's original manuscript with the printed version reveals an interesting omission. In it the composer admitted to feeling 'rather at sea' during his first Committee Meeting. It was, he said, a new experience for him to be faced by an eager group of High Church parsons.

Dearmer was the secretary and very much in his element in that role. He was always neat and methodical. Nan Dearmer (then Knowles), with her mother, was a frequent visitor to the Dearmer home, so she was in a good position to describe Percy's working methods:

> He kept his study in good order with a special place for everything. Rows of small drawers and files, all labelled, kept his papers and letters together. One foible of his was to collect old envelopes and sheets of paper. He rarely bought a new Manilla envelope, all large ones that came for him were carefully opened and preserved under the flap of his desk for future use. There was a stack of half sheets of paper torn from letters and these, together with other scraps such as the backs of old proofs, he used for all his notes. I don't believe he bought a special note pad once during his lifetime. If anyone asked him to do something he invariably said, 'Put it on a half-sheet', indicating the pile on his desk.

Many of the hymns for the new book were tried out for the first time at St Mary's. Congregations are notoriously reluctant to try anything new ('We've never sung that before!'), yet it must be a source of retrospective pride for St Mary's, and a matter of amazement for those of us who take such hymns for granted, that the church folk of Primrose Hill sang for the first time John Bunyan's 'He who would valiant be', Christina Rossetti's 'In the bleak mid-winter', Chesterton's 'O God of earth and altar' and Scott Holland's 'Judge Eternal'. None of these words had ever appeared before in a hymn book. They were also probably the first English congregation to sing the Whittier hymns: 'Dear Lord and Father of Mankind' and 'Immortal Love'. Additionally, there was the new music composed for the book, such as Vaughan Williams's tune 'Sine Nomine', which is now inseparable from 'For all the Saints'; or, in tribute to his birthplace, the tune 'Down Ampney' for the hymn 'Come down, O Love divine'. These were certainly exciting days.

In the preface to the 1906 edition Dearmer wrote that the compilers had attempted to redress those defects in popular hymnody that were deeply felt by thoughtful men:

> For the best hymns of Christendom are as free as the Bible from the self-centred sentimentalism, the weakness and unreality which mark inferior productions. The great hymns, indeed, of all ages abound in the conviction that duty lies at the heart of the Christian life – a double duty to God and to our neighbour; and such hymns, like the Prayer Book, are for all sorts and conditions of men.

He intended that, like *The Parson's Handbook*, *The English Hymnal* would raise and maintain artistic standards at parish church level, while remaining faithful to the principles of the Book of Common Prayer. In this aspiration there was one immediate problem: some Bishops objected to what they chose to call 'direct invocation of saints' in one or two hymns. In fact the Archbishop of Canterbury and the Bishops of Winchester, Exeter, Bristol, London and Oxford threatened to inhibit the book. One particular hymn, 'Ye who own the faith of Jesus', attracted their indignation. It was written by Canon V. S. Stuckey Coles, whom Dearmer had known at Pusey House as one of the Librarians. The hymn contained the couplet, 'For the faithful gone before us, may the holy Virgin pray.' Dearmer protested, 'Does the Bishop [of Bristol] think we should sing "May the holy Virgin *not* pray"?' Another Bishop who took exception to the hymn was his old friend (also from Pusey House) Charles Gore. Percy, rather sadly, wrote to Fr Adderley:

> I know Gore is a strong man and conscientious, but history is full of examples that it has been men of this type who in

their autocratic temper have wrecked the church. It is a very serious move; and must be met at all costs if the church is to be saved.

When the Primate stated that, after a careful examination of the book, he felt bound to express his strong wish that it should not be adopted in any church in his diocese, the situation had obviously become serious. Consequently an 'abridged version' was produced. It was not a success. Dearmer wrote to Henry Frowde at Oxford University Press, giving it as his opinion that the episcopal attacks helped sales, saying that he thought the public 'would resent interferences with our liberties'.

Despite all this 'scandal', the hymn book sold well, and although it never ousted *Ancient and Modern* from its pre-eminent place, it came to be used widely, not least in many cathedrals. An early commentator, the American scholar Louis F. Benson, said in 1915 that although 'handicapped by extreme doctrine, it has created none the less a decided impression of novel charm, and can hardly fail to have a permanent influence on Anglican Hymnody.' History has proved Benson correct.

If the already high musical standards at Primrose Hill, not least the established plainchant tradition, were to be consolidated and advanced, Dearmer needed to find strong musical leadership. Soon after his arrival as Vicar he achieved what must have been acknowledged as a considerable *coup* by persuading George Herbert Palmer, one of the foremost exponents and advocates in the revival of plainsong, to take on the task of choirmaster at St Mary's. Greatly influenced by his father's friend, John Mason Neale, Palmer was ordained priest and served his first curacy at St Margaret's, Princes Road, in Toxteth, Liverpool. There he met G. R. Woodward, whose family came from Liverpool. It was Woodward who managed to entice Palmer to St Barnabas Pimlico, a church whose part in the musical revival in the Church of England we have already encountered. It was at Pimlico with Woodward that Palmer began his life's work in the rediscovery of the true plainsong tradition and the adaptation of the ancient melodies to English texts. To this task Palmer brought a fine musical perception and a natural gift for language. Of his work at St Barnabas it has been said:

> With his unrivalled knowledge of plain-song and his power of training voices, which was equalled if not surpassed by his skill as an accompanist, he soon brought the services to a state of almost perfect beauty.

As his assistant at St Mary's Palmer had Francis Burgess, also remembered as a significant figure in the plainsong renaissance, and who was for many years the guiding spirit of the Gregorian Association. For some reason known as Captain Burgess, he left Primrose Hill in 1902 to become organist at St Mark's Marylebone, where Fr James Adderley was now Vicar, thus maintaining an almost incestuous series of musical appointments amongst this group of friends and acquaintances.

Palmer left Primrose Hill about the same time as Burgess and was replaced by one of his protégés, Dr E. W. Goldsmith. Under him the plainsong tradition remained intact, although one at least of Dearmer's curates thought him too much of a purist, choosing music which was above the heads of the congregation. The next appointment which Dearmer made introduced a more mixed musical diet. Even then he did not stray too far out of the magic circle. The new man in charge was to be Martin Shaw. Shaw, from a musical family numbering many organists, had given up church music to pursue a career in the theatre. He had become involved in a Chelsea bohemian set which included artists such as Augustus John, Jacob Epstein, William Orpen and William Nicholson, as well as the brilliant and innovative artist and stage-director Gordon Craig, son of Ellen Terry. For a few years Shaw and Craig pursued a creative partnership which included the production of Purcell operas, Ibsen, Shakespeare and, finally, organizing a Scandinavian Tour for the extravagantly temperamental dancer Isadora Duncan. These theatrical experiences of Shaw's were later to be valued and drawn upon by Mabel Dearmer.

How did Martin Shaw come to Percy Dearmer's attention? Shaw's autobiography *Up to Now* gives all the clues:

> Curiously enough, I mixed very little with musicians in Chelsea. Most of my friends were painters, actors, and writers. The only musician of whom I saw much was Ralph Vaughan Williams, who lived near by in Cheyne Walk. I thankfully accepted some hack work, as he called it, from him in connexion with *The English Hymnal*, and used to spend hours at the British Museum finding and copying hymn-tunes.

This was during a lull in Shaw's theatrical adventures. Recalling his return to England, from Florence, he wrote, 'Here I was again in the same King's Road and in the same circumstances. I had neither money nor prospects.' Then, in 1909, Percy Dearmer came into this musician's life, as unexpectedly as he had come into Ralph Vaughan Williams's. The story is best told, at length, in Martin Shaw's own words:

> I was now to meet a man with whom I was destined to have much to do. Through him, as will appear, I was to learn things that have been of the utmost value to me, and that have helped to mould the whole of my artistic career. I was far from suspecting this at the time, and only gradually did the new influence find response in me. Ralph Vaughan Williams, through his musical editorship of *The English Hymnal*, had made the acquaintance of Percy Dearmer, who was very largely concerned with editing the words. Dearmer was at that time Vicar of St Mary's Church, Primrose Hill. He happened to mention to Vaughan Williams that his organist was leaving and Vaughan Williams advised me to apply. I did so, and was invited to call at the vicarage. Percy Dearmer offered me the vacant post, which I accepted. It was a most tremendous shot in the

dark for both of us: for him, because he knew nothing about me and was taking me entirely on trust, and for me, because I knew nothing whatever about plainsong. But, unknown to myself, I had it in my blood and reacted to it immediately. I suppose Dearmer was the only parson in the Church of England as by Law Established that would have taken such a risk.

Although possessing no background in plainsong, for a long time Shaw had been interested in folk-song, having also worked with Cecil Sharp. Even so, Shaw said, at St Mary's, under Dearmer, he had opportunities to greatly extend his mental and spiritual horizons. He bears eloquent witness to Percy's ability to harness the skills of artists. The artist's son had rare and unbounded sympathy for the sensitivities of artists, which is still uncommon in the Church today. Martin Shaw's testimony to the widening and deepening experience, to which he was now exposed, is heartfelt: 'It cannot often be said by a creative artist of practical association with a church, but this church had Percy Dearmer as its guiding spirit.'

The musical tradition at St Mary's came as a surprise to many musicians. Shaw tells of a tenor coming to see him at St Mary's in answer to a choir advertisement. He was a very self-possessed young man and examined Shaw thoroughly. 'I suppose now, Mr Shaw, you sing *Messiah* at Christmas?' Shaw had to say they did not. 'Oh, then I suppose you do *Elijah*?' Another negative. Then, hopefully, 'Stainer's *Crucifixion*, no doubt?' Alas, not even that. 'Then, Mr Shaw, what do you do?' He replied that there was the music of the services – the Psalms, hymns, canticles, Mass music and so on. 'Thank you, Mr Shaw, I don't think I need take up your time any more.' And with a flourish he was gone!

They were hectic days at St Mary's. Percy was busy writing and editing, he had a growing family, and he had to attend to all the multifarious duties that go with being a parish priest. Changes were made in order to preserve what was becoming a showcase for the English Use, but he was not a 'fidget'; he tended to stick to his carefully researched decisions. He explained all changes to his parishioners in the *Parish Notes*, believing that he owed them this if they were to accept his innovations.

This was a principle that he held to be true both of the ceremonial changes and the ecclesiastical *objets d'art* that he introduced into the church, all of which had to fulfil the highest artistic standards. It was a stance which had the additional benefit of attracting many artists and writers from all parts of London to the services at St Mary's. One such artist and architect was Peter Anson. He gave it as his opinion (perhaps a little tongue in cheek) that the younger members of the Primrose Hill congregation were almost certain to be Christian Socialists, and possibly vegetarians. With this went an urge to live in Garden Cities or quaint little houses of the 'Simple Life' style, designed by architects such as Annesley Voysey or M. H. Baillie Scott, with white rough-cast walls, low rooms, casements with leaded lights, rose pergolas and crazy paving. If possible, the furniture would be hand-made by Ernest Gimson or Ambrose Heal and the crockery would be 'leadless glaze'. Anson had gone to live in Adelaide Road in the parish of St Mary's, and he would regularly meet Dearmer as he went in and out of the offices and workrooms of the St Dunstan's Society. Dearmer had launched this enterprise, soon after his arrival in Primrose Hill, to make surplices, albs, hoods and vestments according to approved patterns. Anson recalled, sixty years later, seeing Dearmer about his duties, 'a picturesque figure in his cassock and gown, with a square cap covering his shock of rather untidy hair. I cannot recall any occasion when I ever saw him in coat and trousers in this period.'

Anson became a visitor to the Dearmers' home, which he described as setting the pace in the domestic furnishings of the neighbourhood. When Mabel and Percy moved into the new vicarage in 1907 the decoration, furniture and furnishings they chose were all in the latest Arts and Crafts fashion. The drawing-room had cream wallpaper with nine tall rose-trees blossoming on it. There were curtains of natural glazed holland, and rose-coloured chintzes, with a grass-green carpet. It was a house in which 'Beauty was taken very seriously', Anson realised. He said that it 'harked back to the Pre-Raphaelite tradition, although with a faint whiff of Aubrey Beardsley's guttering black candles, and the distant rumblings of the revolt of women'. We can hear in his description the influence of Mabel's *Yellow Book* friends, their shared Socialist enthusiasms, and the cultivated tastes of 'the New Woman'.

Anson's discerning and artistic eye was also able to detect a revolutionary feeling even in the clothes of those who worshipped in the church which had been refurbished according to the principles of *The Parson's Handbook*. In churches like St Mary's which attracted, according to Anson, authors, artists and social reformers, some men defied Sunday convention by wearing baggy suits of home-spun tweed, shirts with soft collars and, quite probably, sandals instead of shoes or boots. Their women-folk tended to look like models painted by Rossetti or Burne Jones and revolted against fashion by discarding corsets. 'Unlike the fashionably dressed ladies with their trumpet-shaped skirts and sway-back carriage, they inclined to droop in a willowy manner, although some adopted a masculine costume, with a practical, though still long, serge skirt, starched blouse and high collar.' Many of the ladies in Mabel's book illustrations would have fitted easily amongst such company as Anson describes.

In this area of clothing, in and out of church, we have noted Dearmer's setting up of the St Dunstan's Society in 1901. It was such a success that, in 1912, he founded the Warham Guild, in co-operation with Mowbrays, to supply vestments and ornaments of the type recommended in *The Parson's Handbook*. It is an indication of Dearmer's outlook at the time, and of his interpretation of the Ornaments Rubric of the Book of Common Prayer, that the Guild was named after the last Archbishop of Canterbury before the break with Rome. William Warham (c. 1450–1532), Archbishop from

1503 to 1532, was succeeded on St Augustine's throne by Thomas Cranmer.

One of Dearmer's first actions after the establishment of the Guild was to form for its guidance an influential Advisory Committee which, over the years, included such powerful liturgical figures as F. E. Brightman, W. H. Frere and F. C. Eeles, with architects and designers like Hermitage Day, Martin Travers and Randoll Blacking. It was a work in which Dearmer retained an active interest right up to his death.

From this period of his ministry there are a number of testimonies to his skills as a communicator, not least to children and young people. Though she could be accused of bias in her recollections, Nan Knowles avows:

> I think it was his absolute integrity that mattered most of all. One felt that he could be trusted to give one the truth as far as he knew it; one would never be put off with half-truths or evasions. I believe that was the secret of his appeal to those of us who were young. The young need to be able to trust and they are so seldom justified in doing it. They are far quicker than their elders to detect a false note and to be alienated by it. For my part I remember the impression his sermons made rather than the actual sermons themselves. Some of the best were based on the teaching he was giving to the *Catechism on Social Questions*. They were simple with the simplicity that is in itself the mark of a master, they were ironical and humorous, and inspired with his conviction that religion and social questions were bound up together.

Another former member of the class wrote, 'Dr Dearmer's influence on my life began when, as a small child, I was taken to the Catechism at St Mary's. His understanding of children was reflected in the large numbers who attended every Sunday.' Indeed, by June 1901, there were 116 children at the Catechism. It took place on a Sunday afternoon, and lasted just an hour. Percy was the Catechist and a succession of curates assisted him. This scheme had a system of monitors, servers and doorkeepers, together with its own organist and an older boy acting as verger. Dearmer's catechetical addresses were factual, descriptive and lively, though couched in the style of their times. An early one, for the Feast of St Philip and St James (1 May), deplores Cromwell's 'robbery' in taking both the holiday and the maypole from the people. Another, on St Peter, concludes with the thought that boys are not always brave and that, in fact, girls are just as brave (though less strong). 'Be about your religion. Stand up for the Church before everyone,' Dearmer said. At Christmas 1903 he told them:

> Remember that it is in quiet things that you will find God. If you only care for excitement, and noise, fine things and pleasure, you will not find him, you will not hear his voice. The Shepherds and the Wise Men when they went to find him, had to seek him in a very lowly humble place. They found him, because they were good. Jesus who was born that day is near you all now. Be loving, and quiet, and reverent; and ask him to make you good and he will bless you and hold you safe.

Among the curates who assisted Dearmer at Primrose Hill the most notable was that unique character, Conrad Noel. The path of Noel's career had continued to be stormy. Eventually ordained deacon in 1894 by the Bishop of Chester, he became a curate in Dukinfield near Glossop, but lasted less than a year, being dismissed, before his priestly ordination, for preaching Christian Socialism. Noel went first to Bradford and then to Manchester, living in Chorlton-cum-Hardy. It was to that address that Dearmer wrote, on a visit to the north, asking for a bed for the night. This was not going to be possible, said Noel's new bride, Miriam. Noel recalled in his autobiography:

> It was impossible because we had no money and no credit. I did not know how to manage, but felt we could not refuse an old friend. My wife fled, quite naturally, for she said if I

insisted on having him, I must shift as best I could. About an hour before his arrival, I went to my bookshelves and took out a book to find some reference or other, and there fluttered from its leaves a ten-shilling note. It was, indeed, a godsend, and I was able to get some food and wine, and we spent a merry evening, what with good cheer and our reminiscences. I think my wife had relented and come back in time for the meal, and was delighted to hear about the miracle of the ten shillings which seemed to have fluttered down as at a spiritualist seance through the ceiling from Heaven. In any case, she returned home for the night and managed to furbish up a dainty breakfast.

It was soon after this that Gore persuaded Edward Lee Hicks, the Rector of St Philip's Salford, to accept 'the most remarkable and difficult of his curates'. As Hicks's recent biographer, Graham Neville, has observed:

> Noel seems almost unaware of the remarkable tolerance of the older priest for a tearaway curate who seemed to be more interested in the stage, good restaurants and socialist meetings on Boggart Hole Clough than the poor of Salford. Noel moved on after a year, with his complaints of poverty, and his occasional fat cheques from rich relations, and his rector looked for another man to succeed him.

In some Christian Socialist circles there was an increasing impatience with the Christian Social Union; they felt that excessive caution and moderation now permeated the organization. It seemed that often the discussion of social ills replaced action about them. One branch of the CSU was reported approvingly as 'vigorously pursuing a policy of discussion'. Perhaps this was not surprising, as many of the members became dignitaries in the Church. The CSU was losing its earlier vitality and vision. For many of the Union's leading members believed little more than that social problems would be solved if the rich were kinder to the poor. In contrast, priests like Dearmer and Noel were convinced that more might be done if the poor were unkinder to the rich. They wanted an England where there would be no longer any poor to patronize nor plutocrats to damn their souls by patronage. They sought to deprive the philanthropist of his prey, they said.

It was while he was on the way towards the creation of a new organization of Christian Socialists that Noel, late in 1904, became part-time curate to Dearmer. Their collaboration at St Mary's was to be a fruitful one and would have much bearing on Noel's subsequent work at Thaxted. Noel said he recognized at Primrose Hill not only the social gospel, but also socially inspired ceremonial. This was a ceremonial based on English medieval usage, and, during his time at Primrose Hill, he realised that it was incomparably superior to that used in Roman Catholic churches on the Continent, at that time foolishly much copied by Anglo-Catholic priests.

During his curacy at St Mary's, Noel and Dearmer spent much time together, not only in church and parish work, but also on the platforms and committees concerned with causes they both held dear. They also spent much time in the company of the Chesterton brothers and, occasionally, Hilaire Belloc. Noel prepared Cecil Chesterton (Gilbert's younger brother) for Confirmation. It was a long preparation, Noel said, in which humour was blended with a liberal interpretation of the creeds. The Confirmation service itself was not without levity, thanks to Noel and Dearmer. Noel tells the story:

> Unhappily, the ponderous and Protestant Bishop of Islington was confirming and gave the address. As the Bishop droned on Cecil's face drooped in dejection and discouragement. The situation was saved by the vicar, Dr Percy Dearmer, handing down from a stall a note which referred us to the Twenty-sixth Article of the Thirty-nine, and Cecil revived with a chuckle when he read: 'The Unworthiness of the Ministers, which hinders not the effect of the Sacrament.'

Dearmer, no less than any of us, valued friendship, and especially when it could be combined with intellectual stimulation. In February 1901, out of the blue, before they had ever met, the Scottish layman Francis Eeles wrote from Aberdeen to Dearmer, just as he was preparing to leave Hyde Park Mansions and move to Primrose Hill. Quickly recognizing a kindred spirit, Dearmer told Eeles that he believed that in liturgical and ceremonial matters, 'the truth will prevail and the present corrupt practices will die out. They have been the result of ignorance in the past: after all, even four or five years ago what else could a priest do?' Then to this stranger, Dearmer made the confession that even in his own case, at first he could do nothing except follow the then existing guides, and that was what made him look into things for himself. 'For the first five or six years of my ordained life I gave no time to these matters and just did as I was told, so that now I am not surprised at finding the great majority of my brethren still in the slough.' Dearmer told Eeles he had high hopes that the younger generation would take up sound ideas. His concluding prophecy did eventually come true after the Constitution of the Liturgy, *Sacrosanctum Concilium*, was published in 1963. Sadly, it proved to be a considerably longer period than he predicted when he wrote in his first letter to Eeles in 1901, 'The present Roman business is becoming even now old-fashioned. In a few years it will die out.'

In his next letter, he told Eeles that he had now moved to Primrose Hill, and apologized for his tardiness in replying, being single-handed and 'deluged with unaccustomed work'. Subsequently a good deal of correspondence passed between them about *The Parson's Handbook*. In April 1901 Dearmer said he was hard at work revising the book, 'in fact rewriting from beginning to end'. He did this because he had decided to put in full ceremonial directions for a Low Mass with priest and clerk, and also for High Mass. Those who only know later editions of the *Handbook* almost certainly do not realise that the original version of the book did not contain the six-column detailed analysis of eucharistic ceremonial which was, for a long period, so beloved of followers of the English Use – and so cruelly mocked by the Romanizing devotees of the Western Use. In fact, the earliest editions contained instructions on how to genuflect – a liturgical gesture which later editions spend seven pages condemning. 'We were many of us misled in the matter, and have now to correct our errors; but it is full consolation to find the Prayer Book and Canons were in the right, and that their restraint as to acts of reverence had been as a matter of fact the universal tradition of the Catholic Church.' No doubt these were the kind of matters he was referring to when he confessed to Eeles, 'My former errors were mainly due to accepting what the older directions and the Society of St Osmund told me: I now see the only course is to start at the beginning right over again.' Dearmer realised the need to supplant the old books altogether, and the only guaranteed way was to give as full directions as possible in his new edition.

The correspondence between them continued, with Dearmer describing his work with Walter Frere and the Bishop of Rochester (E. S. Talbot) on an altar book which would contain 'the Prayer Book service undefiled', but with various appendices of additional commemorations, and other liturgical projects. On May Day 1902 Dearmer suddenly made the suggestion that Eeles ought to 'come to live in Hampstead, it's just as healthy as Scotland, and convenient for the Museum – though alas it isn't often I get among books nowadays'. Otherwise, he suggested Eeles might join the London Library. It would seem that Eeles decided on the wisdom of the former and more decisive course.

Such a move was in fact a return to London for Eeles. Born in Kensington in 1876, he grew up in the West Country and only moved to Scotland in his mid-teens. An inability to pass the necessary arithmetic examinations, despite a number of attempts, meant he was unable to become an undergraduate in Aberdeen. Eeles did not allow this to prevent him attending lectures at the University, even though he could not receive a degree. He had already acquired a deep interest in liturgical and ecclesiological studies, and these he pursued with a voluntary job as Honorary Librarian of Aberdeen Diocesan Library. He was also a Reader at St John's Aberdeen, where Ninian Comper's father had been Rector – a man described as 'one of the most advanced priests in the Anglo-Catholic revival in Scotland'.

Dearmer's befriending and encouragement of Eeles was to be of the greatest possible significance for the care, protection and conservation of the churches in England. As a result of the 1914 Ancient Monuments (Churches) Commission Report, it was realised that a system of advice and control was needed for the Church's buildings and their contents. Eeles had already advocated the creation of an advisory system for protecting English churches and their treasures, and was at hand to take up the significant task of being the first secretary of the Council for the Care of Churches. Dearmer's appreciation and cultivation of the talents and expertise of Eeles, although unsupported by qualifications, was crucial. The system which Eeles was to put in place has, since its formation in 1921, prevented many an aesthetic disaster and much ignorant destruction.

After Dearmer had persuaded Eeles to spend the majority of his time in London rather than Aberdeen, he began to be very active in the fledgeling Alcuin Club. By 1905 Eeles was a member of the Alcuin Committee and was taking a very active part in its affairs. This is demonstrated in *A First English Ordo*, the Alcuin Tract for that year, in which Committee members added their personal comments on the main text (an instruction as to how a priest ought to celebrate the Eucharist) in the notes at the end of the book. By 1906 he was installed as Secretary of the Alcuin Club, with its publications giving an address in Adelaide Road, fair and square in Dearmer's parish.

September 1904 found Dearmer at a meeting called to consider the formation of a society to 'revive the principles and practice of the Ministry of Healing in the Church of England'. An audience of about 400 had gathered in a meeting room in the Paddington Hotel. Dearmer ascended the platform with a large medical textbook into which he had inserted two slips of paper. He announced that he had read the volume through and was amazed to discover that there were only two diseases in which the mental processes of the patient might have an effect on his health. This, he told them, was not now the view of an increasing number of doctors. There were also many others – notably the Theosophists, Spiritualists and Christian Scientists – who found the prevailing scientific determinism unsatisfactory. It was time, Dearmer asserted, for the Church to sit up and take notice. The outcome was the formation of the Guild of Health, with a committee of three: Dearmer as Chairman, B. S. Lombard as Honorary Secretary and Conrad Noel as the third member. The Guild got off to a flying start, and there continued to be impressive attendances at their meetings. In 1909 Dearmer wrote *Body and Soul*, which was an enquiry into the effects of religion upon health. In this book he described 'Christian works of healing from the New Testament to the present day'. It is an amazingly detailed book, which also contains insights into modern discoveries in physiology, particularly neurophysiology. Dearmer wrote, 'Religion, we are seeing, comes with healing in its wings – health for the soul and health for the body; it is harmony, balance, happiness, peace.'

This interest in the Ministry of Healing continued for a number of years. He had another spell as Chairman in 1913, but after the War Harold Anson took the chair. As had psychic research before, this later enthusiasm seems to have slipped down the list of his priorities.

5

Home and Family in Hampstead

Exciting liturgy; fine music; a growing Catechism; visual and artistic improvements; sound preaching (strangers were never let down by the sermon, it was said); all these were the products of Percy's tremendously active and committed ministry at St Mary's. Those interested in questions relating to public worship came to St Mary's, whether they were 'Colonials, Americans, Missionaries or non-Anglicans', Dr Eeles remembers. Equally, intellectual and artistic men and women, often alienated by the dullness of so many churches, found their way to Primrose Hill. Only naturally, a man of such decided views on worship, music and the relationship between the Church and social and political witness was bound to antagonize some. There was criticism and opposition in the parish, both from those who opposed any change, and from those whose conservatism was equally expressed in their political viewpoint. Percy weathered all this with humour. Conrad Noel says that he was always good-tempered under whatever stress of circumstances. Noel recalls, 'The times that Miriam and I spent with him and with Mabel, his first wife, at their vicarage by the church, are among my happiest memories.'

The parish population was not large. The 1901 census stated that there were 2,298 people living in the parish in 342 houses. Together with all his parochial activities and his various extra-mural writing and editorial projects, Percy had the continuing responsibility of a wife and a growing family. On arrival at Primrose Hill they lived in a house shared with Emily Mulholland in Adelaide Road. Next they found a charming house in England's Lane, Chalcot Gardens. Finally, in 1907, they moved to a house in Elsworthy Road which was bequeathed to the church and became the official Parsonage House or Vicarage.

The delightfully named 'England's Lane' was in the parish. It was called this for no other reason than that it was built by a Mr England to ease the workings of his farm. Geoffrey Shaw, who first assisted and then succeeded his brother Martin as organist and choirmaster, wrote a tune called 'England's Lane' for the hymn 'For the beauty of the earth'. By the time the Dearmer family arrived, there was little evidence of farming, but the countryside, and indeed Hampstead Heath, were nearby. The boys, Geoffrey and Christopher, were nine and eight respectively when they arrived. Geoffrey recalled after ninety-five years:

> There was drama, sometimes tragedy, in the streets at the turn of the century, even in England's Lane. There were the singers, often with powerful voices, men and women, solitaries, singing, 'Jerusalem' – I don't mean the version based on Blake's poem – and people would throw coins from the windows at them. And there were the muffin and crumpet men, ringing their bells with one hand and holding their wares on their heads with the other. And the sweep – always a sign of good luck – I remember my mother kissing her hand to one who was as black as a top hat and him acknowledging the tribute with a wave of his hand. And how well I remember the lamp lighter prodding the street lights alight one by one as he walked his evening rounds.

He also remembered hurrying down Primrose Hill Road past the cab-rank of 'growlers' (a four-wheeled cab) which was situated near the church, and the crossing sweeper whose top hat had long ago been discarded by its previous owner:

> That cab rank was to me one of the highlights of the parish. Maybe a hansom or two, like parched and stuck-up aristocrats, honoured the four wheelers. An old lady nearby

used to give the growler drivers a Christmas dinner. It was an event. The female aristocracy of the parish waited on them, and at the end each driver was presented with a bunch of carrots for his horse.

Initially both the boys went for their lessons to the house of a Mr Lacy, next to Lord's Cricket ground. Later they went to West Heath School and then to a school in East Sheen, before separating and going to different Public Schools; Geoffrey to Westminster, like his father and uncle, Christopher to Charterhouse. Meanwhile Mabel was acclimatizing herself to a new life as a Vicar's wife, discovering it to be a different role to that of being the wife of a curate. Not that Percy wished her necessarily to be too closely concerned with his parochial work, but anything less than clear support, and an obvious care and concern for the folk of the parish, would have been widely misunderstood. With Geoffrey and Christopher away at school for a large portion of the year, it did afford her more time and space for her writing, which became increasingly important to her at Primrose Hill.

Stephen Gwynn reckoned that a modest parochial enterprise bringing together parish and literature contained the germ of the future work which was to be uniquely hers. For a number of years Mabel organized a Christmas play in aid of St Mary's Organ Fund. These plays were mostly for children, and through them she developed an extraordinary skill in training children to speak on the stage. As Gwynn says, she taught them to speak and act 'without losing their natural simplicity and grace'. Increasingly the plays took on a new style, as she became more and more interested in the idea of the mystery or morality play. 'Instinctively now, she came into her inheritance,' said Gwynn.

Mabel's work as a book illustrator seems to have ceased at the turn of the century, and there is no positive evidence of her having undertaken such activity at Primrose Hill. However, Jill Shefrin, in a preliminary bibliography of Mabel's work published in 1999, adds a cautionary note: 'This list is far from complete. Mabel Dearmer contributed art work, poems and reviews and other pieces to a number of periodicals throughout her working life.' What we do know is that subsequent to her contributions to *The Yellow Book*, back in 1896, her drawings had appeared in such publications as *The Girl's Own Annual*, *Parade*, *Savoy*, *Goodwill* and *Commonwealth*. She also designed a book cover for Henry Harland and illustrated books for Laurence Housman and Evelyn Sharp. Her drawings in Sharp's book *Wymps and Other Fairy Tales* (1897) were her first illustrations for a children's book. Soon afterwards, in 1898, she did a second book for Sharp. Then Mabel embarked on three children's books of her own: *Round-about Rhymes* (1898), *The Book of Penny Toys* (1899) and *The Noah's Ark Geography* (1900).

At first, writing was her preoccupation at St Mary's, before drama and the theatre claimed her attention. Between 1902 and 1909 she wrote six novels, almost one a year, only failing to produce a novel in 1903 and 1907. They could not be considered great works of fiction. Even Stephen Gwynn, through his rose-tinted spectacles, had to admit that her talents lay elsewhere. 'The novel seemed her obvious field and to the novel she set herself – I advising her. It seems to me now that I was wrong, and a far-seeing critic might have detected her real gift. At all events she laboured with great difficulty at novel writing!' Thus it was first into the writing of drama and then later into what can only be called 'theatre management' that she channelled her ability, brains and energy. She conducted rehearsals, planned the scenery, drew the posters, found and trained the actors, and coped with stage hands, advertising agents, the box office, wig-makers and property stores. And all this with very inadequate means. She was a very busy and preoccupied woman.

These plays, which started modestly as parish fund-raising events, were set to grow. After a series of fairy plays, written by Netta Syrett, she turned her mind to Morality Plays. She believed that the fashion of 'problem plays' was an unhelpful one. The Morality Play, rather than showing the muddle the world has got itself into, 'very quietly, without any preaching or fuss, shows a way out of that muddle'. Mabel went on:

> Surely we are sick of all these despairing plays that hurt one's heart and tire one's head – these plays of jealousy and revenge, of heredity, vice, of morbid imagination – that are like a maze of misery, one crooked path only leading to another – while all the time life is a lovely thing, and the air is full of angels.

In this genre she produced *The Hour Glass* by W. B. Yeats and *The Travelling Man* by Augusta (Lady) Gregory. Then Laurence Housman's *Bethlehem*, followed by her own *The Playmate*.

From this comparatively small start Mabel turned to a much more ambitious enterprise. She had written *The Soul of the World: A Mystery Play of the Nativity and Passion*. It was written with great enthusiasm, but to write it was the least of the trouble; securing its staging meant the provision of money and much organization. It was no small production – it had a cast of between seventy and eighty performers. Over and above these was an army of volunteer helpers. Gwynn describes the atmosphere:

> All was a labour of love, co-ordinated and directed by one driving energy. I never saw anyone with a greater capacity for work than she, and during each of her productions her day was one of fifteen hours. But where she was unapproachable was in the gift of getting 'labour out of other people'.

Mabel founded the Morality Play Society to help produce this and other similar productions. *The Soul of the World* was followed in 1912 by *The Dreamer* (the story of Joseph and his brethren), with music by Martin Shaw. The same dramatic and musical combination created *The Cockyolly Bird* and *Brer Rabbit*. With these she returned to her special ability of providing and producing plays for children. These plays were arranged in partnership with Gertrude Kingston, a pioneer in theatre for children, in a venture called the Holiday Theatre.

While describing all this theatrical and dramatic activity, it must not be forgotten that earlier there had been the pageants. They grew out of a desire by Percy to commemorate St George's Day. The Scots remember Andrew, the Welsh David, the Irish Patrick and the English forget George, he used to say with disgust! The first was 'A Little Pageant of St George', organized in co-operation with the parish of St Mark Regent's Park. It contained a Mummers' Play, Morris dancing and folk-songs, so it was very much of its particular artistic time. The following year there were more ambitious plans, and arrangements were made to stage 'An English Church Pageant' in the grounds of Fulham Palace, the then residence of the Bishop of London. Percy was very much involved in the detailed planning of the event, and he included a number of his friends in the performance. Discerning eyes would have spotted Fr Adderley playing St David; Jocelyn Perkins, Sacrist of Westminster Abbey, as St Ninian; Mabel as Queen Bertha and C. O. Skilbeck as her husband, King Ethelbert. Perhaps the greatest triumph was in persuading G. K. Chesterton to appear as Dr Johnson.

The work on the pageants was an activity which Percy and Mabel could share. When it came to her later and theatrically more ambitious work, Mabel was engaged on her own behalf, with considerable less reference to home and family. For support she was dependent on voluntary labour, supplied by her own power to inspire and her resourcefulness in inventing means by which others could help in her project. Yet she also loved solitude. Gwynn said that she had a contemplative mind strangely wedded to a devouring energy.

Mabel cannot always have been an easy person to live with. It is clear that from 1910 onwards her life consisted of a succession of violent exertions. Geoffrey remembered how, as a boy, he had resented the time his mother devoted to theatre and theatrical things. What then of her husband? How did he cope with a wife of 'devouring energy' given to 'bursts of violent exertion', followed by periods in which she, who could always be the centre of attention at any party, craved solitude? It was not without its problems, even for one blessed with what Conrad Noel described as an ability to be 'good-tempered under whatever stress of circumstances'! In her memoir, his second wife Nan records that Mabel had great success with her plays, 'and Percy took immense pride in all she did'. More privately, in later years, she recalled that the marriage was not always a particularly happy one. It could well have been that Percy, fully occupied himself with his pastoral duties in the parish, his musical and liturgical researches, and his many ecclesiastical, social and political committees, felt the need of a few more degrees of 'home comfort'. Perhaps sometimes he would have preferred to be in his study, and amongst his books, rather than in the middle of the high-octane atmosphere of the theatre and theatre people. We have no strong evidence either way. It would seem from the account of their last days together, when both were hundreds of miles from their previous demands and pre-occupations, that they retained a deep mutual love, unimpaired by the demands of their respective careers. They are days to which we must turn our attention later.

There is no suggestion that Mabel was other than a devoted home-maker. Peter Anson told of the attractiveness of the vicarage. Not only was it pretty, it was also welcoming. Sunday tea was both a happy hour for the family, and one to which parishioners were pleased to be invited. All were welcomed by Mabel – with the exception of Percy's mother. Caroline Miriam still managed to cause trouble in her family. She was the only person of whom Mabel was afraid and in whose presence Percy lost his genial smile. Mabel tried to absent herself when Mrs Dearmer senior visited them. There was one time when this was not possible. Fire broke out in Caroline Miriam's house in Carlton Vale, and the next day she arrived at Elsworthy Road, as the children recalled, 'smelling of smoke'. She was never a popular visitor. Geoffrey, who was perhaps more endowed with the milk of human kindness than most, summed her up as a miserly woman who seemed to be jealous of the happiness of the young Dearmers. She remained wealthy and, when she died in 1911, Percy inherited not only part of her money (the rest going to charity for work among male epileptics, in memory of Edgar, a sufferer) but also her car. A Renault, it was the first of a succession of cars rejoicing under such jokey nicknames as the 'William' Morris and the 'Athelstan' Riley.

The car became an important element in family holidays. Details of these were preserved by Mrs Knowles and retold in her daughter's memoir. Her two sons Jack and Denis and her daughter Nan were often part of the holiday party. Marian Knowles, who lived in St Edmund's Terrace on the south side of Primrose Hill, had become a member of St Mary's congregation during the incumbency of Percy's predecessor, the Revd Albert Spencer. On the Dearmers' arrival the two families soon became friends. Not only are some of the holidays described in the memoir, but more recently a series of plays, written by Nan, dramatizing their holidays, has come to light. On the first of these holidays at Port-na-Blah in County Donegal in August and September 1906 they were also joined by Stephen Gwynn and his son. *The Cottage Home* has characters such as Mrs Dearmer, a distinguished novelist known as Aunt Mabel, the Revd Percy Dearmer, President of Port-na-Blah Golf Links, and Mr Gwynn, a distinguished author and keen fisherman. The following year many of the same party were dramatized in a playlet which Nan entitled *Our Little Collag*. It is set in West Lulworth in Dorset (where their holidays were spent that year). A third drama (for 1908) was located in the vicarage at Painswick, where Percy was doing a 'house for duty' stint. This time there was a darker title for the play: it is called *The Local Demon*. In between these family holidays Percy and Mabel joined the Knowleses at the 1910 performance of the Oberammergau Passion Play.

On most holidays there were frequent excursions by bicycle. Cycling had long been something which Percy enjoyed. Back in 1896 he and Mabel had cycled from London to

Beverley. After completing his Bell's guide to Oxford Cathedral he commenced to write the Wells Cathedral volume in the same series. With this in mind, in 1897, he took a locum tenens at Wrington in Somerset. Every week, sometimes twice, Percy, Mabel and Evelyn Sharp (who, with Laurence Housman and Jo Clayton, was sharing the house with them) cycled into Wells. At the end of the holiday Mabel thankfully put herself, her baby and her bicycle on the train back to London, leaving Percy to cycle back to town. He managed as far as Reading before abandoning the attempt. The venture was spoilt by a detour to see the Saxon church of St Laurence at Bradford on Avon.

A further cycling escapade was undertaken in 1899. Macmillan were planning a series of 'Highways and Byways' books to which Percy was invited to contribute the volume on Normandy. In order to complete his research, Percy and Mabel toured, on their bicycles, all the places mentioned in the book. Mabel found it exhausting because time was limited, and some of the distances were immense. The result is an amazing piece of work, considering the short time available for its research. His command of French, learnt at school in Switzerland, must have been a great boon. The book is a good example of Dearmer's ability to absorb details quickly, distinguishing the important from the trivial, and yet still write in an attractive style. He also had time to provide good practical advice (from his own experience) for any cyclist in France:

> The roads in Normandy are splendid for cycling, the only disadvantage being that the straightness of many main routes hides the beauty of the country, for which reason it is often a good plan, when time is not an object, to pick out the byways on the map. This is the easier, because not only are the byways excellently kept, but the name of a French village is plainly written up, and one does not have ridiculous difficulty (as sometimes in England) in finding out where one is. It is well for the untravelled cyclist to know that he can send his luggage on by train from the hotel

cheaply, safely and easily. I have found it very convenient to combine the two methods, fixing on the stopping-place one or two days ahead, and carrying only enough on my machine for the requirements of a night or two; very often, when a day's run was quite settled, I have packed my bicycle bag with the luggage and ridden with nothing but the tools and a lamp.

In 1902, when Francis Eeles wrote to Percy suggesting a locum tenens in the Orkneys, he had to decline because of his financial situation. 'Being a parson, it is so expensive that I cannot hope for a holiday that involves heavy travelling expenses . . . much as I should love to go to the Orkneys, I simply cannot afford to get there.' As the years went by his finances improved. For one thing, his books began to sell. He reported this good news to Eeles in 1912, not because of the monetary gain, but rejoicing about the fact that so much of his writing on raising the standards of worship was being disseminated:

> Mowbray is going to print 50,000 of *Everyman's Prayer Book*. My penny book on the BCP has gone into its fourth edition of 25,000. All this sort of thing means something and is having its effect.

There was also the not inconsiderable matter of his mother's legacy. Presumably it was in the light of both these factors that Percy and Mabel decided in 1914 that they could afford to rent a place in the country. It was a decision which certainly gave Mabel tremendous delight and satisfaction.

> It must have been early in June [1914] that she climbed for the first time the steep footpath that leads up some three hundred feet from the Chale valley to the ridge on which is the church and village of Oakridge Lynch. The house itself was thatched with grey straw – not the traditional Cotswold roofing. But Cotswold stone made the solid block of its walls, and those mullioned windows which are Cotswold's special charm. The place looked south and east

over a network of steeply cut valleys, rich in timber. All there was green and grey; but nearer the house was vivid colour – a mass of blue creeping veronica under the low windows and white pinks near them. It was an old farm remade by an artist craftsman: the garden was his creation, and the whole thing stood there a finished work – lovelier by far than any picture. Its two acres of steeply sloping ground were an orchard, but in front of the house, girded by a dry-stone wall, was a rolling space of roughly scythed lawn. All one could say was that the place was too pretty to be real.

Mabel spent a good deal of time there, Percy coming and going as his work allowed. She did some writing there, but for the most part she was ceaselessly busy in the cottage and happier, her friends believed, than ever in her life.

Oakridge Lynch in August 1914 was idyllic, but like much else, in what records tell us was a glorious summer, they were not to be enjoyed for much longer. The gathering storm clouds were those of war, and for the Dearmer family, like many another family in England, they were to bring with them many startling changes. By the time the Armistice was signed, Percy would share the grief of thousands of fathers in Western Europe in the loss of a dearly loved son. That the War would also claim the life of the mother of his children, his remarkable and beloved Mabel, was at once the more remarkable and bitterly sorrowful.

6

The War and the Leaving of Primrose Hill

One of Percy's first actions at St Mary's had been to whitewash the walls and vault of the chancel and the Chapel of the Holy Spirit. However, his ambition was to complete the task and have the whole of the interior white. He was uncompromising in his advocacy of whitewash:

> White distemper is one of the most valuable aids to the beauty of church interiors, as architects and other artists well know; and the notion that the whitening of our old churches was due to Hanoverian churchwardens or to the Puritans has no foundation. The whitewash was there before – coat after coat of it is constantly found on medieval stonework; all the iconoclasts ever did was to paint over any pictures with the white that already covered the rest of the interior. The old builders would no more have left brick or stonework bare on church walls than they would have left it in their houses: they plastered their interiors and whitened them. This whitening brings out the lines of the architecture, and forms a beautiful setting for the hangings, ornaments, and paintings.

One Sunday in April 1914, in his notices at the Eucharist, Percy reminded the congregation that this had long been his wish. In a 'wise as serpents, harmless as doves' style of remark he said: 'If I had £100 I could do it. But I shall never have £100 and so the church will never be white.' To mix the biblical metaphor, the seed fell on good soil, and a parishioner sent a cheque for £100 (thousands of pounds in today's money) that afternoon.

Inspired by this gift, many others gave generously so that, along with the whitening, the roof was boarded in to improve both resonance and appearance, and the church's gas lighting was replaced by electricity. The work commenced and continued through the summer of 1914. Meanwhile Mabel was enjoying Gloucestershire and Percy visited her occasionally, when not engaged with the church restoration or other matters. The declaration of war came as a shock to Mabel. She had not seen a newspaper, the only source of information in 1914.

> I hardly touched a newspaper. Every minute was occupied. From early dawn, when, from my outdoor bed, I watched the sun rise through the tangle of flowers overtopped by gigantic hollyhocks to full mid-day, I was busy.

It was a postcard from Stephen Gwynn, in which he laconically stated, 'There is war and we are in it', that first warned her of the coming hostilities. Even so, like many others, she protested, 'I knew nothing of European complications and cared less. The murder of an Archduke meant no more to me than some tale of an imaginary Kingdom in Zenda.' She continued, 'War! The anguish of war was still far from me. I turned to occupy myself with the plums which tumbled now with distressing frequency.'

Geoffrey, her elder son, had graduated from Oxford and was working as a journalist and beginning to show promise as a poet. The younger boy, Christopher, was in France when war was declared. He was in his last year at Christ Church, reading modern languages (both boys had gone to their father's old college). Christopher wrote to his mother: 'I am coming home to enlist. Your loving son, Christopher.' Then it was all very real to Mabel, even though she passionately believed that violence could never be the way to settle international disputes. '"Not by might, nor by power, but by my

Spirit," saith the Lord of Hosts', she quoted. 'It is a method which has never been tried by diplomats.'

The two young men, like so many others of their generation and class, were eager to get into the forces. Christopher was angry that his mother did not share his militant patriotism, but she was not swayed. 'I can't help it, my dear. I can't hate my enemy. I have spent my whole life trying to learn a different lesson.' Then she added, perhaps with a mother's painful intuition, 'If you feel you must go, you must go; it will be right for you to go. You offer your life – that is always good – you can't do more.'

Mabel wrote later that she felt Christopher went unsatisfied, and said she envied the mother who sent her sons, proud of them, proud of the War that called them out, proud of the God of Battles. Sadly she added, 'But that is not my God and my heart is heavy.'

Unknown to her, or to Christopher, another heart was heavy. In her diary for 1915 Monica Duncan Burnett (who, although living in St John's Wood, went unfailingly to Mass at St Mary's) carefully noted each Sunday whether or not Christopher Dearmer was present in church. Nan described Christopher as 'a strikingly handsome young man'. Having outgrown his early delicacy, in many ways he looked like his father. The dark hair of his childhood had become fair. Both Percy and Mabel were very proud of him and of his abilities.

Young Miss Burnett was equally concerned about him. On Sunday 7 March she anxiously confides to her diary that she had 'met Christopher who has had two smash ups and didn't look up to much'. Although she saw him the following week, she made no comment, but on Easter Day 1915 the diary entry reads: 'Christopher looked unhappy. Said goodbye.' This was indeed the day when the Dearmers were saying *au revoir* to Primrose Hill.

In the way it is with all parish priests, Dearmer had his ups and downs at St Mary's. It is tempting to suppose that so famous a ministry, at subsequently so famous a church, must have always been exciting and stimulating. It was not. With our knowledge that he was soon to be left in the wilderness by the Church, a letter he wrote to his old friend and confidant Lord Beauchamp in 1910 makes very sad reading:

> I am getting tired out with the difficulties of Primrose Hill. People imagine that I am inseparably connected with it because I have tried to make the people here do the right thing. But you don't know what it has been like – nearly all the parish is now boarding houses and maisonettes and there are hardly any children left to teach. I can't go on much longer! I am sure I ought to move. This is my eleventh year, and after ten years, in a tiny sphere, one knows one is only marking time, and really wasting one's life. And then when one is about 70, and all one's best working time is over, they put people into Deaneries, as a sort of old age pension! If one could only have the chance of putting life into some cathedral, while one is still comparatively young!

It is known that W. R. Matthews, sometime Dean of St Paul's, believed that Percy would not have been happy in a cathedral. He was almost certainly wrong. It cannot be denied that after Primrose Hill Percy was shabbily treated by the Church of England. They wasted his talents, and there is no doubt that he could have brought one of our cathedrals to life. In a letter from India in 1918 he admits, 'Yes, I should have liked to have been a Dean.' Another possibility, which he himself wondered about, was going to St Martin-in-the-Fields. With typical insight, he saw the potentiality of that church even before it was fully realised during the outstanding ministry of Dick Sheppard. In a letter to his son Geoffrey, Percy said he had told the Bishop of London (Arthur Winnington-Ingram) that he would like a change. 'I said I would like the chance, which I have not had yet, in a church like St Martin's, Charing Cross ... He said he would remember, and that he had almost given me St Paul's Knightsbridge, seven years ago.' Percy adds ruefully, 'But they forget.' As we shall later discover, the true diagnosis was not merely episcopal amnesia.

The catalyst in Percy's decision to seek a temporary, war-

The War and the Leaving of Primrose Hill 97

time change from St Mary's was a letter to *The Times* on 25 March 1915 from the (Anglican) Bishop for North and Central Europe which was entitled 'A Call to Serbia'. In his appeal, Bishop Herbert Bury set out the urgent need for British clergymen (of any denomination) to go out and exercise chaplaincies with the many nursing units working in war-torn Serbia. Bishop Bury made it abundantly clear that it was far from being an easy undertaking and that both typhus and cholera were a continuing threat. He quoted the Military Attaché who said, 'I know it would be immensely appreciated if anyone could come, and I believe be a great source of comfort and strength to those who are working so hard out here.' There was, however, an important financial consideration. 'Anyone going out would have to do so, I fear, at his own charges,' Bury explained. 'The travelling would be entirely by railway, and I think a special car would be put at his disposal.'

Dearmer read the letter on its day of publication and was much moved by it. That morning he told Mabel that he was inclined to volunteer, but, she admitted subsequently, she barely listened. Her mind was full of the problems of arranging a rehearsal for a special matinee performance of her children's play *Brer Rabbit and Mr Fox: A Musical Frolic* on behalf of the Belgian Fund, a charity set up whereby the children of England could help the children of Belgium. The next day, according to her own account of the sequence of events given later in a letter to Stephen Gwynn, Mabel broke off rehearsals to fulfil a promise to go to St Martin-in-the-Fields. Percy had arranged a service there, under the auspices of the Church League for Women Suffrage, to say farewell and Godspeed to the Stobart Serbian Unit. Led by the redoubtable Mabel St Clair Stobart, they were a group of some forty women of varying ages who paraded in the church in a uniform of grey cloth and a round black hat.

Mrs Stobart had always lived an adventurous life. Returning from the Transvaal in 1907, she formed the Women's Sick and Wounded Convoy Corps, which she described as 'Yeomanry Nurses'. The Convoy Corps served in the First Balkan War (Bulgaria, 1912–13), work which she described in her hearty, gung-ho and thigh-slapping book, *The Flaming Sword in Serbia and Elsewhere*. When the Great War broke out in 1914, Mrs Stobart almost immediately fell out with the Red Cross over the restrictions they wished to impose on her work. They told her there was no work for women in the sphere of war. Her reaction can be imagined! Instead she formed her Hospital Unit at the direct request of the Serbian Relief Fund.

On arrival at St Martin's that afternoon, Mabel was just in time for the service and had but the briefest of conversations with her husband, who muttered 'a few hurried words in my ear about Serbia, the significance of which I didn't grasp, and then disappeared.' The full implications of this brief conversation eventually emerged in the middle of Dearmer's sermon. Mabel admitted that, up to then, she had not been giving his words her fullest attention; she was busy weighing up the members of the Unit.

> I had only heard of Serbia as a country penetrated by disease that brought death to those who went to minister to it, and I wondered as I looked at them, how many would return at the end of the expedition. One or two had pretty young faces, and I felt sorry for them and wondered how their parents could possibly let them go. If I had a daughter, I thought. If.

Suddenly she was aware of what Percy was saying from the pulpit: 'This is only *au revoir*,' he was telling them, 'for I myself am to accompany you to Serbia. I have this morning been appointed Chaplain to the British units now working in that country.' Her husband's words took some time to reach her, she recalled. 'Now I know how an ordinary woman behaves in such circumstances. I just sat there with my nose and eyes getting rather swollen, and very red, and dropped tears into my hymn-book.' She realised that her husband was intending to follow her sons to danger and possible death. During the final hymn Mabel became convinced that 'here is the work for which I have waited.' As the Unit filed out of church, she went up to Mrs Stobart and said, 'This is the first I have heard of my husband going to Serbia; Mrs Stobart, you *must* take me with you – as an orderly. My sons are both at the front, and now my husband is going, I must go too.'

Faced by this attractive woman, prettily dressed in green silk and a fur coat, all worn with a decidedly bohemian air, Mrs Stobart admits that she was quite brutal. She pointed at Mabel's ear-rings and delicate chiffons and commented brusquely, 'This kind of thing isn't suitable.' Touching Mabel's fur coat, she said, 'You must leave this at home.' To which Mabel (according to Mrs Stobart) 'bravely' responded that she was an ordinary, sensible woman and could accept discipline, despite any appearances to the contrary. Immediately she was recruited. 'Very well, you can come as an orderly. Call at the office tomorrow morning for a list of clothes wanted and be ready to start in three days.' Mrs Stobart had been converted on the spot and later wrote, 'She was a huge success . . . none of her various roles in life were better played than her role of orderly in a Serbian Camp hospital.' Mabel Stobart admitted that she had been fearful of Mabel Dearmer's artistic temperament, but she found that 'this woman who was an artist, successful in drama, drawing and romance . . . kept scrupulously to her own new part.'

Later, after a meeting in which they were told more about Serbia, husband and wife had the opportunity of a real conversation.

'Well,' Percy said, 'I hadn't time to tell you before.'

'No,' replied Mabel, 'nor I you.'

'Tell me what?' he asked.

Mabel told Percy, 'Only that I am going to Serbia too. I'm a hospital orderly.'

Nothing surprised her husband, commented Mabel. 'He only said, "What fun!" and hailed a taxi. "No," said I firmly, "you are going to endure great hardship in Serbia. You had better begin now and go home in the Tube."' This proved to be grim humour indeed.

Mrs Stobart had overcome her doubt as to Mabel's suitability because of her 'artistic temperament', but she also records further concern about the ability of Mabel's physique to sustain the necessary strains and stresses of the enterprise. In this she was perceptively correct. Hindsight strongly suggests that Mabel ought never to have left England. She had not been completely well since Christmas, and had been under treatment for a swollen knee. On the night before their departure for Serbia she found that the knee was 'suddenly and formidably inflamed'. Knowing that a doctor would most certainly rule her unfit to set out, she decided to go as far as Paris and see how things developed. Gwynn records, in his edition of Mabel's *Letters from a Field Hospital*, 'There was no doubt that a doctor would forbid her to go, in her own interest; but all that troubled her was the fear lest she should become a hindrance to others.' Consequently the Dearmers drove away from St Mary's Vicarage on Easter Day (4 April 1915) to tasks quite different to any that either of them had ever undertaken beforehand.

In Paris Mabel reports that the knee was 'still swollen, but not painful, I am still lying low about it.' Two days later, in Marseilles, as she waited in bed for the chambermaid to prepare her a bath ('the last until – when?') she said, 'The knee isn't right yet.' There is no doubt that she should not have gone further, but the experience (almost a 'vision') in St Martin's lived on in her mind: 'Here is the work for which I have waited. I had no doubt and no hesitation. Every tie that could keep me in England had been cut, every difficulty removed from my path.' Even a lecture, given by a doctor on his way back from Serbia, as they waited for their ship, the *Lotus*, in Marseilles, did not deter her in the slightest. In a letter, Mabel says that he told them that things were pretty ghastly. 'He only remained – all his doctors and nurses had died.'

To add to Mabel's discomfort, her typhoid inoculation gave her 'a horrible arm', as a consequence of which she spent four days confined to her berth. Yet there were consolations for the

Dearmers. Mooring off Malta, Geoffrey came out to see them, and then the three of them went together for dinner ashore (Geoffrey insisting on champagne). Nonetheless, Mabel admitted, 'my arm was torture.' At Athens 'Percy and the Cook's man' took an enormous party to see the Acropolis, but Mabel was not up to it. In a letter from Athens, still not well, she betrays her affection for Stephen Gwynn, which he made no attempt to disguise, including it in his edited version of her letters: 'Oh, I wish you were here.' Footnotes in the book show that Percy had also read the letters before publication, so no impropriety is suggested – just a mutual, deep, admiring friendship.

It was not before 14 April that she could report feeling much better, though her arm was still stiff and swollen. 'I am beginning to feel that I should like work of some kind,' she said, giving a hint of the real 'Mabel of boundless energy'. On Sunday 18 April Percy celebrated the Eucharist in one of the hotels in Salonica, which Mabel attended. This was their last stop before arriving at the Field Hospital at Kragujevatz on 23 April.

Percy and Mabel were accommodated in different tents, because, for military purposes, the Chaplain and an orderly were greatly divided in rank! Mabel comments ruefully:

> Percy and I are in quite different *classes*. Percy sits with the great – the doctors and Mrs Stobart, and I with the common orderlies – that fills me with joy. It is like being at school – and one's virtues are school virtues, and one's sins are the sins of schoolgirls. My knee is much better and I have got the bandage off my vaccination arm. I have got a slight cold but am very fit and well.

Percy was soon busy taking services, arranging a memorial service for the British and Americans who had died there. Meanwhile Mabel was put in charge of the linen tent, where despite 'my synovitical knee . . . it doesn't get painful, only puffed', she was soon hard at work, working sometimes for twenty-four hours at a stretch. Consequently it is no surprise to read on 9 May that she admits that she is rather overworked: 'my knee suddenly got worse, and on Thursday I found I could not walk at all without agony, so now I am a poor thing, crawling and lying about when there is so much to be done'. Surely this is the point at which, despite what would assuredly have been her adamant refusal, the authorities should have *ordered* Mabel home?

No doubt Percy's return two days later from Belgrade cheered Mabel greatly. Percy was Chaplain to all the British in Serbia and had the task of visiting the hospitals and other units in turn. This involved a good deal of travelling, which allowed him the opportunity to write – always one of his favourite occupations. He admired the courage of the local people: 'They are so extraordinarily brave and gentle, and there is a child-like grace about them that is irresistible.' In an article he published in *The Guardian* he anxiously observes:

> The soul of Serbia is still scarred by the agonies of the past. Nor will it recover just yet. She is struggling for the freedom of the Serbs, and the present war is the fourth for her in three years. 'I cannot talk about religious questions, I cannot think of them now', a very exalted Bishop said to me the other day; 'I can only think of my poor country in her sufferings'. But the good future will come.

On 6 July 1915 Dearmer wrote another piece, this time for *The Church Times*, in which he described, in great detail, the funeral the day before of one of the Stobart Nurses, Lorna Ferris. In the article, Dearmer said that he was not intending to dwell on 'our sorrow at the parting of that young life', rather to put on record the fact that Sister Ferris's death had led to a unique occasion – an English service in a Serbian church. Appealing to those among his readers who are learned in precedents, Percy asked if indeed there had previously been an English service in any Eastern Orthodox church. He described the service in great detail. It was performed in Kragujevatz Cathedral by permission of the Metropolitan of

Belgrade, who generously stated, 'Let them do in our church exactly as they would do in their own church at home.' Dearmer was obviously much moved by the service, the setting and the historic significance of the event:

> The Church was arranged for us on July 5, according to the custom here, with a candle surrounded by flowers in the midst under the dome. The hearse was preceded by the Crown Prince's band, and was followed by the members of the Stobart Hospital in their uniforms, by two representatives of the Crown Prince, his Secretary and the Captain of his bodyguard, by three Serbian priests, the British, French, and Russian, as well as by other civil and military officials, the British Chaplain walking in his surplice behind the hearse and holding a taper according to the Serbian custom. The procession, thus composed, walked to the church, and thence, after that part of the Anglican Burial Service ordered by the rubrics for use in church had been said, it proceeded through the town to the cemetery, an hour's march in all.

The Church Times added a note at the end of Percy's article:

> A pathetic interest lends itself to the foregoing letter, for at the time of its dispatch in his covering letter Dr Dearmer spoke hopefully about his wife's condition. As we have learnt since, Mrs Dearmer did not last long after the nurse whose burial he described.

Conditions in the Field Hospital were nearly always far from pleasant. Mabel described them:

> It is not nice when the floor of your tent is a mass of sticky mud which gets on to everything, and when your clothes are wet day after day, but everybody has to have it and none of us women would dream of even *thinking* it wasn't nice.

On 6 June she writes a letter to Stephen Gwynn from her bed, 'as I have a touch of fever.' There is a typhus scare on, she reports. 'But now we have only a silly little fever without a name (it makes you feel rather rotten all the same). I simply feel hot and "soppy" and dissolve into tears at intervals during the day and the night.'

There was a feeling abroad that both the doctors and the nurses were having to cope with a situation for which they had not been prepared – fever nursing instead of dressing wounds. Percy said, 'What are we to do? We are wasting our training here on wounds four and six months old.' Mabel was more phlegmatic and practical:

> The truth is that it always annoys people not to do the thing they set out to do, whatever it is. We do live in odd times – the men go out to kill each other in order to settle some question, and the women, well, if the women can't be ministering angels and brave dangers, they just become horrid little cats and break rules and squabble.

Later Mabel approached the problem of war, and her abhorrence of it, in the typically oblique way of which she was capable. She was greatly troubled by the knowledge that three of the men of whom she was most fond in all the world (Gwynn was now in the army) were involved in killing and maiming others.

> I don't see you and Geoff and Chris hurt, but I see all the men that you and Geoff and Chris are going to hurt as these men are hurt – and that is the unbearable thing. If *you* are hurt you can bear it to death, for you have ideals – but they, poor lambs, they curse and rave and suffer and don't know why it happens, or what it all means. It is this madness of Nationality, this false patriotism, that makes wars.

Mabel despaired of the Serbians around her, who talked of nothing but fighting, as their fathers did before them. 'As soon as they are well, they want to go and fight again.'

News that a new contingent of doctors and nurses was due soon at Salonica meant that they needed to be met and welcomed. 'Percy is going down to meet them. He starts

The War and the Leaving of Primrose Hill 105

tonight,' wrote Mabel. Two days later, on Saturday 12 June, she noted that eleven people were 'down with this deadly fever that has no name'. However, before posting the letter she added ominously in the margin, 'We know now Enteric.' This is the first time that Enteric fever – a particularly virulent form of typhoid had been mentioned.

Some time in the following week Mabel was struck down with fever. On the following Monday she wrote in her little New Testament: 'June 24th. Burning hell. Out of the Deep.' The next day she added a pencil-written postscript to what proved to be the last letter to Gwynn: 'Don't worry about me – it may mean though, that I come back to England at the end of three months. I should be no help unless quite fit.' The truth of her condition was revealed in a telegram she sent to Mrs Knowles the same day: 'Down enteric slight very cheerful.'

At first it was thought that Mabel's attack was a mild one. Percy was away visiting other units, and it was not felt that there was a need for him to return ahead of his plans. A letter was sent telling of Mabel's illness, but this was immediately followed by a wire summoning him back to Kragujevatz. On arrival he found that she was 'distinctly better today, her temperature has remained steady.' Back in Primrose Hill, there was great anxiety. Marian Knowles was acting as the channel through which news was received and distributed to concerned friends. A telegram from Percy on 28 June came as a great relief. It said 'Out of danger' and it was followed by a letter describing plans to stay longer while Mabel recovered. By 1 July she had improved to the extent that she could laugh and read the papers. This improvement in her condition was not maintained, however, and writing on 3 July directly to Geoffrey, still stationed at Malta, Percy told their son that she had suffered another relapse. As late as 9 July Dr Marsden told Percy, 'We shall pull her through now, Padre, I'm pretty certain.' A telegram the next day read briefly, 'Relapse crucial hours', but this message lingered in transmission and was overtaken by another that told Primrose Hill that Mabel had died on 11 July.

Again, as with Sister Ferris, the Serbs went out of their way to provide a suitable funeral. There were differences – notably that this time, as Mabel St Clair Stobart is keen to point out in her account of the funeral, as 'a graceful compliment to Dr Dearmer, the service was to be conducted by the priests of the Greek church, officiating in their own Cathedral.' A chapel in which to lay her, with an altar, was improvised in the doctor's reading tent, and was filled with wreaths and crosses of beautiful flowers sent by friends and sympathizers.

'Four priests, with long hair and gorgeously embroidered robes, three of blue and one of red, said preliminary prayers around the altar,' Mrs Stobart recalled later. 'Again the same frenzied clanging of discordant bells greeted our arrival at the Cathedral; but inside God's house, harmony and reverence reigned.' They persuaded Percy to avoid the procession and the Cathedral service and, with Dr Marsden, to go straight to the grave.

> Outside the graveyard Dr Dearmer was awaiting us. It was a dreadful moment as we drew near, and the band announced to him that she was there, coming to meet him for the last time. I tried to interest myself in the fine view of distant hills, showing purple against the field of ripening corn, near where he stood awaiting us; but I saw only one figure; I thought my heart would burst. He joined us, and we entered the cemetery and moved to the graveside. The coffin, before being lowered, was placed inside a wooden case, to lessen – at Dr Dearmer's request – the harsh clods of earth upon the metal. The final prayers were spoken by the Rev J. Little, chauffeur of one of our ambulance cars; the last terrible moment came; we turned, and left her lying in her lonely Serbian grave.

She is buried in the same city cemetery as her colleague, whose funeral Percy had described, together with a doctor, Elizabeth Ross, from the Stobart Hospital. The inscription is simple:

> Here lies
> Mabel Dearmer
> of The
> Stobart Hospital
> Serbian Relief Fund
> Who Died 11 July
> 1915
> At Kragujevatz

At the base of the three tombstones is the following inscription in Serbian:

> You have given your hearts to the people of Serbia, your deeds are lit by our sun. In memory of Dr Elizabeth Ross and two nurses who laid down their lives in this city in the year of 1915 looking after our sick and wounded soldiers. Grateful warriors of the Thessalonika Front.

One who knows the language, Marina Vasilijevic, has recently observed that the inscription is in a very beautiful, archaic, dramatic kind of Serbian. 'It is obvious from the wording itself,' she says, 'that there is a lot of affection and gratitude for the deceased.' She also says, 'The graves are well looked after and on every occasion of a national holiday or a remembrance day or anything of the kind there are fresh flowers laid on the graves and they are attended by the local officials and citizens.'

Immediately after the funeral, Dearmer returned to England. By sad good fortune he arrived in time to accompany Christopher to Plymouth and bid him goodbye as he set out to join the ill-fated campaign in the Dardanelles. *En route* the vessel called in at Malta, and Christopher was able to meet up with Geoffrey – a great comfort for the brothers in their grief. Geoffrey recalled Christopher being in a resplendent uniform. From Malta Christopher sailed on to Alexandria and thence to Sulva Bay. Because of his proficiency in languages (he was skilled in German, French and Russian), Christopher had been quickly promoted and could have remained in a staff job, far from enemy action, but that was not his wish. He wanted to be at the front. At last he was given three choices, all honourable, but one led to the deadly shores of Sulva Bay. It is said that 'the powers that be' came aboard the ship moored in Sulva Bay to try and persuade him not to join the troops ashore, but he was bored and anxious for action, so reluctantly he was told, 'You can go if you must.'

For ten days he tasted battle, then on 6 October a stray shell hit his tent, falling almost into his lap. He was taken aboard the hospital ship *Gloucester* where he died a few hours later. He was buried at sea. His father received a telegram the same day: 'Regret to inform you Lieutenant Christopher Dearmer reported under date October 6th dangerously wounded any further information received will be at once communicated. Admiralty.' It was not until six days later that a second telegram was received announcing his death in action. He had joined his mother. Gwynn wrote of the mother and son: 'He, too, had followed his vision to the end. Under different inspirations, he by the broad beaten road, she by tracks that few have trodden, reached the same goal.'

Geoffrey's regiment had moved from Malta to Cairo and then on to the Dardanelles, but the two boys never met there. Writing to tell him of his brother's death, Percy said, 'He was so good and so beautiful. But we must not shout or cry: I don't suppose it seems at all important to God, as it does to us, that people should go on living in this plain.' In a later letter giving more details, he told him, 'He had no pain, and was rather inclined to sleep; and that evening at seven he died, and they buried him at sea, before bed-time.' Percy admits, 'I can hardly write about it, my dear.'

In the circumstances we should not be at all surprised to read that his second wife, Nan, thought: 'This second tragedy nearly killed him, but he was very brave and quiet, going steadily on with his work.' Christopher's poet brother expressed his grief and sorrow in the best way he knew, through his verses. The poem he wrote stands as the dedicatory poem in *A Pilgrim's Song*, an edition of Geoffrey

Dearmer's selected poems published in 1993 to mark his one hundredth birthday.

To Christopher
Killed, Sulva Bay, October 6th, 1915

At Sulva when a sickening curse of sound
Came hurtling from the shrapnel-shaken skies,
Without a word you shuddered to the ground
And with a gesture hid your darkening eyes.
You are not blind to-day –
But were we blind before you went away?

Forgive us then, if, faltering, we fail
To speak in terms articulate of you;
Not Death's celestial journeymen unveil
Your naked soul – the soul we hardly knew.
O beauty scarce unfurled,
Your blood shall help to purify the world.

Awakened now, no longer we believe
Knight-errantry a myth of long ago.
Let us not shame your happiness and grieve;
All close we feel you live and move, we know
Your life shall ever be
Close to our lives enshrined eternally.

7

Aftermath

'He was very brave and quiet, going steadily on with his work,' stated Nan, but things could never be the same; different and fulfilling in many respects, perhaps, but the same – never. It also seemed as if the Church was determined to join in a conspiracy to make things as different, and indeed as difficult as possible, over the next fifteen years.

On 5 September 1915, after Mabel's death, Dearmer returned to St Mary's. Our young diarist, Monica Burnett, noted his return and says that she and her father had a conversation with him after Evensong that day but, as we know, any attempt to return to normality was severely hampered, if not made impossible, by the second tragic event in October of that year.

Since 1910, as we have seen, Dearmer had had the niggling thought that it was time to move from Primrose Hill, but no offers or suggestions of a new job had been made. It now appeared that other than ecclesiastical circumstances were to be the sad impetus for deciding upon fresh work. No one could be surprised if the house in Elsworthy Road now contained too many memories of Mabel, Christopher, and equally the daily dangers which Geoffrey faced. When an offer to work with the YMCA was made, Percy immediately considered it with great seriousness. They wanted him to go to France to lecture to the troops. Coincidentally, another department in the same organization asked if he would be willing to go to India on a special year-long mission. He thought the two propositions over carefully, and came to the decision that it was right to leave Primrose Hill completely, to resign the living at Christmas, go for three months to France and then to India in the autumn of 1916. He made his announcement on Sunday 5 December 1915.

It fell to his friend, admirer and colleague, Francis Eeles, to give the first of a series of tributes to Dearmer. At the end of a lecture to the congregation at St Mary's the following Friday, Eeles referred to their Vicar's resignation. He said that since Sunday one subject had occupied the minds of the congregation to the exclusion of all else; that the announcement of Dearmer's resignation had come as a great shock to all. This, he said, was 'in spite of the fact that knowing what we do of all the trouble that has befallen him, we could hardly expect him to remain among the old familiar scenes for very long, with their cruelly insistent message of desolation'. It would be idle to minimize the severity of the blow which had fallen upon St Mary's, and indeed the diocese of London. Eeles then took the liberty of being personal, and said movingly:

> Of all those who are ministering in this church at the present time, I have had the longest connexion with St Mary's, although I have lately been absent for some years, and my recollections go back to the early days of Dr Dearmer's work among you. I have known all his difficulties and they have been many, and with the sanction of successive bishops of the far-off diocese of Aberdeen to which I officially belong, I used to give such help as I could during the first part of his ministry. Associated with him since before that time in a very great deal of his work, I have been in constant touch with him through many years, and he has been – I say it without exaggeration – the best friend I have ever had. When I speak of him and his work, *I speak of what I know*. And he has done a great work, or rather many great works; and it is difficult to realise what Christendom owes to him. I have made a sweeping statement. But I have not made it hastily, for Dearmer's work is known all over the world. His influence has been felt in various ways from here to Petrograd, from the Balkans to

Australia, from Scotland to California, and his name is as well known in the Church in South Africa, as it is in London. And as you know, one of the reasons of his leaving us, is because they want him in India.

Then widening his canvas, Francis Eeles reminded them that the challenge of the future would not be in any way narrowly ecclesiastical:

> We are living in difficult and anxious times, and we all know that in many ways the world will be a different world after the War. Eastern and Western Christianity will meet together as they have not met for many centuries. Social problems will be more acute and greater social and political changes will come among us than either we or our parents have seen. The Church of England, the Church we all love, will be put on her trial, and much of the world's future in religion will depend on what she is. It is, in the judgement of many, very largely Dr Dearmer's point of view that will form the key to the grave problems of the future.

Finally this dedicated disciple could not avoid lambasting those who failed to realise the extent of Dearmer's influence:

> Some of us who feel most keenly Dr Dearmer's leaving St Mary's, have also felt in times past that there were many who did not appreciate his greatness, or realise his tremendous value to the Church. I wonder if you know – perhaps some of you do not know – how many men and women, many of them far away from St Mary's, sickened at the apathy of the Church to those social problems which cut down to the very roots of our life as a nation, have been saved to religion and to the Church by Dr Dearmer? And how many more attracted to the Church, who never thought Christianity had any message at all for them? Too often people think of the Church's mission, especially in great centres, as one to the ignorant and un-educated, to those whose circumstances or whose starvation wages have never allowed them to develop their brains to any large

extent. But the mission of the Church to thinking people, though they be comparatively few in number, is even more important for the future of the world.

Strong stuff from an unashamed admirer, but a reasoned assessment of the enormous importance of Dearmer's ministry at St Mary's. Was any of his subsequent work in any way as significant as that he accomplished at Primrose Hill? Was the lighting of that particular beacon the centrality of his life's work? There is a good deal of evidence to suggest that it was; that the aftermath did not produce as unique and singular a witness as the life and worship of Primrose Hill between 1901 and 1915. In January 1916 it fell to Duncan Burnett (father of the teenage diarist) and W. L. Cooke, the Churchwardens of St Mary's, to arrange 'A Meeting of the Congregation and Friends of St Mary the Virgin, Primrose Hill . . . to express their appreciation of Dr Dearmer's fifteen years' work as Vicar.' They were assisted in the task by Maude Royden, who would certainly have been numbered among those who had been 'saved to religion and the Church by Dr Dearmer'. A devout Anglican, first attracted in her school days to Anglo-Catholicism, she became noted as a Suffragist speaker before the Great War and later clashed with the episcopate about the role of women in the Church. Enthused by the same sentiments as Francis Eeles, she wrote to a number of important Church people seeking support for an address they hoped to present to Dearmer. Some of the responses to her letters have survived. William Temple writes from St James Piccadilly to say he would wish to support a scheme 'trying to show Dr Dearmer how much some of us appreciate him', and offered to help in the drafting. Peter Green, that outstanding Salford parish priest who no one could persuade to accept a bishopric, thought 'he has done a great work and got little or no recognition.' The meeting was duly held with the Bishop of Willesden (the Rt Revd W. W. Perrin) in the Chair. It was no doubt a moving occasion.

In his last letter to the parish in January 1916, Dearmer

hoped that a successor would be appointed who would love the church and all that it had stood for during a quarter of a century, and who would 'make good many things which I ought to have done better.' He went on:

> The ordinary phrases of regret would be so inadequate that I shall be silent. January would have been the last month of fifteen happy years; for I came to St Mary's when this century was but six weeks old; we came with two little boys, and full of hope; and today I can thank God, for it is well with us all. That I know. And the fellowship of St Mary's will endure, and heaven and earth will always be met together within its walls.

Dearmer's anxiety over his successor was natural, even though he realised that he was absolutely powerless in the matter, the decision being in the hands of the Trustees. The name they came up with was that of Arthur Stuart Duncan-Jones, who was born in Oldham, Lancashire in 1879. Twelve years younger than Dearmer, Duncan-Jones started his ministry as Chaplain of Caius, Cambridge, and before going to Primrose Hill he was Rector of Louth. His biographer said of him:

> D.-J. was wholeheartedly for the English Use. Quite soon after his appointment to St Mary's, he had the notable distinction of being chosen to be Hulsean Lecturer at Cambridge. The resulting book, *Ordered Liberty*, is a cogent defence of Anglicanism and of loyalty to the Book of Common Prayer. He developed at St Mary's that close understanding, both learned and practical, of the principles of liturgical worship which he afterwards shewed on a larger scale at Chichester Cathedral.

In the hands of Duncan-Jones all would be well at Primrose Hill. Writing to Martin Shaw, Dearmer said, 'I hope very much that Duncan-Jones will be appointed. I think he would be just the right man. He wrote to me about it.'

Dearmer now turned his attention to the tasks he had

Aftermath

promised to undertake for the YMCA, first of all in France. The work there was already well-established; the Salvation Army, the Church Army and the YMCA all had tents and huts which were used as canteens and recreational centres for the troops. The YMCA huts, in particular, were not only centres for refreshment and recreation, they also provided worship and educational facilities on an interdenominational basis. Some churchmen, not least some of the Anglo-Catholics, were rather wary, to say the least. They feared the creeping advance of what they chose to call 'YMCA religion', because of its interdenominational and non-sacramental character. This was far from just, as YMCA huts were being regularly used for denominational services conducted by each of the churches' chaplains.

Wartime experience at the front in France and elsewhere radically altered the thinking of some of the clergy who went as chaplains to the forces. For many of them, the discovery of the extent of the alienation of the working classes from the Church came as a great shock. They had not realised the extent of the ignorance of the majority about basic Christian doctrines and ways of worship and devotion. This situation obtained even after many years of compulsory education, work in which the Church of England had invested a good deal of time and resources. In an attempt to understand this, the organization with which Percy was now associated instigated a carefully planned interdenominational research project, sponsored by no fewer than eleven churches. Thousands of questionnaires about Christian belief and practice were distributed to everyone, from front-line soldiers to generals, in an attempt to discover the degree of understanding (or misunderstanding) that existed in the forces regarding the Christian religion. A thick book containing the results, *The Army and Religion*, included many facts which were startling. We do not know for certain if Percy took part in this exercise, but it would have been very strange if he had not had some hand in it. Certainly, in one of his publications at the time he referred to the conversations and discussions in which he had become involved in France. In *Patriotism and Fellowship*, published in 1917, he discusses 'Questions men are asking at the front', and later, in the preface to *The Legend of Hell* he refers to question-and-answer sessions on this or other topics. One of his co-workers at Abbeville, where Dearmer was stationed for over two months, gave it as his opinion that these sessions, rather than his lectures, 'did more than any of us to commend the faith to the men thrust into the complexities of the war.'

There is also little doubt that the work with the YMCA in France rekindled his enthusiasm for unity among Christians. He had first glimpsed the potential benefits of reunion as a young student in those weeks in Scotland under the auspices of the Barbours, in the embryo days of the Student Christian Movement. Now, in France, he realised what an enormous barrier to evangelism was the division amongst the churches. He discovered that it was one of the questions they were asking in the YMCA huts: 'Why can't you agree?' He tried to explain that the problems were all man-made. He summed up real unity thus:

> The only real unity is the union of free men, who are at one without any compulsion of force because they have love one to another, and are bound together in the love of love and in the pursuit of truth. This is what we express in religious language by the words Unity in Christ; for Christ means freedom and love, and truth.

Above and beyond his cares about Christian unity, questions such as universal damnation and the worrying ignorance of many in regard to the basic facts of the Faith, there was a most personal and intimate matter (or, indeed, *person*) who was constantly at the front of Percy's mind at that time – Nancy Knowles. We know of the intimacy of the two families and of Nan's charming emulation of the play-writing Vicar's wife by her holiday plays. As a girl she had been a keen and devoted member of the Catechism; Percy prepared her for Confirmation. Her mother was so trusted that she served as the official

Thomas and Caroline Miriam Dearmer

Percy Dearmer in Wiesbaden c. 1880

Twenty Club, Oxford University 1888 (Dearmer front centre, Harold Anson front right)

Percy Dearmer 1889

Mabel Dearmer

St Mary's, Primrose Hill 1903

Geoffrey and Christopher with nursemaid c. 1897

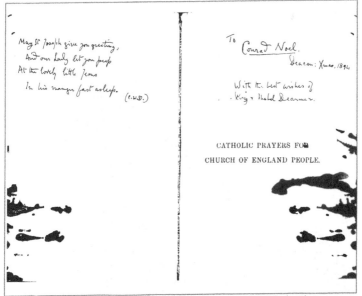

Conrad Noel's ordination present from Percy and Mabel, Christmas, 1894

Percy Dearmer in doctoral gown 1911

Geoffrey Dearmer, 2nd Lieutenant 2/2 London Regiment, Royal Fusiliers

Christopher Dearmer, Lieutenant Royal Navy

The graves of Mabel Dearmer, Dr Ross and Sister Ferris in Kragujevatz, Serbia

Nancy Dearmer 1915

Percy Dearmer 1916

Antony, Gillian and Imogen c. 1924

Nancy, Denis and Marian Knowles 1912

Percy Dearmer, Chelsea 1928

Children's Sunday Service Broadcast 1935 (Gillian and Imogen Dearmer at the back)

means by which information was made available about the tragic sequence of events in Serbia.

In 1916 Nancy Knowles was an unmarried woman of twenty-seven. Already a fond admirer of her family friend and former parish priest, she shared his sorrow at the loss of his wife who had been a very special friend. It is not surprising that Nan promised to write to Percy in France.

Nancy was Arthur and Marian Knowles's only daughter. She had two brothers, Jack and Denis. Arthur Knowles came from a family of wealthy cotton manufacturers who lived in Heaton Grange, Bolton, Lancashire. Heaton Grange, a large and impressive stone-built house standing in its own grounds at a distance from Chorley Old Road, has only recently been demolished. Knowles did not enjoy the best of health and Marian had to assume the sole responsibility for bringing up their children. By the time the Knowleses became involved in St Mary's Primrose Hill, Arthur was completely hospitalized. Nancy was well educated at home by governesses. She had no educational ambitions for herself, nor later for her own daughters. While proud of their achievements, she was anxious lest too much formal education might turn them into 'blue-stockings' – a fate much feared by more conventional mothers in the early twentieth century. The Knowles family fortune ensured a comfortable life, and Nancy was sent to finishing school in Brussels. She had one abiding memory of those days. The headmistress was a friend of Edith Cavell, then matron of the Berkendael Medical Institute in Brussels, who often visited the school. Nancy would recall meeting the heroine who, in 1915, would be executed by the Germans for helping Allied soldiers to escape to neutral Holland.

It was a brave decision by Percy to resign his living and go to France in January 1916. He was forty-eight – even had he not been ineligible because he was in Holy Orders, he was well above the age of call-up for military service. There were to be, as he knew, few creature comforts. Widowed for barely seven months, there was also the daily presence of young soldiers as a constant reminder of the bitter loss of his son Christopher.

Leaving St Mary's, he had written to the parishioners as 'your old parson', telling them how grateful and helped he had always been by 'our cheerful fellowship'. Nan's letters from Norfolk Road in St John's Wood must have served to supply much-needed warmth and reassurance for the (not really so old) parson.

As so often, the biographer has only one side of the correspondence. Nan carefully preserved thirty-three letters from France, dated between 4 January and 21 March 1916. All bear the imprimatur that they had passed the First Censor, and are usually on YMCA notepaper specially printed with the heading, 'On Active Service with the British Expeditionary Force'.

In the first letter Percy describes his billet as 'a quaint little room in a 15th century house with a charming carved front; the room has unspoilt 18th century panelling' – such architectural details were always important to Dearmer. He explains that he is only there to sleep; his time is spent at the Headquarters in the Rue du Molin du Roi. As yet he has done nothing useful except 'dispense refreshments to an endless stream of Tommies who filed past the counter and bought cake, biscuits, Woodbines etc.' The YMCA huts are extraordinarily well planned and efficient and enormously popular, Dearmer says; but the French have nothing of the sort. He doesn't know when he will start lecturing. Significantly, the letter ends merely, 'Good-bye from Percy Dearmer', though the subscription on the next letter moves up a notch to 'Yours affectionately'.

For a while Percy's letters are no more than a record of his work, together with requests for materials: photographs, slides, *The New Statesman* (with a Russian-French conversational book wrapped in it), even elastic bands!

By this time Nan was also working for the YMCA in London and there was also the possibility of Mrs Knowles going to Calais on their behalf. Another of Percy's requests was for some larger photographs of Nan and of his family. He regretted that he had only taken some snap-shots with him

Aftermath

and admitted that if he could have these pictures in his room he would 'feel a little less lonely'. Gradually the letters grew more affectionate, though still signed 'Percy Dearmer'. They contain passages in Russian, an interest they shared. The old, though not always reliable, adage, 'absence makes the heart grow fonder', seems to have applied to Nan and Percy. In his eighth letter, written within three weeks of leaving England, the tone changes and becomes increasingly affectionate, intimate and lovelorn – so personal, indeed, that even the diligent biographer and historian feels it would be unnecessarily intrusive to quote what are increasingly billets-doux. Some of the letters still remained merely factual – the ones Percy knew were going to be read by the censor. Others, he discovered, would be summarily endorsed, and not read – the officers (and equivalent) being left on their honour not to reveal any strategic and logistic details in letters home. In the uncensored letters Nan became 'my own beloved one', and the first tentative plans for the future were discussed. By February they decided what this might be, though Percy asked, 'Are you sure you are not chucking your dear self away? You are an awful little silly to marry me!' Theirs was a courtship conducted by letter, with an intensity which increased week by week, or, given the frequency of their letters, day by day. 'I can realise now how sometimes people have fallen in love without ever seeing one another, because I have fallen in love all over again with the person who writes letters to me.' Again he spoke of 'this wonderful letter-period, with all its growth and new knowledge'. The YMCA officials in France wanted Dearmer to stay longer, until about May, but his anxiety to return to England – and Nancy – defeated him. Is this weakness? he asked himself. The fact is that he could not wait to get back to his new-found love. On 21 March 1916 he wrote his last letter from the BEF: 'I am back on Friday. O how wonderful and lovely.'

As to how the news of their engagement was received at Primrose Hill, we have to rely on memories of remembered family conversations – that is, third-hand sources. Nancy was a little sensitive, it is recalled, about the suddenness of her betrothal to Percy, and there is little doubt that the engagement must have been the subject of much excited and animated conversation over the Hampstead tea-cups. It seems that what actually surprised many of the chatterers was not so much the fact that the former Vicar was planning to marry one of the Knowles family, but the fact that it was the daughter and not the mother who was to be his new bride. Marian and Percy were very much of the same age and had constantly been the best of friends. She had always taken an active part in church affairs, in later years perhaps more than Mabel, who had been preoccupied with her theatrical work. Nonetheless, she wrote regularly to Mabel in Serbia and was, of course, the means of all news. Perhaps few of the congregation realised that Marian was not free to marry; as Nan and Percy's marriage entry makes plain, Arthur Knowles was still alive in 1916.

In later years Nancy told her children that, on at least one occasion, Mabel Dearmer had told her young friend that, if anything happened to her, 'you must take him on.' Percy's remaining son, Geoffrey, admitted that he had found it difficult for a while to accept the place that Nancy had assumed in his father's affections. This is not surprising; they had been childhood friends and there was only four years between them in age. Certainly, in their letters from India to Mrs Knowles after their wedding, Nan and Percy expressed concern about Geoffrey. There was a long period in which the newly-married couple did not hear from Geoffrey, despite regularly writing to him. It was quite a few months before normal communications were resumed.

As was customary for a young woman of her class, Nancy was not engaged in any gainful occupation. Alongside her work for her parish church, she was also involved in other Church organizations such as the Anglican Fellowship. This was a gathering of able men and women who acted as what we might now call 'a think-tank' for those of a radical mind within the Church of England. For a while it was influential in

Church affairs. The founder, first Secretary and then Chairman, was Tissington Tatlow, now remembered for his work as General Secretary of the Student Christian Movement. Tatlow was succeeded as Secretary by Archie Turner, a Fellow of Trinity College, Cambridge. Turner was very much attracted to Nancy. Reading between the lines of Percy's letters to Nancy, it is probable that Turner had asked her to marry him. About 1916 Nancy took over as Secretary and befriended William Temple and his wife who were much engaged in the fellowship. She was involved in a 'gallant attempt to launch a new kind of Anglican weekly – the *Challenge*'. Temple was editor and Dearmer an enthusiastic supporter. The subject crops up in the letters in early 1916. It was because of this joint work and friendship that Nancy and Percy asked Temple to conduct their marriage in August 1916 at St James's Piccadilly. It was a quiet, wartime wedding, Nancy said, with just a few friends and relations present. She was at pains to point out that so early a date for the wedding was necessitated by Percy's agreed journey to India in October for the YMCA.

The newly-marrieds spent their honeymoon at Oakridge Lynch. It might be thought a surprising choice, remembering Mabel's deep emotional attachment to the house; of it Gwynn said, 'She had taken root, she had utterly and unretrievably lost her heart to the place.' Part of the explanation must be that, having left Primrose Hill Vicarage, Percy had no other home to offer his bride. It was no doubt in order that the newly married couple should really feel the cottage was home, that Mrs Knowles purchased it for them as a wedding present. The cottage had been let from the artist-craftsman Alfred Powell and his wife Louise, who painted pottery and china. It remained a place of retreat and renewal for the Dearmers for many more years, until eventually it was sold in 1931.

On 13 October 1916 Nan (so she preferred to be known) and Percy set sail for India on the P & O liner *Kashmir*. Stealing out to sea in complete darkness, mindful of wartime dangers, they commenced a life together very different from that which Percy had known at Primrose Hill. The succeeding years were multi-faceted, often intriguing and nearly always qualifying for that over-used word, 'interesting'. They were to be years spent mainly outside or, at best, on the fringes of the official structures of the Church of England. Many friends and admirers were angry that Percy seemed to have been forgotten, or judged too radical and over-critical of many things in the post-War Church. Certainly, like others who had come through the profound experience of the War, he believed that the Church was being presented with an opportunity which it would ignore at its peril. A number of ex-chaplains, some of whom Dearmer had worked with, compiled a series of essays which summed up the mood of many who had seen active service. These men had heard the surprising and demanding ignorance of many of the soldiers, as well as their appeals for help and guidance in that ignorance. Their prognostications for the future life of the Church were grim indeed, unless it was willing to value what had 'come out of the furnace'. Indeed, they chose as the title of their book *The Church in the Furnace*, and wrote:

> The test has been sterner than any of us can have foreseen. The results we can scarcely formulate yet, as we look forward to returning to the old surroundings. But one thing is certain: we can never again be content with much that we accepted as quite natural in those far-away days before we came out here. We have seen visions and dreamed dreams, and to forget them or to refuse to act upon them would be treachery to the Church we love. Hope and faith have been saved in the trenches, but they have passed through a burning furnace; and there must needs be a difference, made manifest in the fiery process. 'The day' has 'declared it'. They have been 'saved, so as by fire'.

8

The Wandering Scholar

The temptation was to entitle this chapter 'The Wilderness Years', but that must be resisted – for they were years of achievement for Percy Dearmer. That achievement was to be mainly outside the secure and structured boundaries of the Church of England; it was work and activity which does not fit easily into an entry in *Crockford's Clerical Directory*.

For two and a half years the Dearmers were out of England, journeying in India, Burma, Japan and, finally, the United States. The memoir that Nan produced in 1941, after Percy's death, includes what is a travelogue of these exciting days immediately following their marriage. Those pages were based on an even more detailed account of their movements contained in almost daily diary-letters which Nan (and just occasionally Percy) sent to her mother, Marian Knowles. The letters are bound and preserved in the British Library.

In India, where they went first of all, Percy worked for the YMCA, as he had in France. They landed in Bombay on All Saints' Day 1916 and spent the first two months touring in South India, centred around Madras, where Percy was lecturing. Moving on from there, after three days and nights on a train they arrived in Agra for Christmas. Nan wrote to her mother, 'Percy is so happy here, he goes about with a beaming smile.' The following six weeks were spent on a Mission to the Troops, visiting Bombay, then up to Peshawar on the North-West Frontier, then, by stages, back to Calcutta and Delhi. In New Delhi, to Percy's evident delight, they met Edwin Lutyens, who showed them his plans which eventually resulted in his masterpiece, the Viceroy's House. The next stop was Burma, where he found the Diocese of Rangoon 'very good – they are broadminded and tolerant, and Churchmen remember that Dissenters are Christians and co-operate with them.' He wished, he said, that every curate could be sent abroad for five years, in order to have his eyes opened. They returned to Calcutta, where they visited the Oxford Mission.

Next they had a well-deserved holiday in Kashmir before travelling to Simla, where Percy spent two months preparing for the work he had promised to do as Lecturer in English at St Stephen's College, Delhi, starting in September 1917. Nan was glad of the rest and the relief from travelling. She was pregnant. Delhi was enjoyable, and they met up with many old friends and made new ones. On one occasion Professor Rudra, the College Principal, brought Mahatma Gandhi to their bungalow for a chat.

On 19 January 1918 their first child, Gillian, was born, and was baptized in St Stephen's Delhi a few weeks later. The plan was for them to leave India in March on the way to the USA, but the boat they were booked on was commandeered by the authorities for war work. Nan and Percy were keen to take their baby out of the increasing heat of Delhi. It was suggested that they should travel via Singapore, and they were told of a sailing from Colombo in Ceylon, which they joined. They arrived off Singapore on 6 April 1918. Then followed an alarming experience for both parents and child. The ship had anchored at night off Singapore, expecting to dock the next morning. At about 11 o'clock a tremendous storm blew up, striking the ship, which already had a list. They feared it would turn turtle. Nan wrote to her mother of their ordeal:

> We had gone to bed early and when we were summoned on deck there was no time to dress. We only had time to roll Gillian in a shawl and blankets and to collect our life-belts. After some delay we were got into boats, all the time expecting the ship to roll over, but, as we heard afterwards, she had struck a sand bank. We spent the night tossing about in

drenching rain, waiting to be picked up; fortunately it was very hot.

At 5.30 in the morning they were rescued and taken ashore. Apart from stiffness and bruises, they were none the worse – even baby Gillian. Now the best traditions of the Parish Pump took up the story. By the time the news got around Primrose Hill, it had been extensively, and most elaborately, embroidered, with a climax in which Percy swam to the shore holding the baby between his teeth!

From Singapore they sailed to Hong Kong, thence to Japan. There they stayed for six weeks, combining work and holiday, before leaving for San Francisco, arriving – at last – at the end of June.

It was not the west coast of America for which they were bound – they were going to the other side of the nation, to Connecticut. Dearmer had an invitation to Berkeley Divinity School, then located in Middletown. At a conference at Swanwick in June 1914 Dearmer had met, for the first time, William Palmer Ladd, who was then Professor of Church History at Berkeley Divinity School. Ladd was the first prominent leader of the modern liturgical movement in the Episcopal Church in America. In 1917, while still Principal-Elect, he wrote to Percy in India, inviting him to spend some time at Berkeley as a special lecturer. It was not just their shared interest in liturgy that prompted Ladd's invitation, but the fact that they were in agreement about what they believed about the future of Anglican worship. Ladd had made a negative appraisal of the Oxford Movement, going as far as describing its legacy as 'an evil heritage'. In his opinion, Anglo-Catholics had abandoned Anglican tradition by distorting what Ladd believed was its authentic eucharistic theology and practice. Dearmer had found a true soul-mate in the man who could write, in his *Prayer Book Interleaves*:

> They [the Ritualists] made eucharistic worship individual rather than corporate. They brought back to ghastly life all the medieval and Reformation metaphysical wrangles over

the manner of the presence. They took as their standard first the Sarum Use, then the degenerate, legalistic ritual and ceremonial of the Church of Rome, and tried to force the Prayer Book into that procrustean bed.

It has been said that Ladd influenced the Episcopal Church not so much through his writings, as through his leadership of the Berkeley Divinity School. In this context it is of great interest that one of Ladd's earliest appointments to the faculty of the School was this wandering English scholar who had an equally 'High' doctrine of Christian worship – 'High', that is, in its potentiality for good, both for the Church and the world; never a self-regarding, pietistic, 'makes me feel better' sort of worship. Dearmer says in *The Church at Prayer*:

> Here is the instrument of the Kingdom of Heaven, faulty in its working as we all admit, but deep-rooted in tradition and full of enormous potentiality. There is nothing on the remotest horizon that can take its place. And even as it is, the church is a home where we are presented with a different ideal from that of the world with its hard self-seeking: it is a place where men are pledged to charity, pledged to self-offering, pledged to co-operation with the will of God; it is a place where millions are still converted from evil, stirred to personal endeavour, inspired by the thought of great enterprise, and where many are finding at this moment the inspiration which is leading them to a crusade for the Kingdom of Heaven.

The Dearmers stayed in Connecticut from July 1918 until February 1919, throwing themselves into the life and work of the Divinity School with characteristic enthusiasm. Later Dr Ladd remembered how Percy even found time to give public lectures for the people of Middletown, to help design and furnish an oratory at the School, and generally to make a great impression. In fact, the idea of inviting distinguished English clergymen to Berkeley on a regular basis was born out of Dearmer's visit, and has continued to the present day.

When they arrived back in England, they had only Oakridge to go to, but it was too far out in the country. Their need was to be in London to see family and friends – and for Percy to commence new work. Solving the accommodation question was not at all easy. Mrs Knowles had given up her house and was living in Harley Street with her friend Dr Jane Walker. It had been hoped that Emily Mulholland might come to the rescue as she had done twice before, but she was unwell (the 'flu epidemic was raging). It was to a small hotel behind Langham Place that Nan, Percy and Gillian had to go.

As far as a job for Percy was concerned, the Church of England made no suggestions. Percy had said in 1915 that the kind of job that he fancied was something akin to St Martin-in-the-Fields. In a letter to Nan from France, written before they had married, he had said he would ideally like 'a place like St Martin's, with a house that one could turn into offices and enough money for an efficient staff.' Sadly, none of this was on offer. Dick Sheppard had returned from his wartime chaplaincy duties full of fire and determination not only for St Martin's but for the work of the Life and Liberty Movement. There was just one possibility on the horizon, and that through the good offices of an old Oxford friend, Ronald Burrows. Dearmer had written to Burrows from America, telling him that he had absolutely no prospects of work when he arrived home.

Ronald Montagu Burrows was the first lay Principal of King's College London. Hitherto a priest had combined the offices of Principal and Dean. However, after A. C. Headlam had resigned in 1912 to take up the position of Regius Professor of Divinity at Oxford, there had been a separation of the two roles. Burrows became Principal and Alfred Caldecott became Dean. Caldecott was followed by W. R. Matthews in 1918. After taking a double first at Oxford, Burrows had lectured at Glasgow and Cardiff and went to King's from a Chair in Greek at Manchester.

Burrows was a committed churchman who felt for his priestly friend in his dilemma, and thought he could provide at least a partial solution. He came up with the idea of a Chair of Church Art at King's. There had been discussion between Burrows and Matthews about founding a professorship in Church Music, and it was now suggested that, in harmony with this, there might be another Chair in Church Art. Burrows wrote to persuade Dearmer to consider the possibility:

> I very strongly put it to you that if such a Chair was offered to you it would be an ideal thing for you. As you know, I am convinced that Art is your real subject, and whereas you might make a good competent Professor in other subjects, you would on this have the chance of being the leading expert in the Kingdom. I think that you will find plenty of scope for your general views on life by grouping them around Art, and of course if you were a Professor at the College where your lectures would be on week-days, you would have plenty of opportunity of preaching on other subjects on Sundays.

Being an old friend, Burrows was able to speak frankly about money. He warned Percy that most probably, at any rate to start with, the post would be unpaid. 'Please be frank in regard to this in your answer.' Dearmer hardly hesitated and cabled his agreement from Middletown. The Principal had explained that all Theological Professors had a definite and formal method of appointment through an Advisory Board consisting of Members of the College and outside experts. Such a committee (the Committee of the Council on the Chair of Ecclesiastical Art) met under Matthews's chairmanship on 28 February 1919 and decided to seek the advice of W. St John Hope, Professor Selwyn Image, the Revd Dr Frere and the Revd Dr Brightman. There was one other candidate (otherwise unidentified), 'D. Atkinson'.

Favourable replies presumably having been received, on 20 March the Committee resolved to appoint Percy Dearmer as Professor of Ecclesiastical Art (the title had changed since the original suggestion made by Burrows and Matthews). The terms were:

1. An honorarium of £50 p. a.
2. The appointment to be for five years commencing 19 October 1919.
3. Duties: to give general lectures on Ecclesiastical Art and conduct classes for more advanced students.

This recommendation of the Committee went next to the Theological Professorial Board and the College Council for their approval. Incidentally, the funds for a Professor of Ecclesiastical Music were never found, so that Chair was never established.

It was the beginning of a long and happy association with King's which continued right up to Dearmer's death. His lectures were popular and well attended. Some were open to the general public. The College historian, Dr Gordon Huelin, says some of his lantern lectures were 'immensely popular, to which elderly ladies came and fought to get into the front row'. This favourable acceptance of the lectures persuaded the College to widen their scope and appoint Percy to a lectureship in Classical and Medieval Art for the whole College, not just for Theological students. In October 1928 he was appointed to the Theological Professorial Board and he served the College in other ways, a fact recognized by his election to the College Fellowship.

In 1932, after his appointment to Westminster Abbey, the Theological Professorial Board minutes note that he had decided to terminate his duties as Lecturer in Art, since he was not in the best of health, 'but wishes to continue his association with the Theological Department'. He retained his Chair in Ecclesiastical Art until his death. Richard Hanson, Dean of King's (1932–45), wrote, 'He identified with all the College's interests and was respected and beloved by a long line of students.' His own enthusiasm for his King's lectures (he gave ten per term) was such that family holidays were often planned around the acquiring of new photographs which could be made into slides, and the filling of many notebooks in coloured inks, with his own system of 'semi-shorthand'.

King's provided some of the companionship that an ecclesiastical appointment appropriate to his gifts and abilities (most probably membership of a cathedral chapter) would have provided. Among those with whom he worked and talked were Clement Rogers, who taught liturgy, Charles Gore, Professor of Dogmatic Theology, F. R. Barry and Walter Matthews. He had hoped that going to King's would enable him to renew his friendship with Ronald Burrows; unfortunately Burrows became ill in Percy's first term and died in May 1920.

The student world continued to interest him. Building on his involvement in the inception of SCM, and on his friendship with Tissington Tatlow, he was always ready to accept invitations to speak at Swanwick conferences and other student gatherings. Nan Dearmer says that, in the post-War years, he seemed keen to redirect the energies that he had expended earlier on such causes as the Guild of St Matthew and the CSU into support for students and their welfare. Students, she believed, replaced dock strikers, 'sweated' factory workers and voteless women, in his continuing concern for those whom he believed society was not treating even-handedly. Some do not see this as a fair exchange of idealisms, and assert that he had really lost his radical enthusiasms. When we examine some of his other post-War preoccupations, we soon discover that such an assessment is inaccurate. He retained his typical attitude of questioning liberalism in a number of areas, not least theological and sociological.

9

The Church and Art

The work at King's College London was most enjoyable. Burrows was right in thinking that Ecclesiastical Art was Percy's subject and that he could group around it many of his other interests. Not everyone thought he could ever attain the Principal's other suggested putative title: 'the leading expert in the Kingdom' on Church Art. That was something of an exaggeration and a claim that Dearmer never made for himself.

It must be acknowledged that through his work – mainly the various editions of *The Parson's Handbook* and also the practical working out of its principles at Primrose Hill – Percy Dearmer introduced hundreds of clergy and interested lay people to aesthetic ideals which they would never otherwise have thought applied to churches and their furnishings. It is with regard to various details connected with that aim that Dearmer's detractors have concentrated their energies.

The Alcuin Club was formed, in the first place, to offset the influence of those heirs of the Oxford Movement who were intent on 'Romanizing' both their Church and her ornaments and liturgy. Although not a founder member of the Club, Dearmer quickly recognized its potentiality in regard to his own work. His enthusiasm was not welcomed by some members. It is said that it was because of Dearmer that Dr Legg resigned from the Club (although Legg has been described as always quarrelsome and acidulous). Another consistent critic of Dearmer was the distinguished architect Ninian Comper.

From a distance of one hundred years, and considering the scant regard in many places today for those things which

Comper, Legg and Dearmer held dear, it is difficult to recreate the intensity of their disagreement. Even Anthony Symondson SJ, the architectural historian, who is convinced of Comper's immense stature as an artist and as an architect, admits that it is a 'dusty controversy'. The facts are that by the time Dearmer produced the first edition of *The Parson's Handbook*, there were those who had already enunciated the principles which he then introduced to a wider public. Dearmer was in this matter more of a pragmatic popularizer than an innovator, and never claimed otherwise. Comper himself had delivered and published a ground-breaking monograph, *Practical Consideration on the Gothic or English Altar and certain dependent Ornaments* in 1893, to which he added further thoughts over the years. This was six years before Dearmer's *Handbook* made the researches of liturgical scholars easily accessible, and while he was still in thrall, as he later admitted, to much of the Romanizing influence of the Anglo-Catholics. It is clear that it was the arguments and evidence of such people as Legg and Comper that set Dearmer researching in the British Museum. In his own first major survey after *The Parson's Handbook*, *Fifty Pictures of Gothic Altars* (published by the Alcuin Club in 1910), Dearmer pays them tribute. He says, 'the best account of the treatment of the altar in Gothic art is Mr J. N. Comper's *Practical Considerations*', and also states that Dr Legg's various articles 'contain several valuable illustrations, and should also be referred to'.

There was another bone of contention. It would seem that some, while acknowledging Dearmer's skills as a popularizer, believed that he did not always maintain professional scruples. Comper put it thus:

> I think *The Parson's Handbook* may be taken as the most characteristic expression of the change in the Ecclesiological Movement after its first fifty years, when a new phase began, at once more technical and less spiritual. It was no longer out to suffer for the truth but gain by it. It had

a most fatal effect upon architecture, leading to commercial degradation to the level of the church furnisher.

It was this perceived commercialism which had Dearmer's detractors on the raw. Anthony Symondson SJ says:

> What pained these scholars was what they regarded as (a) commercialism (it was Dearmer who suggested that the Alcuin Club's authors should be paid and it was he who established the St Dunstan's Society and the Warham Guild to commercially produce medieval church furniture); (b) vulgarization (c) plagiarism (d) dilution (by wrenching their principles from an Anglo-Catholic context and effectively reducing them to aesthetics). All of this was, of course, seen from a narrow viewpoint, but it explains the coolness that grew between the protagonists.

It would appear that this was not the whole story. There was another kind of division between them which seems likely to have been a crucial factor in the breakdown of relationships. It was not a theological or an aesthetic difference, but a political one. Symondson acutely identifies the stumbling-block. He points out that what probably compounded all other factors was Dearmer's Socialism. 'To describe the school of Legg as reactionary would be an understatement,' he writes. 'They had no sympathy for social justice; the *status quo* was all that was necessary; they saw the liturgy in spiritual terms and the same applied to the Kingdom of Heaven.' They would have had little sympathy for Dearmer's 'purple passage', quoted in a previous chapter, about the priest standing in a 'sweated' pulpit wearing both clothes and robes which were equally products of unfair conditions. As to the charge of commercialism, that is demonstrably quite unjust. He was keen to encourage original designs as his own comments in the first edition of *The Parson's Handbook* bear witness:

> The Church has almost entirely failed to call to her service the great artists and craftsmen of which the last generation produced so large a number.

For Dearmer 'art' was an omnibus word applicable to many aspects of life. In his early ministry he constantly pleaded on behalf of those driven away from the Church on aesthetic grounds. There were those in the Church who had accepted the argument on behalf of music, but stopped there. Music, Dearmer realised, was in a more fortunate position than other arts because it was recognized that bad music drove away people with sensitive ears. Attempting to redress the balance on behalf of the visual arts, Dearmer argued that it was not recognized that people with sensitive eyes are driven away 'by the excruciating faults from which very few of our churches are free'.

Throughout his life Dearmer regularly turned his mind both to the problems of church art (or art in church) and to the more basic issue of the power of art and beauty to reveal God. He edited a series of books entitled *Arts of the Church* between 1908 and 1915. They were intended, Dearmer wrote, 'to provide information in an interesting form about the various arts which have clustered around the public worship of God in the Church of Christ'. They were for the average intelligent man who had not had time to study all these matters for himself. They avoided technicalities, while endeavouring to 'present the facts with a fidelity which will not, it is hoped, be unacceptable to the specialist'. Doubtless Dearmer's critics raised the cry of 'popularism' over this series. His own volume in the series is familiar Dearmer ground: *The Ornaments of the Minister* (1908). It was produced in a new edition in 1920, with a preface written from Oakridge, and illustrated by the photographs of Violet K. Blaiklock, one of his Primrose Hill parishioners. Many of these pictures became familiar from their inclusion in later editions of *The Parson's Handbook*. The 1920 edition of *Ornaments* contained an extra chapter for which Dearmer acknowledged the assistance of F. E. Brightman – a reminder that he was still in touch with the world of academic liturgical scholarship.

After the War Percy produced two further books in which

the emphasis was wider than either church art or ecclesiastical vesture. The first is *Art and Religion* (1924), in which he offered the dictum, 'The artist responds to the glory of God, to the beauty of God and to the divine goodness which he interprets in terms of beauty.' He argued that we need the help of the artist to get us straight, to restore our balance, to help to attain to the complete image of God. That same year, Percy edited a book of essays from the growing SCM Press, *The Necessity of Art*. This collection was an attempt both to increase among artists the sense of their high vocation and to further in the world at large the conviction which Dearmer believed to be already widespread, that art is necessary to the spiritual life. He himself contributed, besides a preface, two essays – one on 'Christianity and Art' and another on 'The Doctrine of Values'. He maintained in the latter that there is a universal conviction that goodness is beautiful, that beauty is good and that truth is beauty. He dared to point out that, for this, it is hard to avoid the word 'trinity', and that if we are theists we cannot but say that such a 'trinity' must be a manifestation of the one God. In his preface Dearmer declared his credo:

> We are less tempted today to regard the arts as a mere pastime; we are discovering that in them we touch the eternal world – that art is, in fact, religious. The object of art is not to give pleasure as our fathers assumed, but to express the highest spiritual realities. Art is not only delightful; it is necessary.

Though always anxious to promote the spiritual values of the visual arts, he never turned his back on the religious significance of music. As early as 1899, Dearmer had said he believed that the importance of getting music in church right was widely appreciated. This did not mean that he was of the opinion that this was always achieved – far from it. He inherited a sound musical tradition at St Mary's but had consistently sought to improve the standard. In this he had been fortunate to have major support from his organist, Martin

Shaw. Writing to Shaw on leaving Primrose Hill, Dearmer warned him that when he had his next church he would be poaching him so that they could work together again. That opportunity never arose in quite the way that he had then in mind, but they were to work together in a different, most creative way. Together they were to make a considerable, if at times controversial, contribution to the improving of church musical standards.

The hymn was an art form which always fascinated Dearmer. His involvement was crucial in the production of *The English Hymnal* in 1906. His next venture in hymn book production was a result of his activities in the Life and Liberty Movement. Percy was not in on the foundation of this, 'one of the most remarkable of Church fellowships which have ever changed a Church's history,' says Roger Lloyd in *The History of the Church of England 1900–1965*. Writing from India in February 1918 to Mrs Knowles, he said he knew little about the movement but he thought that if all the useless dignitaries and all the overpaid bishops, or even a quarter of them, would lay their emoluments at the Apostles' feet, there would be no more difficulty about getting 'Liberty' and the Church might thereby get a little 'Life'. He admitted to Mrs Knowles, 'O! I do love the C of E so much.' He believed that the Church of England might be what no other church in Christendom was or could be, if she 'came right down off her pedestal – down from her thrones and palaces, and laid her jewels at the feet of the poor'.

This was pure Life and Liberty stuff (with distinct echoes of his Christian Socialism), and it was no surprise that, on returning to England, after some initial hesitation, he was quickly involved in their campaigns. Historians suggest that the Movement had its genesis as far back as 1899 in Charles Gore's book, *Essays in Church Reform*. The object was to give the Church of England, through an Enabling Act, more control over its own affairs and legislative standing for the then unofficial Parochial Church Councils and national church assemblies. Among its stalwarts were Dick Sheppard,

F. A. Iremonger and William Temple and a number of leading laymen. Claiming to be 'an unsympathetic but never deliberately unfair observer', the future Bishop, Hensley Henson, then a caustic Dean of Durham, dismissed the Movement as consisting of 'a few shell-shocked Chaplains and young men in a hurry'. He had no patience for them because they were 'Gore's crowd'.

Dearmer was much encouraged in this fresh enthusiasm by a new friendship with Frederick William Dwelly of Liverpool. Dwelly, who was Vicar of Emmanuel, Southport, had come to prominence through the astuteness of Albert Augustus David, Bishop of Liverpool, an early Life and Liberty enthusiast. The Bishop had heard of Dwelly's organizational powers in arranging ceremonial and the words to go with it, whether of a Dickensian pageant or for the dedication of the town's magnificent War Memorials in Southport. Consequently the Bishop later entrusted Dwelly with masterminding a week of services surrounding the consecration ceremonies in 1924 of that massive edifice, the Cathedral Church of Christ in Liverpool. He was given the title 'Ceremonarius'. Dearmer had no part in this work at Liverpool, but he was anxious to recruit the talents of this able priest for a number of projects he had in mind. The first task was the compilation of a new hymn book which, it was thought, Life and Liberty might adopt as their official book. In the event this proved impracticable, but it was adopted for use in Liverpool Cathedral, giving it a valuable early boost.

Dearmer was anxious that his concept of the dignity of the hymn as an art form should be more widely acknowledged. By means of *The English Hymnal*, Dearmer was directly responsible for a considerable improvement in hymn-singing in the Church of England. Roger Lloyd suggests that *The English Hymnal* did even more for the Church than *The Parson's Handbook*. It was a brave attempt to eradicate banalities, and generally to raise the quality of English hymnody both in words and music; but it laboured under a difficulty. The hymnal was widely perceived as a party book, not least because of the atmosphere created by the episcopal threats of inhibition on publication. This was despite the firm denial in the second sentence of the 1906 preface. No one really believed the claim made there, 'This is not a party-book, expressing this or that phrase of negation or excess.' The preface claimed that the book contained only the worthiest expressions of hymnody, from 'those ancient Fathers who were the earliest hymn-writers, down to contemporary exponents of modern aspirations and ideals'. The almost immediate controversies which arose concerning the invocation of saints confirmed the prejudices of many.

That such perceptions continued to hinder the cause of better hymns gave growing concern to Dearmer and a number of his colleagues. They wanted to improve *all* hymnody, and not just in the Church of England. Indeed it was important because, they knew that in many other denominations hymns were even more the staple diet of worship than in Anglicanism. Could there not be a *national* hymn book which might spearhead a national raising of musical and literary standards? It was such idealism which led to a project to compile a hymn book which was originally to be called *Songs of the Spirit* but was published as *Songs of Praise*. From the outset the compilers had schools as well as churches in their sights. An assembly was by then part of the daily pattern in all schools, and hymns were a basic ingredient. It was important that the inculcation of good standards should begin there.

Just as when he tackled *The English Hymnal*, Percy now gathered around him a creative and multi-talented group. F. R. Barry, a member of that group, recalled that Dearmer took, 'as was natural, the leading part. Percy *knew* a great deal about hymnody; most of us merely knew what we liked.' Barry reckoned that the resulting book might almost have been called 'St Martin-in-the-Fields set to music'. By that he meant St Martin's under Dick Sheppard. It was 'avowedly a "liberal production" and is therefore unmentionable among precisionists'. The aim of this new book was to offer congregations, of whatever denomination, a virile, outward-looking presentation of the Christian faith for what they believed was a new age. They were providing hymns, freed from some of the weak, mawkish sentiments which had crept into nineteenth-century hymn books. Barry is quite frank about its objectives:

> It was meant, too, to appeal as widely as possible, reaching out from the inner circle to the fringes – for, as Tillich remarks somewhere, a religion intended only for the inner circle is not the Christianity of Christ – and therefore included a certain amount of material never used before in congregational worship, some of which was frankly more humanist than Christian.

This was a stance which was bound to attract fierce opposition. First in the field were Bishop Chavasse of Rochester, Bishop Wilson of Chelmsford and other Evangelicals. The challenge was that it had 'left out the Cross'. What was Dearmer's position in this? Certainly, during discussion on the contents of the book, Mervyn Haigh (later Bishop of Coventry, and eventually Winchester) protested at Percy's tendency to omit or bowdlerize lines or verses in some well-known hymns which dwelt on the sacrificial elements in the Christian faith and Christian living. Barry explained that this was because Percy was then at a stage of violent reaction against what he called 'the sin obsession'. Percy wanted to help people to look away from their guilt complexes and their introspection, to a more objective vision of God, and find liberty in adoration. This was not some form of Unitarianism – it was Christo-centric. Yet it was a concern which remained with Dearmer. He wrote later:

> Life, light, and love were hidden behind the new symbol in the fourth century of the cross. That symbol, noble as it is, and better understood to-day, ousted the blithe iconography of the earlier Christian art. A system of prescription and damnation fell over the radiant good tidings of Christ.

Once again Percy recruited Vaughan Williams as Musical Editor, but this time he worked alongside Percy's Primrose

Hill colleague, Martin Shaw, by now organist at St Martin-in-the-Fields. For this second hymn book Vaughan Williams decided that there were to be no second bests and no compromises, and in order that this might be so, he cast his net as widely as possible. There was one other change concerning Vaughan Williams's involvement in *Songs of Praise* – he acknowledged his own tunes straight away, whereas in the first edition of *The English Hymnal* his tunes had been given as 'Anon'.

It was thought that *Songs of Praise* would benefit by having a handbook which would serve as a guide to its contents, both to the words and the music. *Songs of Praise Discussed* (1933) was compiled by Dearmer, with notes on the musical contents by Archibald Jacob. This volume is a delight, with many insights into both the compilation of the book and the individual items within it. *Songs of Praise* sold well and was widely used, although that use tended to be confined to churches where the clergy were of a liberal frame of mind. High Churchmen, universally, dismissed it as 'a book of songs and ditties' and condemned its modernist tendencies. We have seen that it was always Dearmer's hope that it would prove to be a national hymn book. He wrote that '*Songs of Praise* is for all churches – not, indeed, for Lot's wife, but for the forward-looking people of every communion.' In *Songs of Praise Discussed* he said:

> We are reaching the time when denominational hymn-books will be recognised as an anachronism and a hindrance to the unity of the Spirit. Why should we thus emphasize and perpetuate our peculiarities? The hymns themselves show how catholic we have already become in spite of ourselves. They represent the whole of Christendom, without sectarian limitations; and the ideal for all the Church is to use the same books, so that the distinction will not be between one denomination and another, but merely the still natural as inevitable one between those who are lingering behind and those who go forward.

An important part of that ideal was never achieved. *Songs of Praise* remained almost entirely a preserve of the Church of England for many years, but now, as *The Oxford Dictionary of the Christian Church* reports, 'Its use in Anglican churches has largely ceased.' Yet there was one element of Dearmer's vision which was realised. A number of simplified versions, including *Songs of Praise for Schools*, were widely used in schools of all denominations and none; in this it was an ecumenical success. More recent developments, the infrequency of school assemblies, and the ubiquitous overhead projector have ousted from its last refuge this, and indeed all hymn books. Until recently *Songs of Praise* only survived as the title of a Sunday evening religious TV programme, but in 1997 it was adopted as the name of a BBC-sponsored hymn book. Its preface briefly acknowledges the pedigree of its title.

Then there was the work Dearmer did on carols. The English carol was rediscovered in the nineteenth century, and Dearmer and friends were part of the process of advancing both their currency and use in the twentieth. What is a carol? Even the redoubtable musicologist Percy Scholes said he found it difficult to frame a completely satisfactory definition. He offered 'a religious seasonal song, of joyful character, in the vernacular and sung by the common people'. By the early nineteenth century, Scholes reports, in many places carol singing had degenerated into a form of petty beggary.

The traditional carol seems to have reached its full development as the popular religious song, of Scholes's definition, by the fifteenth century. What had mostly been forgotten by the nineteenth was that carols were intrinsically connected with dancing. It was J. M. Neale who was one of the earliest to remind musicians of the existence of the carols in his *Carols for Christmas-tide* in 1853. Dearmer describes him as 'the most learned hymnologist and liturgiologist of his time', who lived too short a life. Then H. R. Bramley and John Stainer published *Christmas Carols Old and New* in 1871, and the revival was in full swing. One of the most productive of the writers of 'new' carols, often translations or adaptations, was

G. R. Woodward. He always referred to Neale as 'my master'. Woodward, like Dearmer, served under Fr Adderley at the Berkeley Chapel and had been a member of the original planning group for *The English Hymnal*. Woodward produced his book, also called *Carols for Christmas-tide*, in 1897, but then, more importantly, compiled *The Cowley Carol Book* in 1909. This was probably the most popular English carol book until the publication of *The Oxford Book of Carols* in 1928. The responsibility for this important collection was in the hands of the familiar team of Dearmer, Vaughan Williams and Martin Shaw.

Shaw and Dearmer had already co-operated in the production of *The English Carol Book* in 1913. In this they had attempted to redress the damage that they believed Stainer and Bramley had done to the carol. Finding them quaint and rough, Shaw said, Stainer and Bradley decided that they needed a Victorian shine, so they French-polished the old oak and were content. The result was 'just what one would have expected – either treacly or hopelessly dull'. In Shaw's opinion, hardly one of the collection could really be called a carol, and few had any musical value. Armed with this experience, the three stalwarts aimed to provide real carols, with music of quality; memorable words and tunes you could dance to. From 1928, until the first appearance of the series *Carols for Choirs* in 1961, *The Oxford Book of Carols* was the primary source-book for such marvellous occasions as the world-famous 'Nine Lessons and Carols on Christmas Eve' in King's College Cambridge – as well as more modest carol services in numerous parish churches, schools and colleges. The popularity of the carol service in churches and chapels up and down the land is one of the most significant growth points in contemporary church attendance. For many people, it is their one religious activity of the year. Through *The Oxford Book of Carols* Dearmer and his companions unwittingly provided a stimulus for this somewhat eccentric display of religious observance. The book was also crucial in reminding clergy and musicians alike that 'Carols . . . were always modern'. Dearmer explains in his preface to *The Oxford Book of Carols*:

> The charm of an old carol lies precisely in its having been true to the period in which it was written, and those which are alive today retain their vitality because of this sincerity; for imitations are always sickly and short-lived. A genuine carol may have faults of grammar, logic, and prosody; but one fault it never has – that of sham antiquity.

There was another 'form of art' which, unfailingly throughout his life, Dearmer believed to be of crucial importance to the life, health and true witness of the Christian Church. He believed fervently that public worship was an art entirely worthy of the designation. This conviction was initially to be seen in the 1890s in his compilation of *The Parson's Handbook*, but it continued and developed throughout his life. Before he left the United States, after his work at Berkeley Divinity School, he was invited to give a distinguished set of lectures – the Bohlen Lectures – in Philadelphia in January 1919. These he repeated four weeks later as Lent Lectures in St Martin-in-the-Fields. Dearmer entitled them, and so they were published, as *The Art of Public Worship*. In the lectures he propounded the theory that, 'There can be no public worship without art. However bad it is, the art is there.' Furthermore, he maintained, 'Whatever we do, we cannot avoid the practice of art; but we can avoid beauty, as we can avoid truth. We can have all our arts bad, and sink our worship in misery and humiliation.' He admits that it is not a panacea for 'filling our churches', yet we must, he insists, worship God in the beauty of holiness, and in the holiness of beauty. To do that, it is essential to give up 'all that is unreal and insincere, ugly or depressing, tedious, artificial or mawkish, unsocial, narrow, quarrelsome'. Even so, Dearmer prophesied, 'There will be no sudden response, no flocking back into churches that have been chilled so long. Only if we do what is right, for the sake of the right, all will come right in the end.'

10

Down Among the Liberals

Among those involved in the work of producing *Songs of Praise* were Frederick Dwelly, Arthur Duncan-Jones (Percy's successor at St Mary's), Dick Sheppard, V. F. Storr, Pat McCormick and G. W. Briggs, all of whom came from various shades of opinion within the Church of England's growing Modernist Movement. This was a movement which it is difficult to describe with complete accuracy. There were Evangelical 'Modernists' (such as Storr) and more Anglo-Catholic 'Modernists' (such as Sheppard and Duncan-Jones) and many delicately nuanced positions in between. Students of twentieth-century Christianity in England, while observing that Modernism was the most characteristic theology of the 1920s, have strongly criticized it as not being a faith strong enough or coherent enough to appear as an intellectually convincing option, 'something to which to convert the unbeliever or to rally the unclerical ranks of ordinary Church people drifting towards agnosticism,' says Adrian Hastings in *A History of English Christianity 1920–1985*. It was into these circles that Dearmer was now drawn, almost certainly at further cost to his 'career prospects'.

Looking back, nearly twenty years after the publication of the first edition, Briggs denied that *Songs of Praise* set out 'to dilute Christian doctrines'. 'Indeed the truth is exactly the opposite,' he argued. He admitted that the original book, which appeared in 1925, was deficient in the confession of sin, but the Revised and Enlarged Edition (1931) made the subject more prominent. Sensitive to the many criticisms of the book, Briggs was anxious to explain that some of the perceived problems had arisen out of misunderstandings. As an illustration, he took the example of the omission of the verse, 'There was no other good enough' from Mrs Alexander's well-known and well-loved hymn, 'There is a green hill'. Briggs explains that the particular verse in question was omitted because it is 'a quite unworthy description of the Atonement':

> 'There was no other good enough,' is surely inadequate; and there is no 'price of sin'. There is a penalty of sin, and a price of redemption; but 'the price of sin' would only fit the gentlemen who went up and down Europe peddling indulgences.

In this, and in other such matters, Briggs recalled that Dearmer 'had a righteous passion for truth, and a wholesome hatred both of false doctrine and mawkish sentiment.' Yet Dearmer had his own weaknesses, such as too much love for what is 'gay' and 'jolly'. Briggs reckoned that they were at least more wholesome. He was less tolerant about some other details of Dearmer's methods as editor, believing that he did use *Songs of Praise* to express his own new and developing theological outlook. Although admitting that, to some extent, such modifying is humanly almost inevitable, Briggs and others argued that the ideal hymn book should be wide enough to include all reasoned views, and certainly should not offend legitimate convictions.

In some of the hymns in *Songs of Praise*, as well as recognizing what we noted earlier that Russell Barry characterized as his reaction to 'the sin obsession', we can detect a distinct change in Dearmer's sacramental theology. In his unashamedly High Church days his was a theology which he shared with friends and colleagues such as Walter Frere, Charles Gore and Conrad Noel. This was now beginning to be modified in the 1920s, and can be seen to be moving in a distinctly more 'liberal' direction.

One of his oldest friends, Harold Anson, himself a speaker at the famous (some would say infamous) Modern Churchmen's Girton Conference in 1921, explained that Dearmer had been led, in the first place, to value sacramental religion because he also cared deeply for the reconstitution of society on the basis of Christ's love and self-sacrifice. 'Apart from this Christian Socialism, public worship had for him little interest, except for his love of colour and drama.' Dearmer, said Anson, saw the Eucharist as a gathering of neighbours for a friendly meal, filled with the sense of Jesus present as the true leader, wherever, and in whatever cause they met. This meal should be surrounded by all that is beautiful in colour, in ceremony, and in music. That is why he cared so intensely for these matters. Yet the meal was not a substitute, but a focus for the common meals in which neighbours meet to affirm their mutual love. It was this which led him to devote so much time, effort and research, in the British Museum and elsewhere, in order to produce *The Parson's Handbook*. The book did not arise from any love of ecclesiasticism. It was, in Anson's words, 'a handbook to the hallowing of the true socialism'.

G. W. Briggs saw this particular sacramental theology as being formularized during the editing of *Songs of Praise*. He put it down to the fact that Dearmer tended more and more to regard the Eucharist as the *Agape*. So 'supper' becomes very prominent in the hymns, sometimes being used as a substitute for 'sacrament'. Briggs grants that there was some virtue in this emphasis and that Dearmer was underlining an aspect of the Eucharist which had previously been somewhat ignored in hymns, but Dearmer's views were changing.

About the same time, Dearmer became involved in another 'eucharistic' matter. This new concern was neither to do with the shape or form of the rite, nor was it regarding any matter of ritual or ceremony. It was a matter of discipline and, at first sight, might seem a strange sphere for him to get involved in, but it proved to be of great importance in the campaign of bringing the Church and the Eucharist to people. This was a cause to which Dearmer was still committed, even if his method of expressing it had taken on a revised and Modernist tone.

Down Among the Liberals

One of the manifestations of the second, 'ritualistic', stage of the Anglo-Catholic Movement (that is, from the 1860s onwards) was a growing insistence, by the clergy, that the Holy Communion should always be received after fasting. The Anglo-Catholics were now teaching their congregations that the 'Holy Food' of the Eucharist must not be preceded by the consumption of ordinary food. Furthermore, they taught that it was the discipline of fasting which helped to produce the correct mental and spiritual attitude in which the worshipper should receive Communion. With these principles in mind, Anglo-Catholics developed, in their parishes, a pattern of worship to accommodate this discipline. There was an early Mass (or even many Masses) before breakfast for the receiving of Communion, and then the faithful were bidden to return to church, after having 'broken their fast', in order to 'worship' at the High Mass held at 10.30 or 11 a.m. At the High Mass there would be no communicants (or at least only the sick and the elderly who, like the officiating priest, would have fasted up to that time.)

In the last quarter of the nineteenth century there had grown up a concern about the increasing fixation by practically all Anglo-Catholics on this strict rule of fasting, but little or nothing was done about it. Dearmer described the situation:

> Bewildered people in one parish after another were told that they ought not to communicate at noon, but must come to the newly invented 'early Celebration' at eight in the morning, an hour which to the great majority of our people is almost impossible. This was because of the introduction of fasting-communion, which has now been taught with great and insistent earnestness for two or three generations, till even at Evangelical gatherings an early Celebration has come to be taken for granted.

It was into this controversy that Dearmer entered – with all guns blazing. In 1928 he published a polemical volume, provocatively entitled, *The Truth about Fasting – with special reference to fasting-Communion*. He said all agreed that it was good for Christians to receive the Holy Communion together; that reception should be more general and more frequent, and there was no argument that preparation was essential for so important an act. However, any way of preparation should not be a hindrance but a help to the reception of grace.

By 1928 the question of fasting-Communion had assumed a growing practical importance as an increasing number of parishes began to experiment with a different pattern for their programme of Sunday morning services, in order to accommodate what we would now recognize as the precursor of the Parish Communion.

Evidence suggests that the first two pioneers of the Parish Communion Movement were Walter Frere at St Faith's Stepney in 1890 and John Burns at All Saints' Middlesborough in 1893. It is intriguing to note that both of these priests were Christian Socialists. Of Frere it is recorded that, 'Before he left Cambridge he was drawn to Socialism'; and of Burns, his biographer says, he was 'commonly regarded as a Socialist, and in fact called himself one'.

This fact, that the roots of the Parish Communion are in Christian Socialism, has been fully argued elsewhere. Here it is sufficient to point out that, as a Christian Socialist, Percy Dearmer also saw the potentiality of the Parish Eucharist. In the earliest edition of *The Parson's Handbook* he speaks of the importance of the main Sunday Eucharist being 'fixed at the time when people can best attend', but later, in the same paragraph, mentions the Eucharist being 'at the usual church hour (say at eleven)'. It was not a position he defended for long. The seventh edition of 1909 speaks of 'reverting to the old canonical hour of nine'. His overall principle on this subject had been first enunciated in the 1902 fourth edition when he coined the phrase: '"The Lord's Service on the Lord's Day" must be our watchword.' After the Second World War this phrase became one of the slogans of the highly influential

'Parish and People Movement' formed to advocate the introduction of the Parish Communion in parishes.

In his 1928 book on fasting, Dearmer said that to the ordinary Englishman it might appear to be a subject too unimportant to bother writing about, and he would have tended to agree, if it were not for the apparently insoluble problem of Sunday morning services. Granting, somewhat reluctantly, the possibility of an early celebration of the Eucharist, Dearmer was clear that a later hour for the main service of the day, which would always be a Eucharist, was essential, and then examined the authorities, beginning with apostolic and sub-apostolic evidence, and continued through the centuries. His conclusion was that fasting before receiving Communion was not laid upon communicants as a binding and inflexible rule of the Church and that, within the Church of England, there was no authority for the practice. He concluded:

> I would venture to suggest that fasting-communion as a *tabu* has had a profoundly demoralising effect upon the corporate life of the Church, and that to the individual the danger lies in the unconscious response within us of the Pharisaism in the struggle against which our Lord laid down his life.

Dearmer's help in the removal of this shibboleth was crucial to clearing the way for many High Church parishes to introduce a mid-morning Eucharist, with full ceremonial, music and general Communion, in good conscience.

None of these activities – the work on *Songs of Praise*, his book on fasting, various writing projects, together with many other tasks – were undertaken, as we know, from any sort of official base, parochial or elsewhere, apart from King's College. He had the problems, difficulties, opportunities and freedom of being freelance. Although some of his writings, not least the hymn books, provided him with an income, the comfortable financial position of his wife meant that he was free from any acute pecuniary anxieties. But he was a 'churchman', in every sense, and he missed the task of planning and organizing worship. He needed his own church. It was through the renewal of his friendship with Maude Royden that an opportunity arose, if not to care for his *own* church, at least to have a major stake in a worshipping community.

Agnes Maude Royden, the youngest daughter of Sir Thomas Royden of Mossley Hill, Liverpool, was educated at Cheltenham and Lady Margaret Hall, Oxford. There the Cowley Fathers had reinvigorated her love of High Church ways, which she had first discovered at All Saints' Cheltenham. It seemed at one time that they would lead to her becoming a Roman Catholic. After working at the Victoria Women's Settlement in the Scotland Road area of Liverpool, she became Parish Worker at South Luffenham, Rutland. Soon afterwards she became involved in work for women's suffrage and came to be an inspiring platform speaker for the cause. She helped form the Church League for Women's Suffrage, of which Bishop Edward Hicks was president, and William Temple and Scott Holland were members. At the time of the National Mission of Repentance and Hope, in 1915, there was considerable opposition (led by Athelstan Riley) to women speaking at Mission Services in churches. Riley wrote, 'If this innovation is to be imported into the methods of the National Mission, disaster must inevitably follow.' It was in the context of this debate that serious discussion of the ordination of women first arose.

Having first given the impression that permission for women to speak would be granted, the Bishops in fact refused to lift their ban. Maude Royden had come to believe that her powers of oratory were intended not only for the platform but also for the pulpit. As Percy Maryon-Wilson put it, 'the pulpit rather than the platform was to become her *métier*'. In 1917 she was invited to preach at the great London Nonconformist church, the City Temple. After some turmoil, she decided to accept. It was not the first Nonconformist chapel she had preached in, she explained, but the City Temple was a different thing – a 'real' church even in Anglican eyes. With its great white pulpit (the gift of the City of London) and its long line of notable ministers, it was something very special for a woman to be invited to preach there. It was an action which quickly caused battle-lines to be drawn up, for and against Royden. Some Anglicans realised that her action would perforce deprive the Church of England of a strong and influential voice at the moment when it was most needed – for example, by the Life and Liberty Movement. Not pulling his punches, Francis Eeles wrote to her, 'You are too valuable to the church to waste your influence by prejudicing your position in this way.' Nevertheless, although Royden spoke at the Queen's Hall at the launch of Life and Liberty, the Principal of Cuddesdon (the Revd J. B. Seaton), himself a keen member of that movement, would not allow her to sleep under the college roof, only to attend a meeting of its Council and then leave. All this was exacerbated by her acceptance of an invitation to take the Three Hours Service on Good Friday, 1921, at St Botolph's in the City. She preached to a packed church.

It was into this boiling cauldron that Dearmer stepped – with a surprising suggestion. A long-time suffragist, with successive wives keenly supportive of the movement, he had known Maude Royden for many years. She had stayed at Oakridge on a number of occasions, both before and after her membership of the Primrose Hill congregation. In 1918 she 'adopted' a daughter, Helen, and the Dearmers had looked after the child for two months. Even so, it was a remarkable proposition he made to her. He suggested that she should start a place of her own, and that the two of them should run it. She and Dearmer made it clear from the beginning that they were not setting up a new church, 'adding to the weakness of the Church Universal', as Royden put it. The experiment was intended to spring from the Church of England and remain within the Church of England. They even hoped, naïvely, that the Church of England might encourage the experiment.

The services started in Kensington Town Hall in 1920 and were called 'Fellowship Services', and were only held on Sunday afternoons and evenings, so that communicant members might attend their own churches in the morning. However, the work always focused on those who, for one reason or another, had lost touch with organized religion. In a sermon Royden said:

> I speak to those who are outside the Churches, but I also speak, as you will have realised, to those who, like myself, are still members of a Christian Church, and I say that, whatever form the religious needs of this and the coming generation will take, if religion is to live at all (and it cannot fail to live) it will be by concentrating upon Christ. The centre of it must be Christ, the ruling principle the love of Christ. There must arise a Church or Churches, or a movement, whatever that is, which shall have the courage to realise that it is not faith, but love, that is the supreme content of the Christian gospel.

In 1921 they moved to a disused Congregational Chapel in Eccleston Square, to which Percy applied his artistic skills. Royden describes his immediate reaction to the building and its possibilities:

> While I was groaning over the ugliness of the building which was to become the Guildhouse, he was delighting in its goodness! He pointed out that it was good – honest and well-built, no sham Gothic, no shoddy work. The painting and 'decoration', we agreed, was hideous. He applied his favourite remedy – whitewash – and the place was transformed.

Dearmer, as we know, judged that it was not solely high standards in the visual arts which were needed for inspiring worship – the music must also be of the very best. Having warned Martin Shaw that he would most probably need his services after the War, he now called upon him for that help, albeit for a less than conventional project. Although directing the music at St Martin-in-the-Fields, Shaw found it possible to combine his duties there with the Guildhouse:

I was called in to do the music. The whole thing was to be congregational, varied with the unaccompanied singing of a vocal quartet, and we decided not to use the organ. A brainwave of Percy Dearmer's produced the title 'Five Quarters' for the afternoon meetings; meaning, of course, an hour and a quarter.

They used *The English Hymnal* at first, and later *Songs of Praise*. Dearmer employed his liturgical skills in drawing up the order of service. It was a notable and worthwhile experiment, reaching out to the unchurched. In a joint statement Royden and Dearmer declared:

> Our feeling is that the Church of England, like other Churches in this country, is at present appealing to that minority of English people who go to church on Sunday – a minority which appears to be decreasing. She ought to appeal to the public at large, by means of addresses and informal gatherings for discussion, and to speak to the great body of people who are not at home in church, or who do not even know their way about the Prayer Book. Very probably there should be a centre of this sort in every district of our great cities, and certainly several in London.

Yet both he and Royden were constantly pointing to the mainstream Church. 'I have never left my own church,' Maude Royden regularly reminded people, and certainly Dearmer still hankered after the services and surroundings in which he had been nurtured.

When, in the autumn of 1924, another old friend, Christopher Cheshire, moved from the Wardenship of Liddon House in Mayfair to be Rector of Holy Trinity, Sloane Square in Chelsea, he invited Dearmer to work with him. They had been colleagues twenty or more years before, producing the CSU's journal *Commonwealth*. Dearmer decided to accept the offer and remained part time on the staff at Holy Trinity until 1931. It was a happy arrangement, much appreciated by

Percy. In 1930 he accepted a similar post with Gordon Arrowsmith at St Luke's Chelsea.

The Dearmer family moved from Radnor Place, the house they had purchased on their return to England, to 9 Embankment Gardens in 1923. There was a growing family. Anthony had joined Gillian in the nursery in 1920, and Imogen was born in October 1923. Geoffrey was again living at home, having left the army in 1920. He worked in India for a year as a tutor before returning permanently to England. Later he worked in the censorship office of the Lord Chamberlain, followed by a long period of outstanding service for the BBC, mainly as an editor and a highly imaginative contributor to *Children's Hour*. He was made a Member of the Royal Victorian Order in 1955. During the inter-War years Geoffrey published a continuous flow of verses, plays and novels. A selection of his poems was published on his hundredth birthday in 1993. He married Margaret Proctor in 1936 and died in 1996. His daughter, Juliet Woollcombe, was one of the first women ordained priest in 1994; a fact which would have given her grandfather great joy.

Imogen inherited her father's and grandfather's artistic talents and is a respected water-colourist with many exhibitions to her credit. She married William Nichols, Clerk of the Salters Company in 1946. Anthony, who followed his father to Westminster, was killed in action with the RAF in April 1943. Few families have suffered more in the two World Wars of the twentieth century than the Dearmers: Mabel and her son Christopher in the First War, and in the Second War, Anthony, and also Richard Addis (husband of Anthony's elder sister Gillian), who was lost at sea. In 1950 she married Michael Warr, a diplomat.

In 1946 Nan married Sir John Sykes KCB, who died in 1953. Lady Sykes (as Nan was then) died in 1979.

11

Worship: Conformity or Change?

To be interested and concerned about the nature and performance of public worship was not an unusual occupation for a Church of England priest in the latter part of the nineteenth century. In fact it sometimes appeared as though a large proportion of the clergy were involved in little else beside concerning themselves with the various, often violent and certainly vitriolic, controversies regarding differences of opinion on ritual and ecclesiastical furnishings. Dearmer's entry into these stormy waters was not, in itself, remarkable. Ritual controversy at that time was a favourite spectator sport for both Catholics and Protestants within the Church of England. John Shelton Reed has recently said, 'From working class tenements to the pages of *Punch* to the very Houses of Parliament, the Victorian Anglo-Catholic Movement provoked bitter debate and even violence throughout Victorian times.' And no sub-section of the 'bitter debate' was as likely to provoke 'even violence' than that about the style in which worship was conducted. It was a sorry scene. Services which were intended to be *ad majorem Dei gloriam* were frequently reduced to what resembled a beargarden. The history of the Church of England in those days is besmirched by ritual riots and all kinds of ritual controversies. Reed has suggested that the Anglo-Catholics seemed to thrive on confrontation, even to seek it; that the word 'compromise' did not figure large in their vocabulary. It often seems as though that was true. In 1874 a deliberate attempt was made to stamp out the ritualists when Parliament passed the Public Worship Regulation Act. Unfortunately for its supporters, the most immediate result of that legislation was the prosecution and imprisonment of a number of priests, producing a most undesirable fresh phenomenon – the ritual martyr. One might have thought that things could not get worse, but they did.

It may be difficult for a largely non-churchgoing generation to comprehend the decision to set up the 1904 Royal Commission on Ecclesiastical Discipline, with all the concomitant expense of such an exercise. The task of this high-powered Commission was:

> To inquire into the alleged prevalence of breaches or neglect of the Law relating to the conduct of Divine Service in the Church of England and to the ornaments and fittings of Churches; and to consider the existing powers and procedures applicable to such irregularities and to make such recommendations as may be deemed requisite for dealing with the aforesaid matters.

A good deal of the Commission's time was spent in examining witnesses (in Anglo-Catholic eyes 'spies'). These were in the main agents of the Church Association, formed in 1865 by leading Evangelical churchmen, to maintain the Protestant ideals of faith and worship in the Church of England. They also considered the material accumulated by the Joint Evidence Committee of the Church of England League and the National Protestant Union; both specially formed to collect evidence for presentation to the Commission. The evidence, the witnesses' statements, and the Commission's report are contained in two large volumes. The Report is at once fascinating, repetitive and deeply sad. Worship should never be the object of such forensic examination. A good majority of the 118 meetings of the Commission were occupied with listening to such sordid and often clandestine evidence.

The Commission, realising the long haul ahead of them and the daunting nature of the evidence, expressed themselves willing to listen to the views of other informed commentators. On their sixth day of meeting (23 June 1904) Dearmer appeared before them, with W. H. Frere immediately following as the next witness. They must have been in cahoots: Dearmer deflected some of the questions put to him as ones which Frere was better qualified to deal with.

The beginning of the verbatim transcript for that day records Dearmer's modesty:

> *Chairman:* You have devoted a great deal of attention, I believe, to the question of ritual and ceremonial?
> *P. D.:* Some little attention.

Dearmer's 'evidence' covers over 200 paragraphs of the report of proceedings. It is detailed and persuasive. He did not deal with the finer points of rite and ceremonies, as some might have expected, but concentrated on more substantial issues regarding worship according to the Book of Common Prayer. 'He being dead, yet speaketh.' For the biographer to have in transcript the *ipsissima verba* of his subject, detailing the depths of his convictions at that juncture of his life, is of inestimable value in evaluating his sentiments. It is also strangely moving.

The Commission material reveals Dearmer as being very nearly a Prayer Book Fundamentalist – the stance of the earliest Tractarians. In Tract No. 3 Newman addressed to the clergy his 'Thoughts on the Alterations in the Liturgy', in which he counselled them to petition the Bishops to resist any alteration. Just like the leaders in those early days of Tractarianism (R. H. Froude, in Tract No. 9, wrote critically of those who complained that the services of the Church were too long), Dearmer wanted a full and complete observance of the Prayer Book provisions. It was a position which he later modified.

Curiously at his appearance before the Royal Commission in June 1904 Dearmer was questioned about auricular Confession. He adopted the classic Anglican position summed up in the aphorism, 'All may, some should, many do, none must.' Then he was pressed on the subject of the reading of the Exhortation during the Communion service which, unsurprisingly, in view of his 'fundamentalism', he believed ought to be read more frequently. More striking is his advocacy of 'fencing the table'. This was a use of the Prayer Book system by which intending communicants submitted their names at least the day before making their Communion. A slightly unreal discussion arose over the practicalities involved in receiving Communion while on holiday at the seaside. This section of his submissions was summarized by Dearmer:

> The Prayer Book prescribes a discipline which is strict, and her character in this respect has been changed by long-established slackness in carrying out her direction. Whether for good or for evil, her character has been largely changed, and it has been left, I believe, very often to Nonconformist bodies to try and revive a discipline which was found to be necessary in some form or another to Christian life, which, I believe, is illustrated by the rise of Methodism and by other bodies.

Next the discussion turned to the question of guaranteeing the position of the centrality of the Holy Communion in the worship patterns of the parish churches of England. In the nineteenth and early twentieth centuries Morning Prayer, in perhaps the majority of parishes, usurped the place of the Eucharist. Percy had consistently maintained that, according to the clear directions of the Book of Common Prayer, the central place belonged to the Eucharist. It was that service, not Mattins, which should always be the heart of Sunday morning worship. The Commissioners took Dearmer through this matter in great detail, questioning him closely about the various rubrics and directions of the Prayer Book. Dearmer stated with conviction:

> The Prayer Book follows the custom of the primitive Church, which undoubtedly was that the Lord's Supper was the principal service on the Lord's Day, and the custom also of what is called in the Preface 'the whole Catholic Church of Christ', in retaining this service, so far as there are a convenient number of communicants, as the principal

service of the Lord's Day; but that in practice a great deal of the common use reverses this custom.

Drawn out by the Rt Hon. J. G. Talbot MP on his view of perfection in this matter, he replied:

> Well, my ideal, would be a Communion service at which everybody should communicate at about nine o'clock in the morning to be the service of general Communion – but only I think in the average parish. In parishes of course where there are large congregations and many clergy it would be extremely convenient to have other earlier celebrations.

A reply which he reinforced in another response, this time to the Chairman (the Rt Hon. Sir Michael Edward Hicks-Beach, Bt. MP):

> My own wish is, in so far as is practicable, to have the Sunday morning services altogether earlier. I should like them to be, say, about nine or half past; Mattins perhaps at nine, followed at half past nine by the Litany and the Communion, if it were found to be practicable. That would be my ideal.

While talking about Sunday morning patterns of service, Dearmer reminded the Commissioners of the fact that Baptism should always be Public Baptism, as laid down by the Prayer Book. In this Dearmer revealed himself as an unwitting advocate of another of the foundation principles of the Parish Communion Movement, that Baptism should not be performed at a hole-in-the-corner service on a Sunday afternoon in the almost total absence of a congregation. 'The Prayer Book undoubtedly makes much of the Sacrament of Baptism, and intends it to be a very public service, whereas in practice it has become a semi-private service,' he told them.

Closely connected with Baptism were his submissions on Catechising and Confirmation. Having particularly emphasized the virtues of the revival of Catechising on a Sunday, he was challenged on the subject and asked whether or not he believed the Sunday school had taken its place.

> I do not think Sunday school teaching has taken the place of catechising; it filled the vacancy which had been left by the fact that the clergy had given up catechising. About 125 years ago, I think it was, Raikes started Sunday schools, at which time catechising had fallen into disuse, and therefore the laity endeavoured to do what the clergy had neglected to do.

Dearmer was then asked if he thought that Sunday school teaching was irregular, to which he responded:

> I should not like to use the word 'irregular', only that it was a substitution for the expert teaching – the teaching of the clergy, who are trained in the work.

Finally there was a long series of questions and answers on the subject of the Daily Office. Was it 'of obligation' for the clergy; was it a waste of time if no one came; would it not be better if the clergy were to spend their time taking part 'in social work of all kinds which keeps accumulating upon them?' asked one MP. The same man (George Harwood) suggested to Dearmer that the compulsion of having to be in church twice a day was a physical strain. There appear signs of righteous anger in his reply to this surprising suggestion:

> I should say that far from being a physical strain, the daily service is a physical rest, and a spiritual rest; and also I should have thought, it is the experience of most of the bishops, that it is just those clergy who are most active in social things who are also most regular in the use of daily services.

Dearmer's session with the Commissioners ended with a bizarre conversation with the Archbishop of Canterbury as to whether 'preaching and study of divinity' are a preventing cause for priests and deacons not to fulfil their daily duty of reciting Morning and Evening Prayer. Dearmer told his Grace that such cannot be regarded as an adequate excuse; only sickness is an acceptable extenuation. Whether Archbishop Davidson agreed with that answer or not, it served to conclude Dearmer's appearance before the Royal Commission.

In the Commission's final report they adjudged the omission of the daily services, disregarding the rubric on the Catechism, non-observance of the rubric on Public Baptism and that on signifying names before receiving Communion, as being 'non-significant breaches of the present law' and 'practices which have resulted from negligence or inadvertence'. None of which can have pleased Dearmer in the slightest.

The Commission was more concerned about celebrations without communicants; the use of the Canon of the Mass from either the Roman or Sarum Use; omission of the invitation to the Confession; the absence of the Creed and the Gloria at a Requiem; the Elevation of the Host; genuflexions; the singing or saying of the *Agnus Dei*; Reservation of the Blessed Sacrament; the Mass of the Pre-Sanctified on Good Friday; and Benediction.

Dearmer would have supported the Commissioners in condemning such things where it was clear that the rules and regulations of the Church of England and its Prayer Book were being openly flouted, and he would have equally supported the general tenor of their main conclusion that:

> The Law relating to the conduct of Divine Service and the ornaments of churches is, in our belief, nowhere exactly observed; and certain minor breaches of it are very generally prevalent. The Law is also broken by many irregular practices which have attained lesser, and widely different, degrees of prevalence. Some of these are omissions, others err in the direction of excess.

The Royal Commission realised that the situation was brought about not simply by lawless clergy and came to the conclusion that 'the law of public worship in the Church of England is too narrow for the religious life of the present generation', and continued,

It needlessly condemns much which a great section of Church people, including many of her most devoted members, value, and modern thought and feeling are characterised by a care for ceremonial, a sense of dignity in worship, and an appreciation of the continuity of the Church, which were not similarly felt at the time when the present law took its present shape.

Dearmer certainly would have warmed to this, feeling (not unreasonably) that he had personally made a significant contribution, in *The Parson's Handbook* in particular, towards a 'sense of dignity in worship and a care for ceremonial'.

It was in order that a standard of liturgical practice should be established within which 'the machinery for discipline' could operate, that the Commissioners' Report recommended Letters of Business should be issued to the Convocations in order that 'the existing law relating to the conduct of Divine Worship and to the ornaments and fittings of church may tend to secure the greater elasticity which a reasonable recognition of the comprehensiveness of the Church of England and of its present needs seem to demand.' Despite a certain degree of reluctance from the Prime Minister (Sir Henry Campbell-Bannerman MP), Letters of Business were issued on 10 November 1906, the Government stating that they would hold themselves free to judge the course of events that they ought to adopt – whatever view might be taken by the Convocation. With that warning ringing in their ears, the work was put in hand. This is not the place to describe the complications which ensued due to the fact that the process of producing the Reply to the Royal Letters of Business had to be discussed by both the Upper and Lower Houses of the Convocations of both Canterbury and York, but it proved to be a long and tedious procedure.

Things should have been helped by a resolution of the Upper House of Canterbury on 6 July 1911 establishing 'a committee of scholars of acknowledged weight, whose advice can be sought with regard to liturgical and other proposals

Worship: Conformity or Change?

with which Convocation is now dealing.' This 'Committee of Experts', as it was to be known, first met at Lambeth Palace on 22 October 1912. Dearmer was not at that meeting, as he was not appointed to membership until November. The Committee included three other members of the Alcuin Committee – Frere, Brightman and Christopher Wordsworth, but its potential was never utilized. Ronald Jasper – an admirer of Dearmer's work, a late-twentieth-century member of the Alcuin Committee and Chairman of the Liturgical Commission which prepared *The Alternative Service Book* – was fearful in 1958 that his Commission would suffer a similar fate. Calling the Committee of Experts 'this first Liturgical Commission', Jasper said it failed 'not because of the incompetence of its members, but because no satisfactory method was devised for collaboration with the Convocations.' That was true; it met fitfully until 1918, and then was summoned no more. Their historian summed up the work of the Committee: 'Its life, on the whole, had not been a happy one: its usefulness had been restricted by the severe limitations of its terms of reference: and some of its most valuable advice had been rejected.' Dearmer shared with his fellow liturgists in an unhappy experience.

This was not to be the end of Dearmer's work for a revised Prayer Book. There was now no official 'Liturgical Commission'; the Convocations were working on their own. It was in other places that a good deal of fevered liturgical composition would be undertaken. This work eventually resulted in the Bishops (by whom the ultimate decisions had to be made) being faced with three other sets of proposals and suggestions, beside the official Convocation-produced document. This advice to their Lordships was slow in coming from each source, but for different reasons. The first in the field was the Alcuin Club. They hesitated because:

> The Alcuin Club takes no side in the discussion as to the advisability at this time of Prayer Book Revision. The Committee recognises, however, that liturgical knowledge

should be put at the service of the Church as a whole with which the decision must ultimately rest, and that a body of students, such as the Club is, should contribute so far as it can to the solution of the questions, both ritual and ceremonial, which are involved. Whether the Book of Common Prayer is revised by this generation or not, nothing but good can come from the spread of sound knowledge upon liturgical subjects, and the consequent growth in the mind of the English Church of a high and consistent ideal of worship.

Overcoming their reluctance, they initiated a series entitled 'Alcuin Club Prayer Book Revision Pamphlets'. The first, in 1912, was a new edition of T. A. Lacey's *Liturgical Interpolations*. Lacey stated that, although he believed revision of the Prayer Book at that time to be inopportune, there certainly was a case for the repairing of the 'lamentable dislocation of parts, for which there is no justification in reason or history' in the Prayer of Consecration. Dearmer was a member of the Committee encouraging this and the subsequent fourteen pamphlets in the series. In one of them E. G. P. Wyatt defended the English Use and criticized those who seized on the name of Dr Percy Dearmer as the author and originator of the English Use. Wyatt explained, 'There is no one who would disclaim authorship of the English Use more indignantly than the author of *The Parson's Handbook*, who only considered himself the mouthpiece of the liturgical experts.'

The English Church Union, the principal Anglo-Catholic society in the Church of England, was equally slow off the mark with liturgical proposals. Their reason was disapproval of the whole process. Darwell Stone, Dearmer's erstwhile companion at Pusey House, and a doctrinaire Anglo-Catholic liturgical scholar, had written deploring the whole business. Back in 1899 he was arguing, 'In the present circumstances ... it is a wise course to use every effort to maintain the Prayer Book unaltered.' It was a position Stone found hard to move away from. In this attitude the Anglo-Catholics shared a common ground with Evangelicals, over against the central churchmen. Towards the end of the First World War it became clear that the reply to the Royal Letters of Business could not be delayed much longer. The time was approaching when a final decision would have to be taken. Consequently, in 1917 the English Church Union made a decision which was effectively an abandonment of its previous anti-revisionist policy. They asked a group of liturgiologists 'to prepare a detailed statement of the alterations in the Prayer Book which we ourselves would approve.'

From the outset the Alcuin Club produced their pamphlet series in conspicuous orange covers; the Anglo-Catholic proposals (mainly the work of Darwell Stone and N. P. Williams) came out bound in green; the stage was ready for the appearance of 'the Grey Book'.

More precisely, it was entitled *A New Prayer Book* and contained the proposals of these 'liberals' for Prayer Book revision. Dearmer was in on the discussions from the start. His main allies were Russell Barry, Fred Dwelly and Mervyn Haigh; others involved included Leslie Hunter, Dick Sheppard, F. C. Eeles, Guy Rogers and Edward Woods. William Temple (now Bishop of Manchester) contributed a foreword, and actively encouraged the enterprise, but did not take any part in the framing of the proposals. Of them, Temple said:

> At a time when the revision of the Prayer Book is occupying the minds of all Church people suggestions are to be welcomed from every quarter, provided they are offered in sincerity and spring from a desire for the highest welfare of the whole Church. Many men of very different ecclesiastical traditions who have seen the forms here set forth have preferred them to any others that have been put before us. It is possible that here we have proposals on which something like an agreed solution of a specially delicate and important problem might be found.

The arguments and impetus behind the Grey Book's proposals

can best be seen in a series of Grey Book pamphlets. Barry, Dearmer, Haigh and others recorded their motives in one such pamphlet, *Principles of Prayer Book Revision, being a reasoned preface to A New Prayer Book*. There was an attractive evangelistic thrust about their suggestions which was absent from the arguments put forward by the supporters of other proposals. The Grey Book advocates wrote:

> Inarticulate multitudes need, even if they do not demand, freer, more varied, and more homely forms of devotion, which will not only avoid excessive repetition, but bring within the immediate scope of Church worship the more everyday thoughts and activities of lives as commonplace as a Galilean carpenter's.

In these Grey Book pamphlets important issues regarding worship were tackled, many of which prefigure the vigorous debates that have surrounded more recent proposals for liturgical revision. Neither the orange nor the green book advocates seem to have given any thought, for instance, to the issue of a twentieth-century liturgical language. By contrast, the Grey Book advocates' pamphlet asks a pertinent question:

> Can we imagine Jesus, our Lord, talking to parents and mourners and talking to God before them in the way in which the priest in these two offices [Baptism and Marriage] is sometimes made to speak? Lack of his humanity in services which belong to the most human passages of life is indefensible.

There were those, like Dearmer and some of his Grey Book colleagues, who feared the prospect of an imposed conformity as a result of the proposed new Prayer Book. Indeed, it was said that the process was always going to be flawed because it was more about discipline than liturgy. Fred Dwelly made the point:

> The old idea of rigid uniformity has led in the past to disruption. Its failure is made manifest in the present disorders

which we all alike deplore. Is not diversity itself an essential element in the Christian ideal of Fellowship? And if it is, may we not well hope that an ordered variety in worship will lead us to a truer and stronger unity than uniformity is ever likely to achieve.

Although part three of the substantive proposals remained in print for a further sixteen years – it was a book of services of praise and prayer for occasional use in churches, drafted by Mervyn Haigh – the Grey Book proposals in general, sad to say, made little impression on the process of revision. By the time of the final examination of the texts by the House of Bishops, Mervyn Haigh was senior Chaplain at Lambeth and had first-hand opportunity of observing the episcopate at their liturgical work. It was not an inspiring sight, nor did it augur well for the contents of the final product. Haigh put down his impressions:

> Most of the bishops, many of whom had taken part in the early discussions of Revision in the Convocations between 1906 and 1914, seemed weary of the subject before they started this, as it was hoped, final consideration of it. Few took much, if any, notice of the Green, Grey and Orange Books with which they were also supplied; and few indeed seemed to have any vision of a Book of Common Prayer which, while remaining in essence its own glorious self, would yet be more appropriate for use by, and better adapted to the needs of, people living not in the seventeenth but in the twentieth century.

Despite this, Dearmer supported the Revised Prayer Book when it was given the episcopal, if not Parliamentary, go-ahead after 1928. The Revised Prayer Book, devised by the Convocations and approved by the Bishops, twice failed to receive Parliamentary approval in 1927 and 1928. The Bishops of the Church of England decided that, in the future, deviations from the Book of Common Prayer would be judged according to the criteria of the 1928 Prayer Book – an anomalous situation. Of it Dearmer commented, in one of his last books:

> What seemed at first to many a blow to the Church of England, and to the Establishment that has brought so much good both to Church and State, may well prove to have been a blessing in disguise. It was of enormous significance that the Houses of Parliament should have devoted so many days to the discussion of public worship, and 'with such sincerity that cavilling was silenced'; Continental observers were astonished, and it was well said among them, 'We envy you your controversies'. The people of England care about their Church, and are profoundly interested in its ways of worship. Indeed it may be said that the failure of the book was really due to the Bishops having sometimes forgotten the Nation in their preoccupation with small groups of partisans in the Church.

Dearmer and Christopher Cheshire wrote a joint letter to *The Times* in August 1927 – that is, before the first Parliamentary débâcle occurred in December of that year. They said they thanked God that the Church had preserved the old services, 'and yet has relieved thinking men by just such alterations as were most urgently needed, and has at the same time given us ways of expressing the aspirations and ideals of the twentieth century'. With misguided optimism they concluded their letter, 'A new age for the church has begun.' It was not to be, and no further official progress in liturgical reform was possible in Dearmer's lifetime.

12

At the Abbey

It was not that Percy Dearmer had turned down offers of jobs, nor had he been choosy or difficult about any appointment – the plain fact is, that after he returned from the United States in 1919, there were no suggestions of a new post. The sole exception, as we have seen, was the work at King's College, London. Rumours that something was in the offing occurred from time to time. Nan shared her husband's constant disappointments:

> From time to time Percy's name was mentioned when various positions in the Church became vacant. We were told that he was to be a Canon of St Paul's, Dean of a certain cathedral in the north, but as nothing ever came of these rumours we ceased to take much interest in them.

The waste of his talents and the ignoring of his many gifts infuriated his friends and admirers. Obviously 'the powers that be' did not share their estimate of his abilities. Davidson, we know, was far from appreciative of Percy's work. The Archbishop retired in 1928, after his long stint at Canterbury, and was followed by Cosmo Gordon Lang. Dearmer and Lang do not seem to have been personally acquainted, but at the beginning of his primacy there was one tangential link. George Bell, the Dean of Canterbury, was anxious to simplify the accumulated complications of enthronements. In order to justify the changes he had in mind, Bell asked learned advice from liturgical experts: Armitage Robinson (Dean of Wells), Walter Frere (Bishop of Truro), F. E. Brightman, F. W. Dwelly and Percy Dearmer. It is intriguing that, in the middle of these apparent 'years in the wilderness', Dearmer's advice should be sought and taken for this most significant of Anglican ceremonies. At that point he was no more than an Honorary Curate at Holy Trinity, Sloane Square. One of the suggestions Dearmer made was that Ralph Vaughan Williams should be asked to compose a setting of the *Te Deum* for the occasion which did not include the final suffrages which are additional to the original text. He volunteered to make the first contact with his musician colleague over the matter. The offer was accepted, and the resulting composition was sung at the Enthronement. Dearmer carefully and at great length answered Bell's enquiries, finally submitting a full and detailed order of service for the Dean's consideration.

This seems to have been the beginning of Dearmer's restoration to official favour. A further push by his friends was required to bring about some positive action. We know that about this time a letter was sent to the Prime Minister by a group of clergy headed by William Temple, and including Russell Barry, asking that some form of preferment might be found for Percy. The situation was also improved by the knowledge that, in addition to the removal of archiepiscopal prejudice at Lambeth, there was now a sympathetic ear in Downing Street in the Labour Prime Minister, Ramsay MacDonald. MacDonald was not a churchman and cared nothing for creeds or ritual. It is said that he mourned the disappearance of 'the old austere heroism in worship, the simple Covenanter's psalm, the silent Quaker meeting', and found the true spirit of Protestantism existing in the Ethical Movement, rather than in the churches. Regardless of these personal preferences, he had the task, over seven years of premiership, of making episcopal and other ecclesiastical appointments. This he did with great care. Archbishop Lang remarked that he had never known a Prime Minister take his responsibilities in the matter more seriously than did MacDonald. One of his very earliest Church appointments, during his first administration in 1924, was that of the Christian Socialist F. L. Donaldson to be a Canon of Westminster. Faced now by a letter from such politically rightly thinking clerics (in his eyes) as Temple and Barry, the Prime Minister showed himself not averse to giving consideration to the candidacy of another stalwart of the Christian Socialist Movement – Percy Dearmer. There is a Dearmer family tradition that also whispering in MacDonald's ear was Dr Jane Walker, a long-time friend of Marian Knowles, a veteran of the Suffragist movement, and one of the Prime Minister's medical advisers.

The papers of the Archbishops of Canterbury, housed in Lambeth Palace Library, contain a considerable amount of correspondence, *aide-mémoires* and memoranda on the subject of ecclesiastical appointments (some of which do indeed have those legendary notes attached, such as, 'unmarried – some means'). These documents mainly concern episcopal appointments, the more senior deaneries – and appointments to Westminster Abbey. Despite it being a 'royal peculiar', and consequently outside the jurisdiction of the Archbishop (or perhaps perversely because of that!), Lambeth always seems to have been very anxious to add its advice to the sovereign, via the Prime Minister, on the selection of both Deans and Canons of Westminster. Sadly, there is a gap in the early papers of Archbishop Lang, so we cannot peruse the details of Dearmer's appointment there. In the Westminster Abbey muniments, just part of an intriguing letter from the Archbishop of York, William Temple, to the Dean of Westminster (the Very Revd Foxley Norris) has survived. It is most revealing, and shows that the enthusiastic advocacy of Temple, Barry and others among Dearmer's admirers was not shared in the Deanery at Westminster. It was necessary for the Archbishop of York to make plain his own position on the matter:

> I must not leave you in any doubt about what I can do. Dearmer is one of my oldest friends and his wife was a great friend of both of us before they married. They chose me to marry them at St James' Piccadilly. I consider that he has

been passed over repeatedly when he ought to have been given a fuller position in the Church. The fact that you do not feel him to be the right man weighs with me immensely, but in any ideas I put before the Prime Minister I should not feel able to let them appear as being in competition with Dearmer, and I am presumptuous enough to believe that you will find both Dearmer and his wife a real acquisition when you get them! His freakishness is only skin deep.

It requires no astute reading between those lines to discern that Foxley Norris did not want Dearmer as a member of the Chapter at Westminster, seeming to think that he would not be able to make a significant contribution to the Collegiate body. It was an opinion which Foxley Norris came to believe was eventually amply justified.

In 1929 Robert Henry Charles, Archdeacon of Westminster and renowned biblical scholar specializing in the Apocrypha and the inter-testamental literature, had a road accident. He was gravely handicapped for eighteen months, and died at his home in Little Cloister on 30 January 1931. Now at last the Prime Minister was minded to suggest the name of Percy Dearmer to the King as the successor to Charles in his Abbey Canonry. Having obtained notification of his willingness to accept such an offer, it was announced, on 11 March 1931, that Percy Dearmer had, after a long delay, been found a position within the official structures of the Church of England – almost sixteen years after he had left St Mary's Primrose Hill. The new Canon was installed in the Abbey on 1 May 1931 (the Feast of St Philip and St James). It was a most appropriate choice of day. May Day had long been a festival day for Christian Socialists. Indeed, Dearmer had himself written a May Day hymn for *The English Hymnal* which begins:

> The winter's sleep was long and deep,
> But the earth is awakened and gay;
> For the life ne'er dies that from God doth rise,
> And the green comes after the grey.

So God doth bring the world to spring;
And on their holy day
Doth the Church proclaim her Apostles' fame,
To welcome the first of May.

Dearmer no doubt felt that with his appointment to Westminster, green shoots of hope were about to succeed the grey days of frustration, not perhaps realising the far-from-untroubled atmosphere into which he was entering. The Dean's misgivings apart (never revealed to either Dearmer, or his family, then or later), it was, as Russell Barry was to discover when, two years later, he succeeded C. S. Woodward at the Abbey, 'not a very happy ship'. Barry acknowledged that the Dean (known as 'Old Bill') 'was always kindness itself', but the Dean's irritations were all too obvious.

Foxley Norris's considered estimation of the abilities (and disabilities) of his capitular colleagues is revealed in a letter to Archbishop Lang five years later, in 1936. Looking back on Dearmer's ministry, he was dismissive of the concept that an Abbey canonry should be treated as a suitable reward for a man who, in the Dean's view, had already completed his best work. He believed that to have been the case with Dearmer. 'However much his friends may wish to say otherwise, he has been practically no use to us at the Abbey,' he told the Primate. This harsh judgement is hardly supported by the facts. It may very well be that Foxley Norris was looking at the matter narrowly, only assessing what he considered Dearmer to have done for the Abbey. Dearmer was not the only victim of Dean Foxley Norris's cutting judgements. Canon Carnegie, he said, 'can no longer be heard owing to age and infirmity'; Barry did what he could to help, 'but is always tired out before he starts'; Storr is so busy organizing the Evangelicals 'that he is practically never available'. Then there is Donaldson; 'You know his limitations', the Dean tells the Archbishop. Storr was a particular target of the Dean's displeasure. On arrival at the Abbey, Barry quickly discovered that one of the major problems was a long-standing tension between the Dean and Storr. 'Ostensibly it was about Chapter Finances. But it was due, I fancy, to some deep and half-irrational clash of personal temperament.'

It seems, then, that Dean Foxley Norris's personality made a not insignificant contribution to the tensions at Westminster Abbey. Lawrence Tanner, who was the Abbey's Keeper of the Muniments from 1925 until 1966, spoke of him as 'a pugnacious man . . . autocratic by nature, he was never afraid of a fight.' *The Times*'s obituary of Foxley Norris goes further and says he was 'distinctly autocratic'. As incumbent of various parishes, and again as Dean of York, he had been able to do as he pleased. At Westminster, as the obituary says, he discovered that the statutes governing the College of St Peter are far from granting the Dean complete independence, and for many purposes the Dean and the Canons have joint powers and responsibilities. *The Times* commented, 'Foxley Norris was apt at times to forget this'; which serves to emphasize another of its comments, that he was 'intolerant of opposition'. In the 900th year history of the Abbey Dr Adam Fox (Canon 1942–63) said there was 'a refreshing individuality about Dean Foxley Norris', but added, 'he sometimes irritated people.' That seems to have been a considerable understatement.

Certainly, Dearmer shared with his brother Canons an anxiety about the future of the Abbey's ministry and even of Foxley Norris's leadership. Storr, also writing to the Archbishop of Canterbury, tells how three days before Percy's death, 'Dearmer met Barry and myself and we were talking about what might be made of the place, if we had keen leadership and a good team.' Storr added gloomily, 'At the moment the Abbey is in low water.' Woodward (a Canon when Dearmer arrived and later Bishop of Bristol) offered his assessment, again in a letter to the Primate, telling him, 'new blood is very badly needed', and says, 'Of course the Dean would be horrified, he can't be in the saddle much longer.' All of which serves to emphasize the depth of the unhappiness into which Dearmer entered in 1931.

How wrong was Foxley Norris about the value of Dearmer's contribution to the Abbey? Dearmer's major work at the Abbey was as Librarian, where there was important work to be done as a result of the Library's refurbishment. In 1932 the Pilgrim Trust gave a generous grant which enabled the Library in the East Cloister to be connected with the Muniments Room. Percy worked happily, and established a valued friendship, with Lawrence Tanner who, in addition to his duties as Keeper of the Muniments, was Sub-Librarian and in charge of the day-to-day affairs in the Library. Dearmer was also Canon Steward, the member of the Chapter traditionally responsible to his colleagues for the Abbey's grounds and gardens. This he also enjoyed, having known the Abbey precincts since his school days. Another bonus enabled Dearmer to work alongside a fellow member of the Alcuin Club Committee, whose artistic and liturgical tastes he had long shared. Jocelyn Perkins had been appointed to the office of Minor Canon and Sacrist at the Abbey in 1899, so had already served there for over thirty years when Dearmer arrived. There was no resentment between them, however. In his recollections, *Sixty Years at Westminster Abbey*, Perkins hailed Dearmer as a remarkable person who was 'a brilliant writer and a first-rate ecclesiastical journalist'. He lavished praise on Dearmer's work:

> No doubt he did a good deal of original work himself; but the glory of *The Parson's Handbook* is that it brings masses of material which otherwise would have remained unread on the shelves of libraries into the sight of all men by weaving it into an impressive connected narrative of the utmost value to all shades of opinion.

It was a happy convergence, and Dearmer was able to encourage and support his friend in his unceasing campaign to improve the ornaments and furnishings of the Abbey. Perkins had built up a wonderful collection of plate, banners, altar frontals, copes and such like, and revolutionized the dignity of the ceremonial of the Abbey's worship, based on the English Use – another enthusiasm he and Dearmer shared.

Was it perhaps Dearmer in the pulpit that the Dean wished to criticize? On his preaching in the Abbey, his ever-loyal wife Nan is surprisingly frank. She gives it as her opinion that he was not always at his best in those years in the Abbey pulpit.

> He had always been an unequal preacher, often giving his best when the occasion seemed least to demand it and sometimes missing fire disappointingly when it was important that he should succeed. He was at all times greatly influenced by his hearers and if he felt that they were out of sympathy with him, he lost power, whereas when he and they were of accord, he could rise to great heights.

Percy Dearmer was still 'a name to conjure with' in Church circles, and there were always good congregations in the Abbey when he preached. Additionally, the press loved to quote him. He may have spent years apparently forgotten by the Church, but his name was still well enough known to attract column inches in the secular, as well as the religious, press. The additional fact that he was preaching from the pulpit in the Abbey, and dealt from time to time with unusual subjects, gave his words an extra *frisson*: when, for instance, he criticized the printing and presentation of the Scriptures, calling the Bible 'the worst printed book in the world'; when he told the Conference of Educational Authorities that knowledge, like leisure, is ill-distributed and that the school leaving age should be raised; again when he pleaded for people to put 'Church before Party' in a sermon on Ash Wednesday. He declared that he believed:

> The Church is at this time in danger from the pressure of highly organised parties, which have taken advantage of its comprehensiveness to overstress particular points of view, and themselves represent neither the general aspirations of the English people, nor the learning of scholars, nor the mind of the Church of England as a whole. I am convinced,

therefore, that an effort must be made to represent that mind, to rally church people to understand what their church really is.

On another occasion, in an Abbey sermon, Dearmer attacked gambling and hoped that 'England would now be released from the moral contagion that comes from outside in the form of sweepstakes'. Again, Dearmer told them from the Abbey pulpit that the Christian religion had often been caricatured, brutalized or vulgarized, 'but the actual teaching of Christ has seldom either been fully preached or sincerely practised'. In yet a further sermon he deplored the emerging methods of dictatorship: 'hate, violence, suppression of free thought and action, control of education', and prophesied, 'It will be for England again to save democracy.'

Hospital Sunday 1934, *The Times* reported, drew from him a return to warnings regarding the dangers of gambling:

> To secure peace required more imagination than we yet possessed. To prevent disease and accidents also required more imagination. But everyone now has enough to see that the sick must be looked after and that hospitals must not only be supported but must have the best. Let us support the hospitals, but without defiling them by gambling, by demoralizing the people of other countries with sweepstakes.

Among the sermons Dearmer preached in the Abbey were a number which concentrated on the lives of particular famous people. It is a type of sermon he obviously enjoyed preparing and delivering. Consequently there were sermons given on Cowper, Lewis Carroll, Locke, Wren, Bishop Heber, George Herbert, Ruskin, Coleridge and General Gordon. This last subject attracted a good deal of slightly shocked press coverage on delivery. *The Times* rather soberly headlined its news item on the sermon 'The Martyrdom of Gordon'. In contrast, *The News Chronicle* ran it as '"Damned Lie" Denied in the Abbey: Canon Dearmer defends Gen. Gordon'. Dearmer was referring to the accusation that Gordon was a secret drinker, and said in the sermon, 'Kitchener called it a damned lie, and for once the theological adjective is justified.' Other papers also adopted a stance of mock prudery about the use of the word 'damned' from the pulpit. However, nothing equalled the reaction of the press (and others) to the content of Dearmer's sermon on 10 January 1932. He preached on the subject of birth control.

In that sermon, after describing the way in which the population had been restricted in the past by wars, pestilence, famine, infanticide and abortion, Dearmer showed the necessity for a fresh consideration of the whole question of birth control in the light of modern science, especially biology, and of what he spoke of as 'a higher ethic'. The fact of one of the Canons advocating birth control from the Abbey pulpit was in itself surprising, but what fed the newspaper headlines with additional ammunition was his condemnation, in the sermon, of the Roman Catholic attitude towards the subject:

> The majority of educated Christians now take a different position from that of a few years ago. But many do not. Yet no Christian Church forbids birth control. The Roman Catholic community is commonly supposed to, and the poor and ignorant often believe this . . . There are very important exceptions, and apart from these exceptions, the control is always allowed by the Roman Catholic community if it takes the form of abstinence, permanent, or even (though reluctantly) of periodical discretion. Therefore, it is not birth control that is really disallowed by the Christian Church, but only certain forms of it.

The sermon was attacked by *Osservatore Romano* as 'erroneous' and *The Tablet* stated that 'the churlishness of this Protestant dignitary has been proved to us more than once'. Dearmer was not willing to leave it there. The matter became something of an obsession with him. Writing or speaking on the Roman Catholic stance on birth control, Dearmer continued to reveal a level of intolerance towards that church which does not fit easily with his general conviction regarding Christian unity. In a letter to Dr Marie Stopes, the birth control pioneer, he is quite uncompromising in his condemnation of Roman Catholic methods. He spoilt his reasonable advocacy of birth control by including remarks which can only be judged as being both irrational and bigoted.

> Slowly, and reluctantly, I have been forced to the conclusion that the Roman Catholic Church is not so much a religious community as a great political machine endeavouring to control our newspapers and other sources of information and to acquiring a dominating position through a small but highly organised minority vote, over the affairs of Great Britain. Many good Romanist laymen do not realise how they are being used, trained as they are in habits of submission and excluded from the free access to literature through censorship imposed by their authorities. It is not possible any longer to doubt that an attempt is being made through immigration from Southern Ireland, gradually to drive the English out of England and the Scots out of Scotland.

How is this invasion to be brought about? Dearmer provides a ludicrous explanation. Through the denial of birth control to Roman Catholic parents in order that they may 'flood England with Irish papists'. In a further letter to Marie Stopes he counsels her always to use 'the good old English word "Papist" rather than "Catholic"', in order not to offend a huge body of Anglican opinion.

One of the results of the sermon in the Abbey was that Dearmer became much in demand as a speaker for the Birth Control Movement. In June 1932 he was the guest of honour at the first Campaign for Birth Control luncheon held at the Criterion Restaurant Piccadilly. In his speech on that occasion, he again referred to 'celibate people in search of power'. Dearmer contrasted this with the Anglican situation:

> You know at the Lambeth Conference the bishops, with a

necessary amount of caution, came down on the right side. And that was very remarkable. I was relieved and quite a little surprised that after all the Conference pronounced a perfectly legitimate opinion, due to the fact that our bishops and clergy are married. Thinking it over at home a bishop might have said, 'I am going to vote against birth control,' and his wife would have said, 'Don't be a fool, John.'

Thanking Dearmer for his address, Dr Stopes said:

> It is my duty and pleasure in a few words to thank Dr Dearmer both for his presence here and for the many gallant efforts he has made on behalf of enlightenment, and of that greater beauty of life of which he has spoken so eloquently. How whole-heartedly we agree with him with regard to the dangers of Roman Catholics in our midst, old members of our Society need hardly be reminded.

Later that year Dearmer contributed a preface to Marie Stopes's *Roman Catholic Methods of Birth Control* in which he repeated the allegations he had made in that letter to her in which he had written of the Roman Catholic 'great political machine'.

Such high-profile 'extra-mural' work was in the best traditions of Canons of Westminster. Nan Dearmer said that there were those who hoped Percy would use his influence to revive the tradition of Christian Social preaching in the Abbey, and were disappointed when he did not. That does not seem an altogether accurate assessment of what happened. Dearmer was still concerned about 'issues' and was willing to tackle them in the pulpit – and in more practical ways. Predecessors such as Canons Kingsley, Gore, Donaldson and Barnett would have approved, not only of the content of many of his sermons, but also of his willingness to engage in 'hands-on' social action. In January 1933, writing to Dr Stopes, he apologized for his tardiness in submitting an article, giving as an excuse that he had been 'running a Canteen for the Westminster unemployed, devoting the whole of every morning to the work'. The account he gives of this admirable work is blemished by an uncharitable reference to 'Irish unemployed taking bread out of the mouths of unemployed'. This otherwise kind and generous priest seems to have had an insensitive blind spot when it came to surveying the Roman Catholic Church of his day.

From whatever assessment, there is ample evidence that, until his illness in 1935, Percy Dearmer remained active, and much in demand, both as a speaker and writer. It may be, as his colleague, friend and obituarist Russell Barry put it, that in his later life his reputation as 'an original, independent thinker, informed by a thorough scholarship in his own subject' tended to be 'dissipated by an over-great and somewhat ephemeral output', but that did not deter the invitations to speak or to write. He was an adornment to the Abbey and rightly allotted his energies in the time-honoured way of his predecessors. This seems to have been agreed as: sufficient to fulfil capitular duties, while coincidentally being available to the Church, and indeed the secular world, as priest, prophet or evangelist. It is difficult, at this distance, to identify where the Dean felt his colleague was deficient in either of these regards. Could it have been that, like Archbishop Davidson, the autocratic (if not aristocratic) Dean disapproved of Dearmer's (and Donaldson's) still far from abandoned 'left of centre' approach to matters of social concern?

Amongst the writing which Dearmer completed while at the Abbey, there was the somewhat curious *A Short Handbook of Public Worship*. In many ways it is a return to where he started with *The Parson's Handbook*. The volume is described as being for the clergy, church councillors and laity of the churches of the Anglican Communion. A preliminary note states that the Archbishops of Canterbury and York cordially approved of the motive and aims of the book. It was produced for the Worship and Order Group, a varied and unusual gathering of talents. Of the thirty-two contributors, many have already featured in this narrative: F. R. Barry, Christopher Cheshire, F. C. Eeles, W. R. Matthews and

Jocelyn Perkins, with F. E. Brightman assisting in the editing. Others were well-known in Church circles: E. J. Bicknell, B. K. Cunningham, J. W. Hunkin, S. L. Ollard and E. S. Woods. The Dean of Bristol (H. L. C. V. de Candole) chaired the Group and Jocelyn Perkins was Secretary, but Dearmer, having produced the book on their behalf, is described as 'author'. In it very visible traces of *The Parson's Handbook* remonstrances remain – even the advocacy of the priest's gown worn over the cassock, a defence of the Ornaments Rubric, and such anti-ultramontanisms as 'A priest of the Church of England has no more right to wear a biretta than a coronet or a fez!' A kind of potted *Parson's Handbook*, it has less than one hundred pages but much sound sense, including a classical Dearmer *cri de cœur* at its end:

> Perhaps our past mistake – in church as in the study – has been mainly that, given poetry to handle in the text of our common worship and in its ceremonial, we have used it all as if it were prose; and this is only another way of saying that we have made a material use of spiritual things. But the past is over and done; and we are looking forward with confidence and with hope. For the light of a new dawn is already in the sky.

A rather different book from Dearmer's Abbey period is a collection of essays he edited entitled *Christianity and the Crisis*. The book starts with W. R. Matthews describing the intellectual and moral confusion of the times, followed by particular chapters on 'the current situation in industry', 'literature in the judgement of history' and 'confusion in international relations'. Next there is an analysis of what Christianity *really* is, contributed by Dr Charles Raven, calling his chapter 'The Secret of Christ'. It is followed by supportive sections by J. S. Bezzant, George Bell, E. S. Woods and others. In the third part 'The Christian Solution' is applied to such subjects as personal and family life, education, the social and economic order, and the world of international affairs. Now it is the turn of A. A. David, Hewlett Johnson,

Maude Royden, Cosmo Gordon Lang, Maurice Reckitt and F. R. Barry to have their say, with William Temple providing 'The Conclusion of the Matter'. It was a weighty and worthy document – very much an earnest child of its time. The establishment had fully welcomed Dearmer back into its inner sanctums by entrusting the preface and editing of such a volume to his pen.

Neither the embrace of the establishment nor the respectability conferred by the Westminster Canonry meant that the old radical was willing to be gagged, as we have seen from his sermons. There was another regular opportunity to recall and renew the critical spirit, in meetings of Club. The name of this society is not preceded by the definite or indefinite article – it is simply 'Club'. It was a group of what was then known as 'progressive clergy'. The 'official' history of Club is delightfully vague about its beginnings and says it was formed on a Monday or a Tuesday in mid-December 1927. Edward Woods, then bishop of Croydon, with Pat McCormick, who had followed Dick Sheppard at St Martin-in-the-Fields, called a meeting at St Martin's Vicarage to discuss 'The Position of Christianity among those outside organised religion'. Among those who attended were Tissington Tatlow, Harold Anson, Gordon Arrowsmith, B. K. Cunningham, Dick Sheppard and Percy Dearmer. The meeting lasted two days and at the end it was decided to meet again – with Dearmer proposing the name 'Club'. It was a society which Percy much enjoyed. When he went to Westminster he took the opportunity of injecting it with a little new life. It met in 4 Little Cloister in the Abbey, and he became its chairman. One of its first members has written:

> Christian argument it was, and it is a pity it is not more common. I think 'Club' has always stood for that. To be able to come up two or three times a year and be in that atmosphere has been to me what a week's retreat is to some people. It is a group of people who, though I hardly dare believe it, put a very few first things first; and a large

number of what I (in the face of an apparently large majority of my fellow clergy) consider to be second things, 'Club', thank heaven, also puts second.

In 1941, after his death, Nan Dearmer wrote that 'Percy believed whole-heartedly in the need for such a group' and that nothing would have made him happier than the knowledge that it was then still continuing. Percy would no doubt be even happier to know that 'Club' has survived, with just the occasional hiccup, into the twenty-first century.

Another extra-mural activity came almost literally 'out of the blue'. F. A. Iremonger, who had been in at the beginning of Life and Liberty in 1917, became Director of Religious Broadcasting at the BBC in 1933. On arrival he discovered the poor quality of religious programmes for children. It appeared to Iremonger that there was little imagination to hand. He asked Percy if he would undertake a series of services for children to be broadcast on Sunday afternoons. It was a unique opportunity and one which aroused the enthusiasm of the catechist in Dearmer. In order to give the programme an authentic feel Percy recruited what he called his 'Crew' from among his own family and their friends. The result was that Gillian, Tony and Imogen all became regular broadcasters. It was a half-hour service and went out monthly. The broadcasts attracted a large post-bag and must be regarded as a further important extension of the Abbey's ministry.

Liverpool had long had a particular place in Dearmer's affections. His friendship with Fred Dwelly was always stimulating; and he continued to take a great interest in the building of the Cathedral. The tradition remains there that Percy was involved in the design of the distinctive robes of the Cathedral Vergers and the members of the Cross Guild, but that cannot now be fully substantiated, though Nan says they 'were planned on the occasion of our last visit there in 1935'. That final visit was undertaken at the invitation of the General Assembly of Unitarian and Free Christian Churches, who had asked him to deliver the Essex Hall lecture. The Dearmers stayed with the Bishop of Liverpool (A. A. David) and Mrs David. The subject of the lecture was 'Christianity as a new Religion'. His style in this lecture is provocative, reiterating a favourite theme, that Christianity has never really been tried – only imitations, substitutes or plain distortions of the faith. In his peroration he is scornful and challenging:

> 'Follow me.' And we say, 'May we not follow an image of thee? There are so many helpful suggestions: the despairing Enigma of Albert Schweitzer, the *Mysterium Tremendum* of Rudolph Otto, the transcendent Thunder of Karl Barth.' And many follow where Loisy failed, and say, 'The Church can take thy place.' And some who are very modern say, 'Alas, we cannot. You lived so very long ago. But we will follow the best of the saints; for your spirit is revealed in them.' And all of us have said in our hearts: 'We can follow a system, a theory, a metaphysic, a mystery, and when that is too difficult, a mythology. Bid us be orthodox, or bid us be heterodox; but do not ask us to be simply Christian. For that is something new!'

Foxley Norris's criticism that Dearmer had gone to the Abbey too late in his career is perfectly sustainable; that his contribution during his time there was insubstantial and insignificant is not. Nan Dearmer agrees that his contribution could have been greater 'if his health had not been rapidly failing'. Before he arrived at the Abbey he had been suffering from rheumatism, and this, it later transpired, had affected his heart. The five years at Westminster were a gallant struggle against increasing disability. He would not allow illness to hamper his work, but was unable to hide his increasing infirmity. An old acquaintance, Hensley Henson (by then Bishop of Durham), was at the Mansion House for the Lord Mayor's Dinner for the Archbishops and Bishops on 20 June 1934. He saw Dearmer there and was shocked at the difference he saw in him.

Percy Dearmer was there, and his face arrested my notice,

and haunted my memory. He does not look either well or happy. I had not seen him for many years, and this change in his look was distressing. He always had in his countenance a suggestion of recklessness, such as might befit an undergraduate, but it was never an unhappy face, now it is not a pleasing countenance to look on. He was, when I knew him first, an advanced Anglo-Catholic, he is now a rather irresponsible 'Modernist', who gives much copy to the pressmen.

The visit to Liverpool proved to be his last major undertaking. In July 1935 he had a serious breakdown in health and the doctor told the family that his heart was badly affected. His advice was that Percy should go to their cottage at Gasson, Peaslake, near Guildford (Oakridge had been sold years ago), in order to see what a compete rest would accomplish. In September he became gravely ill and, for a month, was not expected to live; but he rallied and was able to return to Westminster in October and, by the end of January, was able to do a little work.

George V died in January 1936, which plunged the Abbey into a maelstrom of activity. Nan had taken Gillian to a family in Berlin to learn German. Percy wrote telling his daughter, 'The streets are dense – about a million have filed past: the Abbey crammed all day – nave packed for Monday Mattins!' The Sacrist took the Dearmers to see the lying in state. 'Perks took us (Grannie, Imogen, Tony and me) to West[minster] Hall at 7. It is wonderfully impressive – very simple and very rich.'

He was also able to resume preaching, broadcasting the children's services, and happily was able to assist at his son Geoffrey's wedding in March. He wrote to Gillian in Berlin and said that the marriage service was 'simple and beautiful, with a jolly family feeling as if all the little congregation were relations'. But his friends could see he was a sick man and watched him with increasing concern. Barry records they felt his work was nearly done; yet, often obviously in acute pain, he carried on and 'never allowed his physical suffering to spoil the charm, humour and generosity, which made him so delightful a host'. Barry also says that only the week before his death, he was 'actively making suggestions for perfecting details at the Coronation'. He did live to take part in that ancient and unique liturgical ceremony.

In mid-May he spent three days at Gasson, returning for a meeting of Club at Little Cloister. On Thursday 28 May Nan and Percy drove down again for a day in the country at Gasson. While there he told his wife, 'This is the day I look forward to each week.' Both in her memoir, and in a letter to Martin and Joan Shaw, Nan tells how, although he was 'so brave and so good in his illness he had such depression to struggle against.' It seemed as though he was getting stronger. She told the Shaws, 'He thought he was getting better and indeed lately he seemed much more himself that I hoped, with care, we might keep him perhaps for a year or so.' In her letter to the Shaws, written five days after the funeral, Nan is frank about what the previous winter had taken out of her. It was terrible, she tells them. To Martin Shaw she says, 'I haven't written so fully to anyone else, but you and he loved each other.'

On the afternoon of 29 May, the Friday before Whitsunday, Dearmer took a party of his King's College students around the Abbey. Nan was with him and thought that he seemed 'very much his old self as he discoursed on the history of the place, and pointed out its beauties'. It was planned that Nan should take a short break – she was very tired – and spend Whitsun in the country, leaving Mrs Knowles to look after Percy. She told the Shaws, 'I don't think he had anything to suffer at the end. He was talking gayly to my mother at 6.30 and at 7 they found him in the study – gone.'

Whether Mrs Knowles sent for him, or he had providentially called, his next-door neighbour and brother Canon, Russell Barry, found him dead on the floor of his study. Nan says, 'I found pages of the book he was writing and his pen without the cap on, lying on the window seat. I know he started to write and felt tired and just lay down and went. We couldn't wish better for him. I wish I had been there.'

Indeed, it was a happy release for one who had been much frustrated in his time of illness. Nan is surely right in saying, 'It is so much what he would have wished – to be working right up to the end. What we both dreaded, I know, was another awful illness or for him to go on unable to work at all.' In her memoir Nan says, 'In the middle of work on his book, he laid down his pen and pipe for a moment's rest, and died.' He was in his seventieth year.

He was cremated on Tuesday 2 June and his funeral took place in a packed Abbey at noon on the following day. The Prayer Book service was ordered lovingly by his friend Jocelyn Perkins. It included two of Percy's own hymns, 'A brighter dawn is breaking' and 'Jesus, good above all other', and a Bishop Heber hymn from *The English Hymnal* (and *Songs of Praise*), 'When spring unlocks the flowers to paint the laughing soil'. He was buried in the north walk of the Cloisters, the 'place where the monks had studied', immediately by the Great Garth, the scene of many a Westminster boys' fight.

13

The Man and His Message

On a dismal January Sunday in 1905 or 1906 (he could not remember which) a Harrow schoolboy, bitten, on his own admission, by a fascination for church ritual and ceremonial, entered St Mary's Primrose Hill for the first time. He justified his ecclesiological obsession as being 'as respectable a hobby as the collection of the varieties of moths or postage stamps'. He was at St Mary's to 'collect' a specific example of High Churchmanship, of which he had previously only heard, and as yet, not seen; it was the species 'Dearmerism'. The High Celebration of the Eucharist, which the young man attended that Sunday, impressed him enormously. There was, first of all, the setting: 'An ugly red-brick church turned into a shrine of beauty' with the vestments, plain-chant and incense relieving 'the banality of a prim suburban neighbourhood'. But there was one thing, over and above all else, that lingered for ever in the schoolboy's memory: 'The form of Percy Dearmer in the pulpit, the handsome face like a Florentine painting, the cutting blade of the incisive voice sedulously washed from clerical unction.' From that morning on, David Murray was hooked.

The death of Dearmer, not surprisingly, occasioned a number of obituaries. *The Times*, as one would expect of that newspaper of record, was the first in the field, printing an obituary the day after the death. Although anonymous, it is clearly the work of 'an insider', even detailing Percy's last hours at the Abbey: 'shortly before his death walking and talking with Canon Barry'. From tone and content (for it 'damns with faint praise'), it could well have been the work of Foxley

Norris. On Tuesday 3 June, there appeared two further 'appreciations' – one anonymous and the other written by Canon Donaldson. Both of these are kinder, and more balanced, than the original. The anonymous contribution, which employs the word 'colleague' when referring to Percy, is almost certainly by Russell Barry. Further evidence of this is in a surviving letter of Barry to Marian Knowles in which he says, 'I hope the note in *The Times* today made some amends for the too-unappreciative notice on Saturday.'

In the following days more assessments appeared in *The Times* and the church newspapers. After this initial flurry of tributes there then followed, as might be expected, a few years of public silence about Dearmer, his life and his work, until, in 1940, memories were stirred and stimulated by the publication of Nan Dearmer's *Life*. The reviewers of her book took the opportunity to offer critiques of her tentative assessment of Percy's achievements. Among these, the most informed and sophisticated essay comes from the pen of David Murray, the erstwhile Harrow schoolboy.

After leaving Harrow, Murray went up to Balliol, Oxford, where he obtained a first in *Literae Humaniores* in 1910, and further added to his distinguished academic career by becoming both the Brackenbury History Scholar and the John Locke Scholar. During the First World War, he was employed in the Intelligence Department of the War Office and then afterwards went to work on *The Times* as foreign sub-editor. In 1920 he became a member of the editorial staff of *The Times Literary Supplement*, rising to become a highly successful editor of that journal in 1928. When Nan Dearmer's *Life* of her husband arrived on his editorial desk at the *TLS* in 1940, it would have been no surprise to those who knew Murray well that, rather than allocating the review to one of his staff or one of his bevy of contributors, he chose personally to undertake the task – although still published, in those days, without attribution. The result was a concise, well-argued, authoritative piece, elegantly written, as one would hope of the editor of one of the world's leading literary journals.

Murray had already written elsewhere that he regarded himself as 'one who cannot be called a close friend, but who was very proud to be any sort of friend of such a man'.

Murray's opinion of Dearmer, a man whom he had known for over thirty years, is the finely honed judgement of a deeply erudite and cultured man. In the first place he, and other obituarists, were agreed that Dearmer was unique, a 'one off'. Murray claims the experience of one who has spent long years in Church circles and in the study of ecclesiastical problems, and asserts that of all the many striking figures with whom he had been brought into contact, 'Percy Dearmer stands out in my memory as the most salient and vivid of all.' Yet, he goes on, when an attempt is made to formulate his characteristics, neither his ideas nor his personality seem susceptible of definition. Was it the artistic temperament which he seems to have inherited from his father in such full measure which made him so hard to capture?

David Murray said of Dearmer that he was always going to be a difficult subject to categorize – or indeed (for the Church) to employ. The Church can cope with pastors and preachers, scholars, philosophers, historians, educationalists, administrators – even statesmen, social reformers, journalists and novelists – within its ordained ranks, but the priest as artist is a much rarer bird, and, it would seem, a more disconcerting one. This is perhaps the main reason why no adequate sphere of activity was ever found to put to proper use his undoubtedly remarkable gifts. Dearmer loved his mother, the Church of England, Lewis Donaldson said in *The Times*, but she was a cruel parent and refused him her embrace. 'He was a true son . . . she was a somewhat harsh mother to him.' This rejection was a sad and damaging repetition of his childhood and adolescent experience with Caroline Miriam, an experience of which Donaldson would almost certainly not have known.

This 'artistic temperament' manifested itself in a number of ways, Murray opined. Dearmer was capable of being 'wayward, incalculable, contemptuous at least of all the minor orthodoxies, refractory to regimentation, dowered with a searing tongue, disrespectful towards dignities, and what was worst sometimes, towards dignitaries'. Of the 'searing tongue' allegation, the copy of the *TLS* review preserved in the Dearmer family papers has an added hand-written note by his mother-in-law, Marian Knowles, which states, 'He was never prickly to his family. His best side was for them.' The appreciations in *The Times*, by his Abbey colleagues, also bear witness to the paradox that, while at times, he was unable to 'suffer fools gladly', having 'a characteristic laconic manner' and a capacity for a cutting remark, yet he was more often a humorous companion and a generous and entertaining host. In another *Times* tribute he is spoken of as being 'always genuine and invigorating'.

'Far more prickly characters [than Dearmer] have risen high in the Anglican hierarchy', Murray reminded the *TLS* readers. Was his failure to obtain the promotion, which so many of his admirers believed to be his due, more likely to have been caused by his seeming ability, in later life, to change his opinions with rapid regularity? Certainly, that is what one of the other *Times* contributors believed to be the case. 'His constantly shifting views and certain personal idiosyncracies made his promotion in the Church difficult.' Barry even goes as far as posing, for readers of *The Times*, the question, 'Does anyone know what Dearmer really believed?' This question is partly answered by a fellow member of Club who likened Dearmer to Wordsworth's Newton, 'voyaging through strange seas of Thought, alone'. On this voyage he accepted fearlessly every discovery of modern science and thought, and laid claim to new and forgotten realms of beauty, truth and goodness in the Christian gospel and in Christian art and worship, however much that might mean the sacrifice of his previous opinions or his personal popularity. He taught people, his friend maintained, to love God with their mind.

The Church newspaper *The Guardian* said, at his death, there was in Dearmer always much of the child: naïvety, sensitiveness, an eager thirst for new experiences, and a direct vision of the objective and the concrete. 'He was a Peter Pan,

The Man and His Message

the boy who never grew up, with his charm and mischievousness.'

Nan Dearmer hints that, because he ended being what Murray describes as 'the supreme ecclesiastical individualist', he could never have been a really convinced High Churchman. Murray vigorously disputes this, and says that Dearmer's early years are unintelligible if he was not a Tractarian in those days. As if to anticipate this coming debate, Donaldson, in his piece in *The Times* in June 1936, emphasized the importance of those High Church years and praised the tremendous contribution that Percy had made in the first days of the Christian Social Union. He drew attention to Dearmer's part in the lively protests against the evils of poverty, social deprivation and other contemporary evils. It would seem, from what we have examined of the contents of his sermons in the Abbey, that 'sociological questions', as the Dean chose to call them, still dominated his mind and disturbed his conscience to the end. Murray argues that 'Dearmer's Christian Socialism was no mere offshoot of his religion, it was of the essence of it.' For Dearmer, he said, the Church meant the people bound together in a brotherhood for sacred and secular purposes. Sadly, experience brought him to a realisation that Anglo-Catholicism was little more than just another party, and one which, Murray alleged, Dearmer apprehended as 'ineradicably sacerdotally dogmatic'. This failure of the Movement made it increasingly repugnant to him. His hope for the future of the Christian Church in England lay in the eventual reincorporation of English Nonconformity with Anglicanism, 'while clinging (with apparent inconsistency) to the principle of the Establishment, as at any rate the symbol of a comprehensively national Church'. How appropriate, then, that he should end his days, the *TLS* Editor declared, as 'a Canon of Westminster, the most national of all Anglican shrines'. Murray makes no reference to Roman Catholic non-conformity, which is as well, remembering Dearmer's intolerance of that communion.

Many years after Dearmer's incumbency at Primrose Hill,

one of his successors there felt unmistakably that Percy's time as Vicar had been 'the best of times' for him. Along with so many positive memories and flourishing traditions was a clear understanding, shared almost universally by the obituarists, that the First World War had changed everything for Dearmer. This was more even than the obvious distress caused by the death of his first wife and a beloved son; it does not deny or underrate the obvious happiness and contentment of his second marriage and the love and joy he had in the children. It was another sort of death.

He shared this other 'death' with fellow priests and prophets such as Dick Sheppard, Pat McCormack and Studdert Kennedy, whose characteristic it was that they all died too young and generally greatly frustrated. It is too easy, too glib, merely to say they wore themselves out. It is far nearer the truth to say they were each victims of the disappointment that afflicted many post-War churchmen. They had believed that, given its 'life' and its 'liberty', a Church from which the furnace of War had burnt off its sinful preoccupations with trivial and petty concerns, could (and now would) concentrate on essentials – proclaiming the fundamental truths of the gospel, and boldly witnessing to the Kingdom. During the War these men had seen the depths of wickedness to which humanity could descend, while, at the same time, glimpsing a vision of the heroism and dignity to which the human race could aspire. But hopes were dashed, things did not change and such fine phrases as the occasional rallying calls we have heard Percy Dearmer utter, were to little or no avail. The Church returned to trivialities and petty concerns: to flower rotas, tedious services, lifeless sermons and interminable Church assemblies.

Dearmer himself was never going to bring about, on his own, a major change in the direction of the post-War Church. He did have the insight and imagination needed to provide some of the wherewithal for new directions. First of all, there was his attempt to rescue the Church's rites and ceremonies from continental captivity, and to affirm the dignity essential in liturgy. Alongside this was his concern to incorporate art and beauty, artists and craftsmen, within the Church's offering of what must never be less than the very best when it assembles for worship. Against all discouragement, F. L. Donaldson affirmed, Dearmer stood his ground on this matter. His aesthetic taste was among his greater gifts and was acute and sensitive. The Philistines, his colleague said, 'naturally regarded him as a dilettante. They were wholly wrong. He recognised the beautiful with the keenest perception, wherever it was to be found – in poetry or prose, in art or life. He worshipped beauty as an attribute of God – and could not bear its violation.'

Having successfully tackled the visual, Dearmer passed on to raising the standard of the Church's sung praises, expressly the corporate art of hymnody. It is a fact worthy of note that in the early years of the twentieth century Percy Dearmer and his friend Conrad Noel recruited to the service of Church music the two leading composers of the day. Vaughan Williams was part of the team around Dearmer who produced *The English Hymnal*, and he was willing to be equally involved in *Songs of Praise*. Vaughan Williams also encouraged Gustav Holst to contribute to both hymnals. But more significantly, Noel persuaded Holst to undertake the task of organist and choirmaster at Thaxted. It is hard to imagine a corresponding twenty-first-century situation.

Dearmer's idealism was not bounded by the walls of any church building. Along the way, he was one of the first churchmen to affirm the unity of body, mind and spirit and to seek to extend the Church's ministry of healing to each part of the human experience. Also as he continued his life's pilgrimage, he found himself a pioneer in recognizing the contribution that women were capable of making in the ministry of the Church.

It is also true that Dearmer received few of those honours that reflect an appreciation of work done and aims achieved. For most of his life he was pleased to be addressed as 'Doctor' Dearmer, but this dignity was a result of his academic work:

an Oxford Doctor of Divinity awarded, as the Register of Divinity Examinations states, after reading 'two dissertations as exercises for the degrees of Bachelor and Doctor of Divinity on Wednesday 7 June 1911'. Christ Church, his Oxford college, did not award him its Honorary Studentship, but its present-day historians maintain that it was mainly Prime Ministers rather than clerics who were so honoured by their college. However, King's College, London, with which he had such a long association, did elect him as a Fellow. His work in Serbia was recognized by the award of the Serbian Red Cross Medal. But there was one distinction of which he was particularly, and rightly, proud; it was rarely conferred on clergymen. This was his appointment, in 1924, as an Honorary Associate of the Royal Institute of British Architects in recognition of his services to ecclesiastical art and architecture.

Dearmer's life's pilgrimage contained many surprises. After the somewhat peremptory departure of the young aesthetic priest and his bohemian wife from the gaseous surroundings of South Lambeth, who could have guessed what would come next? In the event a short, sharp series of assistant curacies climaxed in a securely Anglo-Catholic parish in Hampstead, which will forever be connected with his name in the minds of the ecclesiologically minded.

St Mary's proved to be the beginning of many miles of the journey, before War and tragedy intervened. That the established Church would find him a difficult square peg for which they only had available conventional round holes, perhaps took him time to absorb, but the pilgrim continued his journey, while writing and lecturing, inspiring and stimulating on a variety of subjects. During these years Dearmer was deprived of any continuing pastoral responsibility. To his dismay, having employed in the title of his most seminal work the very English word 'Parson' (meaning the one who, in their own *persona*, represents before God the people of the parish), he found that he had no such sphere in which to do just that. Yet he journeyed on.

Dearmer never claimed to be a poet (occasionally others

The Man and His Message

described him as such) and was conscious of the inadequacy of some of his hymns. But he was rightly proud of his achievement in adapting Bunyan's words from *Pilgrim's Progress* for inclusion in *The English Hymnal*. He himself described it as a daring thing to do which had never been attempted before. Combined with Vaughan Williams's version of the tune of the Sussex folk-song 'Our Captain calls all hands aboard', it has been an inspiration to many for over ninety years. It also provides a suitable epitaph for Parson Dearmer on his pilgrimage. Valiantly, despite many discouragements, nothing made him relent his avowed intent.

> Who so beset him round
> With dismal stories,
> Do but themselves confound
>   His strength the more is.
> No foes shall stay his might,
> Though he with giants fight:
> He will make good his right
>   To be a pilgrim.

Appendix

Bibliographical Note on Sources Used

Because of the disparate nature of the material used in this biography, and its comparative inaccessibility, the judgement was that it would be better to give this account of sources used, rather than provide footnotes which, of necessity, could only be of a general nature.

First of all, I could do no other than acknowledge the incalculable value of Nan Dearmer's *The Life of Percy Dearmer*, 1941, during the writing of this book; it has been constantly at my side. Sadly, few of the original sources she used have survived. The exceptions are Dearmer's travel diaries of 1890 and 1891, and three holiday plays, which his family still retain. Percy's and Nan's diary-letters (1916–18) to Marian Knowles are now in the Oriental and India Office Collection at the British Library.

There is, however, further documentation of the greatest importance for any contemporary study of the life of Percy Dearmer still in the possession of the Dearmer family. I am assured it will, eventually, be deposited in a suitable archive. I have had unlimited access to this material, consisting of manuscript sermons, addresses, lectures and broadcast scripts, some contained in books, others loose. There is a large family scrapbook (substantially pre-1914) with mementoes of Mabel's productions; many photographs; a large collection of newspaper cuttings dating from the 1920s and 1930s, together with odd copies of *The Guildhouse Monthly*, *New Generation* and *Birth Control News*. Dearmer's letters to Nan

Bibliographical Note on Sources Used 199

from France (1915–16) are still in these family papers. There is also a good deal of correspondence relating to Martin Shaw, *The English Hymnal* and *Songs of Praise*.

For extra details of Mabel Dearmer's life and work, I have depended upon: Dearmer, Mabel (with a memoir of the author by Stephen Gwynne), *Letters from a Field Hospital*, 1915; Gwynne, Stephen, *Experiences of a Literary Man*, 1926; Krippner, Monica, *The Quality of Mercy, Women at War, Serbia 1915–1918*, 1980; Shefrin, Jill, 'Dearmerest Mrs Dearmer', Friends of the Osborne and Lillian H. Smith Collections, Occasional Paper, no. 2, Toronto, 1999; Stobart, M. A. St Clair, *The Flaming Sword in Serbia and Elsewhere*, 1916.

It is a convention to thank libraries and librarians, but in this case it is very necessary, for often they have gone to great lengths to unearth further material for me. So, I am anxious to express my gratitude to the House of Commons Library (particularly Dr Chris Pond and Andrew Parker); St Deiniol's Library, Hawarden (the Very Revd Peter Francis); the London Library; the British Library (for Add MS 56690, Add MS 585549 and the Oriental and India Office Collection); Lambeth Palace Library (Miss Melanie Barber) for guidance through the Davidson, Lang, Jenkins and Bell papers; and, not least, Westminster Abbey Library (Dr Tony Trowles). I also received particular help from the archivists at the Church of England Record Centre (Edward Pinsent) for NRA 25406 Eeles; Westminster School (Peter Holmes and Edward Smith); King's College, London; Oxford University Press (Dr Martin Maw) for NRA 27790 OUP (OUP/PUB/30); St Mary's Primrose Hill (John Hawes); Oxford University Archives (Simon Bailey); The British Architectural Library of the Royal Institute of British Architects (Susan Harris); and the Archivist of Christ Church, Oxford (Judith Curthoys). The Revd Dr Martin Dudley provided access to the (incomplete and unsorted) files of the Alcuin Club housed at St Bartholomew the Great, Smithfield.

Others who gave of their time, patience and advice are:

Monica Holmes (Guild of Health); Canon Alan Luff; Bernard Braley; the Revd Professor Robin Barbour (for a copy of the pages of the Bonskeid visitors' book containing 'The Second University Gathering'); Dr C. J. Kitching (Royal Commission on Historical Manuscripts); the Revd Michael Edge (Secretary of Club) for Ralph Stevens, *Notes on the history of 'Club'*, 1984; Professor David Smith (Borthwick Institute of Historical Research); Canon Alan Wilkinson; Peter Kennelly (Liverpool Cathedral); the Ven. Martin Draper; Dr Thomas Coke (Council for the Care of Churches); Canon Arthur J. Dobb (Diocese of Manchester) and the Sub-Dean of Christ Church, Oxford (the Very Revd Robert Jeffery). But in this category I must express my especial gratitude to Jill Shefrin, who generously shared with me details of her researches on Mabel Dearmer, and Fr Anthony Symondson SJ, who gave advice from his unique knowledge of the life and works of Sir Ninian Comper. (See also Anthony Symondson, '"Unity by Inclusion", Sir Ninian Comper and the planning of a Modern Church', *Twentieth Century Architecture 3, The Journal of the Twentieth Century Society*, pp. 19–42, 1998.)

The Church Times and *The Guardian* have provided many details. Disappointingly, in the official file copies of *The Church Times* in the Church of England Record Centre page 696, containing Dearmer's obituary in the issue of 5 June 1936, has been removed.

Hitherto unknown material and information was supplied by: David Addis (Dearmer's grandson), details of Mabel Dearmer's grave; the Revd Juliet Woollcombe (granddaughter), particular help with photographs; the Revd Michael Thompson, the diary of Monica Duncan Burnett; the Revd Michael Ainsworth, 'Grey Book' pamphlets; John Ridgeway Wood (Church Union) and the Revd G. M. Ikin, various items of Dearmer's correspondence; and the Revd Richard Rowe (former Vicar of Thaxted), Noel's copy of *The Parson's Handbook*. Reg Reading of the Gale Group kindly unearthed the authorship of the anonymous *Times Literary Supplement* review of 1 June 1940.

Bibliographical Note on Sources Used 201

It may be useful to list the printed sources which I have relied upon to provide both further details and background to the various incidents and events in Percy Dearmer's life, and I would recommend the following works for any further reading:

General Church history: Edwards, David, *Christian England*, vol. 3, 1984; Hastings, Adrian, *A History of English Christianity, 1920–1985*, 1986; Lloyd, Roger, *The Church of England 1900–1965*, 1966.

Anglo-Catholicism: Chadwick, Owen, *The Mind of the Oxford Movement*, 1960; Hughes, Dom Anselm, *The Rivers of the Flood: A personal account of the Catholic Movement in the 20th Century*, 2nd ed., 1963; Hylson-Smith, Kenneth, *High Churchmanship in the Church of England*, Edinburgh, 1993; Nockles, Peter B., *The Oxford Movement in Context, Anglican High Churchmanship 1760–1857*, 1994; Pickering, W. S. F., *Anglo-Catholicism, A Study in religious ambiguity*, 1989; Reed, John Skelton, *Glorious Battle – the Cultural Politics of Victorian Anglo-Catholicism*, Nashville TN, 1996; Yates, Nigel, *Anglican Ritualism in Victorian England, 1830–1910*, 1999.

Christian Socialism: Adderley, J., *Christian Social Reformers*, 1927; Bryant, Chris, *Possible Dreams: A Personal History of British Christian Socialists*, 1996; Gray, Donald, *Earth and Altar*, ACC 68, 1986; Jones, Peter d'A, *The Christian Socialist Revival, 1877–1914*, Princeton NJ, 1968; Norman, Edward, *The Victorian Christian Socialists*, 1987; Pinnington, Judith, *Kingdom and Commonwealth: the Christian Social Union and its legacy to radical social thought in the Church of England, 1899–1941*, Jubilee Group, 1997; Reckitt, M. B., *Maurice to Temple*, 1947; Reckitt, M. B., ed., *For Christ and the People*, 1968; Wagner, Donald O., *The Church of England and Social Reform since 1854*, New York, 1930; Wilkinson, Alan, *Christian Socialism: Scott Holland to Tony Blair*, 1998.

Westminster Abbey: Carpenter, Edward, ed., *A House of*

Kings: *The Official History of Westminster Abbey*, 1966; Perkins, Jocelyn, *Sixty Years at Westminster Abbey*, 1960; Tanner, Lawrence, *Recollections of a Westminster Antiquary*, 1969.

Westminster School: Carleton, John, *Westminster School: A History*, 1965; Field, John, *The King's Nurseries*, 1987.

Guild of Health: Harding, Geoffrey C., *The First 75 Years of The Guild of Health*, Guild of Health no. 42, 1983; Maddocks, Maurice, *The Christian Healing Ministry*, 1981.

Anglican Modernism: Smith, Eric A., *Another Anglican Angle, The History of the A.E.G.M.*, 1991; Stephenson, Alan M. G., *The Rise and Decline of English Modernism*, 1984.

The First World War: Macnutt, F. B., ed., *The Church in the Furnace*, 1918; Marrin, Albert, *The Last Crusade: The Church of England in the First World War*, Durham NC, 1974; Wilkinson, Alan, *The Church of England and the First World War*, 1978; *The Army and Religion. An Enquiry and its Bearing Upon the Religious Life of the Nation*, 1919.

St Mary's Primrose Hill: Anson, Peter F., *Fashions in Church Furnishings 1840–1940*, 2nd ed., 1965; Franglen, Geoffrey, ed., *England's Lane*, 1988; Ovenden, John, *St Mary's Primrose Hill: A Visitors' Guide*, 1985; Stephen, Francis, ed., *St Mary's Primrose Hill – A Guide and History*, 1972; Yates, Nigel, *Buildings, Faith and Worship: The Liturgical Arrangement of Anglican Churches 1600–1900*, 1991.

St Dunstan's Society and Warham Guild: Schoeser, Mary, *English Church Embroidery, 1833–1953*, 2nd ed., 1998; *The Warham Guild Handbook*, 2nd ed., 1963.

Alcuin Club: Davies, Horton, *Worship and Theology in England*, Vol. V, Princeton NJ, 1965; Jagger, Peter J., *The Alcuin Club and its Publications*, 1986.

Prayer Book Revision: Cuming, G. J., *A History of Anglican Liturgy*, 2nd ed., 1982, and *The Godly Order*, ACC 65, 1983; Headlam, A. C., *The New Prayer Book*, 1927; Jasper, R. C. D., *Walter Howard Frere, His Correspondence on Liturgical Revision*, ACC 39, 1954, *Prayer Book Revision* in England, 1954, and *The Development of the Anglican Liturgy 1662–1980*, 1989; Joynson-Hicks, William, *The Prayer Book Crisis*, 1928; Lowther Clarke, W. K., *The Prayer Book of 1928 Reconsidered*, 1943; *Minutes of Evidence taken before the Royal Commission on Ecclesiastical Discipline* (Cd 3069), 1906.

King's College, London: Hearnshaw, F. J. C., *The Centenary History of King's College, London 1828–1928*, 1929; Huelin, Gordon, *King's College, London, 1828–1978*, 1978.

Religious Broadcasting: Wolfe, Kenneth M., *The Churches and the British Broadcasting Corporation 1922–1956*, 1984.

The English Hymnal: The First Fifty Years: A Brief Account of the English Hymnal from 1906 to 1956, n.d.; Benson, Louis F., *The English Hymn: Its Development and its Use in Worship*, 1915; Draper, M. P., 'Percy Dearmer and the English Hymnal', *Alcuin Occasional Journal*, 1980; Watson, J. R., *The English Hymn: A Critical and Historical Study*, 1998; Music, D. W., 'Americans in the English Hymnal of 1906', Neil, A. J., ed. *With Ever Joyful Hearts*, New York, 1999.

Songs of Praise: Briggs, G. W., 'The Criticisms of *Songs of Praise*', in *The Hymn Society of Great Britain and Ireland Bulletin*, January 1941; *Songs of Praise Discussed*, compiled by Percy Dearmer with notes on the music by Archibald Jacob, 1933.

Plainsong: Barnes, John E., *George Ratcliffe Woodward 1848–1934, Poet, Priest and Musician*, 1996; Hughes, Dom Anselm, *Septuagesima, Reminiscences of the Plainsong & Mediaeval Music Society*, 1959.

Biography feeds on biography. The careful perusal of biographical and autobiographical material concerning those who were Dearmer's contemporaries, acquaintances, colleagues and friends has been of great benefit during the preparation of this biography. Books which have provided information are (in alphabetical order of subject): Stevens, T. P., *Father Adderley*, 1943; Anson, Harold, *Looking*

Forward; Barry, F. R., *Period of My Life*, 1970, and West, Frank H., *F.R.B. - A Portrait of Bishop Russell Barry*, 1980; Jasper, R. C. D., *George Bell, Bishop of Chichester*, 1967; Nichols, Bridget, 'F. E. Brightman' in Irvine, Christopher, ed., *They Shaped Our Worship*, ACC 75, 1998; Chesterton, G. K., *Autobiography*, 1936; Ward, Maisie, *Gilbert Keith Chesterton*, 1944, Ffinch, Michael, *G. K. Chesterton*, 1986, and Pierce, Joseph, *Literary Converts*, 1999; Peart-Binns, John S., 'Albert Augustus David, "The Liberal Autocrat"', in Smout, Michael, ed., *Four Bishops of Liverpool*, 1985; Bell, G. K. A., *Randall Davidson*, 3rd ed., 1952; Carpenter, S. C., *Duncan Jones of Chichester*, 1956; [on F. C. Eeles] Findlay, Donald, *The Protection of our Churches, The History of the Council of Churches 1921–1996*, 1996, and Scott, Judith D. G., 'Memorial of Dr F. C. Eeles', in Simpson, W. Douglas, ed., *King's College Chapel Aberdeen*, 1955; Phillips, C. S., and others, *Walter Howard Frere*, 1947, and Leggett, Richard G., 'Walter Howard Frere', in Tuzik, Robert L., ed., *How Firm a Foundation: Leaders of the Liturgical Movement*, Chicago, 1990; Prestige, G. L., *Charles Gore*, 1935; Barry, F. R., *Mervyn Haigh*, 1964; Henson, Hensley, *Retrospect of an unimportant life, 1863–1939*, 1943, and Chadwick, Owen, *Hensley Henson, A Study in the friction between Church and State*, 1983; Neville, Graham, *Radical Churchman, Edward Lee Hicks and the New Liberalism*, 1998; Paget, Stephen, *Henry Scott Holland*, 1921; [on W. Palmer Ladd] Moriarty, Michael, *The Liturgical Revolution*, New York, 1996, and Myers, Ruth A., *Continuing the Reformation*, New York, 1997; Lockhart, J. G., *Cosmo Gordon Lang*, 1948; Matthews, W. R., *Memories and Meanings*, 1969; Marquand, David, *Ramsay MacDonald*, 1977; Noel, Conrad, *Autobiography*, 1945; Groves, Reg, *Conrad Noel and the Thaxted Movement*, New York, 1968, and Leech, Kenneth, ed., *Conrad Noel and the Catholic Crusade*, 1993; Paget, Stephen, and Crum, J. M. C., *Francis Paget*, 1913; Richards, Grant, *Author Hunting by an old literary sportsman 1897–1925*, 1934; Taylor, T. F., *J. Armitage Robinson, Eccentric,*

Scholar and Churchman, 1858–1933, Cambridge, 1991; Fletcher, Sheila, *Maude Royden, A Life*, 1989; Shaw, Martin, *Up to Now*, 1929; Scott, Carolyn, *Dick Sheppard*, 1977; Cross, F. L., *Darwell Stone*, 1943; Maude, Aylmer, *The Authorized Life of Marie C. Stopes*, 1924; Harris, G. H., *Vernon Faithful Storr*, 1943; Anson, Harold, *T. B. Strong*, 1949; Iremonger, F. A., *William Temple*, 1948, and Lowry, Charles W., *William Temple, An Archbishop for All Seasons*, Washington DC, 1982; Vaughan Williams, Ursula, *R.V.W.: A Biography of Ralph Vaughan Williams*, 1964; Hoggart, Simon, *Vaughan Williams*, 2000.

(All books published in London, except where otherwise stated. ACC = Alcuin Club Collection. NRA = National Register of Archives.)

Index

Abbeville, 116
Aberdeen, 79, 80, 111
Adams, Cyril Crofton, 10
Adderley, Fr James, 2, 24, 35, 67, 69, 87, 142
Albert, HRH Prince, 12
Alcuin, 51
Alcuin Club, ix, 38, 48, 50–6, 63, 80, 131, 163, 175
Alcuin Club Prayer Book Pamphlets (Orange books), 164
Alexander, C. F., 145
Alternative Service Book, 1980, 163
Anglican Fellowship, 120
Anglo-Catholicism
  Cambridge Movement, 17, 39
  Hackney Phalanx, 38
  High Church, 17, 34, 40, 58, 63, 193
  Nobody's Friends, 38
  Ritualists, 17, 18, 39, 41, 125, 155
  Tractarians, 17, 21, 38–9, 49, 62, 157, 193
Anson, Harold, 14–15, 21, 26–7, 29, 32, 38, 81, 145–6, 183
Anson, Peter, 55, 72–3, 88
Army and Religion, 115
Ancient Monuments (Churches) Commission Report, 80
Arnold, Matthew, 21
Arrowsmith, Gordon, 154, 183
Art and Religion, 135
Art of Public Worship, 143
Arts and Crafts Movement, 54, 72–3

Athens, 101
Atwell, Robert, ix

Barbour, Robert and Hugh, 22–3, 116
Barnett, Canon Samuel, 180
Barry, Bishop F. R., 130, 138–9, 145, 165–6, 170–4, 181, 183, 186–7, 189–90, 192
Beamish, Selina, 28–9
Beardsley, Aubrey, 33, 37, 73
Beauchamp, Lord, 96
Beerbohm, Max, 33
Bell's Cathedral Guides, 36, 90
Bell, Bishop G. K. A., 169–70, 182
Bell, George, 57–8
Bell, George William, 57
Belloc, Hilaire, 72
Benson, Archbishop E. W., 27
Benson, Louis F., 68
Berkeley Divinity School, Connecticut, 125–6, 128
Bezant, J. S., 182
Bicknell, Prof. E. J., 182
Birkbeck, W. J., 63
Birth Control, 178–81
Blacking, Randoll, 174
Blaiklock, Violet K., 134
Blair, Rt. Hon. Tony, MP, 4
Bodley, G. F., 60
Body and Soul, 81
Bombay, 123
Bonskeid, Perthshire, 22–3
Book of Common Prayer (1549), 40
Bouverie's Bank, 6
Boys' Home, Hampstead, 57–8

Briggs, G. W., 144–6
Briggs, Henry, 35, 48, 50
Brightman, F. E., 20–1, 51, 74, 128, 134, 163, 169, 182
British Library, 36, 54, 70, 79, 123, 132, 146
"British Museum Religion", 2, 46, 59
Browning, Robert, 21
Bunyan, John, 66, 197
Burgess, Captain Francis, 69
Burma, 124
Burne-Jones, Sir Edward, 30, 73
Burns, John, 148
Burnett, Duncan, 110, 113
Burnett, Monica Duncan, 95, 110
Burrows, Ronald, 15, 127–8, 130–1
Bury, Bishop Herbert, 97

Calcutta, 123
Caldecott, Alfred, 127
Cambridge University
  Caius College, 114
  King's College, 142
  Trinity College, 121
Campbell-Bannerman, Sir Henry, MP, 162
Carnegie, Canon W. H., 173
Carols, 141
Carter, John, 24
Catechism, 24, 75, 82, 116, 159–60
Cavell, Edith, 117
Chair of Ecclesiastical Art, 127–31
Challenge, 121
Charles, Archdeacon R. H., 172
Charterhouse, 50
Chavasse, Bishop Christopher, 139
Cheshire, 153, 168, 181
Chesterton, Cecil, 72
Chesterton, G. K., 1–2, 37, 66, 77, 87
Chichester Cathedral, 114
Children's Broadcast Services, 184, 186
Christian Social Union (CSU), 24–6, 30–2, 57, 76, 130, 193
Christian Socialism, 4, 16–17, 19–20, 24, 34, 36, 43, 57, 62, 64, 76–7, 136, 146, 148, 171, 193
Church Association, 156, 172
Church in the Furnace, 122
Church League for Women's Suffrage, 97, 150
Church Reformer, 19
Church Times, 3, 45, 102–3
Church, Dean R. W., 63
Churches:
  All Saints', Middlesborough, 148
  St Anne's, South Lambeth, 25, 27–9, 31–2, 34, 36, 196
  St Augustine's, Kilburn, 12
  St Barnabas, Pimlico, 64, 68–9
  Berkeley Chapel, Mayfair, 34–5, 142–3
  St Botolph's, Bishopsgate, 150
  St Edmund's, Lombard Street, 31
  St Faith's, Stepney, 148
  Holy Trinity, Sloane Square, 153, 170
  St James's, Piccadilly, 113, 121, 171
  St John's, Great Malborough Street, 32
  St John's, Richmond, 29
  St Laurence, Bradford-on-Avon, 90
  St Luke's, Chelsea, 154
  St Matthew's, Bethnal Green, 18–19
  St Margaret's Princes Road, Toxteth, 68
  St Mark's, Marylebone Road, 35, 37
  St Martin-in-the-Fields, 96–8, 100, 127, 138, 140, 143, 152, 183
  St Paul's, Knightsbridge, 96
  St Peter's, Vauxhall, 27
  St Philip's, Salford, 76
  St Savior's, Eton Road, 58
City Temple, 150–1
Clarke, Somers, 50
Clayton, Jo, 19–20, 90
Club, 163–4, 187, 192
Cole, Sir Henry, 12

Coles, Canon Stuckey, 20–1, 67
Columbo, 124
Community of the Divine
  Compassion, 35
Committee of Experts, 162–3
Comper, Sir Ninian, 51, 80, 130,
  132–3
Cooke, W. L., 113
Council for the Care of Churches,
  80
Craig, Gordon, 69
Crockford's Clerical Directory, 123
Cromwell, Oliver, 75
Cunningham, Canon B. K., 182–3
Cycling, 89–91

Daily Office, 160
Dardanelles, 107–8
Dat Boexken Vander Missen, 52
David, Bishop A. A., 137, 182, 185
Davidson, Archbishop Randall,
  26–8, 31–2, 36, 56, 160–1, 169,
  181
Davies, Dr Horton, 61
Davson, Dr, 13
Day, Hermitage, 74
de Candole, Dean H. L. C. V., 182
Dearmer, Anthony, 154, 184, 186
Dearmer, Caroline Miriam, 6–7,
  9–10, 12–13, 16, 20, 28, 88–9,
  191
Dearmer, Christopher, 31, 83–4,
  92, 94–5, 104, 107–8, 110, 117,
  194
Dearmer, Edgar, 7–10, 12, 84, 89
Dearmer, Geoffrey, ix, 31, 83–4,
  87–8, 94, 96, 101, 104–5,
  107–10, 120, 154, 186
Dearmer, Gillian (Mrs Warr), ix,
  124–5, 127, 154, 184, 186
Dearmer, Imogen (Mrs Nichols), ix,
  154, 184, 186
Dearmer, Mabel Jessie Pritchard,
  28–9, 30, 33, 35, 43, 54, 72–3,
  82ff, 120, 154, 194
Dearmer, Nancy, 7–10, 15, 31, 60,
  66, 74, 88–9, 108, 110, 116ff,
  172, 176, 184ff

Dearmer, Thomas, 6–9, 13, 20, 191
Dickens, Charles, 8
Donaldson, Canon Lewis, 191,
  170, 173, 180–1, 190–1, 195
Douglass, Fr F. W., 15
Down Ampney, Glos., 63, 67
Drummond, Henry, 22
Duncan, Isadora, 70
Duncan-Jones, Dean Arthur Stuart,
  114, 144
Dwelly, Dean F. W., 137, 144,
  165–6, 169, 184
Dykes, J. B., 62

Eastbourne, 13
Eeles, Dr Francis, 38–9, 49, 74,
  78–9, 80, 82, 91, 111–13, 151,
  165, 181
Ellis, Havelock, 37
England's Lane, 83
English Altars, 3, 53–5, 132
English Carol Book, 142
English Church Pageant, 89
English Church Union, 164–5
English Hymnal (1906), 2, 62ff,
  136–8, 140, 142, 153, 172, 188,
  195, 197
English Use, 44–5, 47, 71, 77, 79,
  114, 164
Epstein, Jacob, 69
Essex Hall Lecture, 184

Fabian Society, 31, 64
Ferris, Sister Lorna, 102, 106–7
Fifty Pictures of Gothic Altars, 53,
  132
First English Ordo, 80
Florence, 23
Fortescue, Adrian, 3
Fox, Canon Adam, 174
Frere, Bishop W. H., 51, 74, 79,
  145, 148, 156–7, 163, 169
Froude, R. H., 157
Fulham Palace, 87
Fuller, Charles James, 58
Fuller, Morris, 35

Gandhi, Mahatma, 124

George V, 34–5, 186
Gifford, Jane, 64
Gimson, Ernest, 71
Goldsmith, Dr E. W., 69
Gordon, General Charles George, 177–8
Gore, Bishop Charles, 20–5, 29, 33, 67, 130, 136–7, 145, 180
Grasson, Peaslake, 186–7
Green, Canon Peter, 113
Gregory, Augusta (Lady), 86
Grey Book, 165–7
Guardian, 46, 102, 192
Guild of Health, 4, 81
Guild of St Matthew, 18–19, 24, 26, 31, 34, 57, 130
Guild of St Raphael, 4
Guildhouse, Eccleston Square, 152
Gwynn, Stephen, 28–9, 35, 84–9, 94, 97, 100–1, 103–5, 108, 121

Haigh, Bishop Mervyn, 139, 165–7
Hanbury Tracy, Hon. A. F. A., 62–4
Hanson, Canon Richard, 129
Harland, Harry (Sydney Luska), 33, 85
Harwood, George, MP, 160
Hastings, Adrian, 144
Headlam, Stewart, 18–19, 26, 127
Heal, Ambrose, 72
Henry Bradshaw Society, 49–50
Henson, Bishop Hensley, 137, 185
Herbert Herkomer's School, Bushey, 29
Hicks, Bishop Edward Lee, 76, 150
Hicks-Beach, Rt. Hon. Sir Michael Edward Bt., MP 159
Highways and Byways, 90
Holland, Canon Scott, 24–5, 32–5, 64–6, 150
Hollis, Howard, ix
Holst, Gustav, 195
Hope, William St John, 48–51, 53, 128
Housman, A. E., 37
Housman, Lawrence, 33, 85–6, 90
Huelin, Dr Gordon, 129

Hughes, Dom Anselm, 45, 50
Hughes, Thomas, 57
Hunkin, Bishop J. W., 182
Hunter, Bishop Leslie, 165
Hurstpierpoint, 49
Hymnal Noted, 62–3
Hymns Ancient and Modern, 62–3, 68

Image, Professor Selwyn, 128
India, 121ff, 136
International Socialist Congress, 1896, 34
Iremonger, Dean F. A., 137, 184

Jackson, Bishop John, 58
Jagger, Dr Peter, 52
Japan, 125
Jasper, Dean R. C. D., 163
Jay, Arthur, 11
John, Augustus, 69
Johnson, Dean Hewlett, 182
Johnson, Stuart, 23
Joint Evidence Committee, 156
Jones, Charles Alfred, 10
Jones, Professor Peter d'A, 19

Keble, John, 38, 58
Kensington Town Hall, 151
King's College London, x, 127ff, 149, 169, 187, 196
Kingsley, Canon Charles, 180
Kingston, Gertrude, 87
Kipling, Rudyard, 21
Knowles, Arthur, 117, 120
Knowles, Denis, 89, 117
Knowles, Jack, 89, 117
Knowles, Marian, 66, 89, 105, 116–17, 120–1, 123, 127, 136, 171, 186–7, 190, 192
Knowles, Nancy (see Dearmer)
Kragujevatz, 101ff

Lacey, Canon T. A., 63, 164
Ladd, William Palmer, 125–6
Lambeth Conference, 179–80
Lambeth Palace Library, 171
Lang, Archbishop Cosmo Gordon,

169–71, 173–4, 183
Lathbury, D. C., 63
Latimer, Bishop Hugh, 2, 30
Le Gallienne, Richard, 33
Legend of Hell, 116
Legg (see Wickham Legg)
Letters from a Field Hospital, 100ff
Letters of Business, 162, 165
Liddell, Dean Henry George, 15
Liddon House, Mayfair, 153
Liddon, Canon H. P., 15, 20
Life and Liberty Movement, 127, 136–7, 151
Liturgical Movement, 3
Liverpool Cathedral, 137, 184, 186
Lloyd, Canon Roger, 136–7
Lombard, B. S., 81
London Library, 79
Lowder, Charles, 32
Lutyens, Sir Edwin, 123

MacDonald, Rt Hon. Ramsay, MP, 170–2
Malta, 101, 103, 107–8
Manning, Cardinal H. E., 39
Marsden, Dr, 105–6
Marseilles, 100
Maryon-Wilson, Percy, 150
Matthews, Dean W. R., 5, 96, 127–8, 130, 181–2
Maurice, Frederick Denison, 17, 57–8
Maynall, Elizabeth, 37
McCormick, Pat, 144, 183, 194
Messiah, 71
Methodists, 41, 62, 158
Micklethwaite, J. T., 48, 50, 52
Milford, Humphrey, 37
Ministry of Healing, 4, 80–1, 195
Ministry of Women, 4, 195
Mirfield, Community of the Resurrection, 20, 33
Monk, W. H., 62
Morality Play Society, 85–6
Morris, W. A., 27, 29, 31–2, 34
Morris, William, 16–17, 29, 89
Mullholland, Emily, 32, 82, 127
Murray, David, 189–93

National Mission of Repentance and Hope, 150
Neale, J. M., 39, 62–3, 68, 141–2
Necessity of Art, 135
Neville, Graham, 76
New English Hymnal (1986), 2, 70
Newman, Cardinal John Henry, 29, 157
Nicholson, William, 69
Nockles, Dr Peter, 39
Noel, Conrad, 27, 34, 75–7, 81–2, 88, 145, 195
Noel, Miriam, 75–6, 82
Norman, Canon Edward, 57
Norris, Dean William Foxley, 171–5, 181, 185, 189–90, 193

Oakridge Lynch, 91, 94, 121, 127, 134, 151, 186
Ollard, Canon S. L., 48, 182
Ornaments Rubric, 40, 42, 73, 182
Orpen, William, 69
Osservatore Romano, 178
Ouseley, Sir F. A. Gore, Bt., 62
Ovenden, Canon John, ix
Oxford Book of Carols, 142–3
Oxford House, 35
Oxford University:
  Balliol College, 190
  Christ Church, 13, 15, 32, 36, 94, 196
  Dramatic Society, 16
  Palmerston Club, 16
  Pusey House, 20–5, 36, 37
  Twenty Club, 16
  University Press, 37, 47, 66, 68

Palmer, George Herbert, 68
Parish Communion, 148–9, 159
Parson's Handbook, x, 2–3, 35, 37, 41, 43–8, 52, 55, 59–60, 68, 73, 78, 131–4, 137
Pearson, J. L., 50
Perkins, Dr Jocelyn, 87, 175, 182, 186
Perrin, Bishop W. W., 113
Pilgrims' Trust, 175

Index

Plainsong and Medieval Music Society, 50
Pocknee, Dr Cyril, 44
Pope Pius XI, 49
Powell, Alfred and Louise, 121
Powell, York, 13–14, 16, 19
Prayer Book Catholic, 2
Prestige, Canon G. L., 21
Priest's Crown, 1, 72, 182
Primrose Hill, St Mary's, ix, 56ff, 82–4, 93ff, 136, 196
Primrose League, 14
Public Baptism, 159, 161
Public School Act, 1868, 7
Public Worship Regulation Act, 1874, 40, 58, 155
Pusey, Dr Edward, 15, 20, 39, 58
Putney Hill, 12

Raven, Dr Charles, 182
Reckitt, Maurice, 183
Reed, John Shelton, 155
Revised Prayer Book (1927–28), 167–8
Reynolds, J. B., 22
Richards, Grant, 37, 42
Richmond, Wilfred, 24
Ridley, Bishop Nicholas, 30
Riley, Athelstan, 63, 65, 89, 150
Robinson, Dean J. Armitage, 169
Rochester Cathedral, 26
Rogers, Canon Guy, 165
Rogers, Clement, 130
Roman Catholic Church, 78, 178–81, 193
Ross, Dr Elizabeth, 107
Rossetti, Christina, 66
Rouse, Ruth, 23
Rowton House, Lambeth, 34
Royal Commission on Ecclesiastical Discipline, 1906, 54, 156–62
Royal Institute of British Architects, 196
Royden, Maude, 4, 113, 150–3, 183
Ruskin, John, 21

Sacrosanctum Concilium, 78

Sarum Missal (Use), 43, 44–5, 49, 53, 161
Scholes, Dr Percy, 141
Scott, Charles Broderick, 7
Scott, George Gilbert, 50
Scott, M. H. Baillie, 72
Seaton, Bishop J. B., 15, 151
Serbia, 97ff, 196
Serbian Relief Fund, 98
Sharp, Cecil, 63–5, 71
Sharp, Evelyn, 35, 85, 90
Shaw, Bernard, 37
Shaw, Dr Martin, 69–71, 86, 135–6, 140, 142, 152, 187
Shaw, Geoffrey, 83
Shaw, Joan, 187
Shefrin, Jill, 84–5
Sheppard, Dean H. R. L. (Dick), 96, 127, 136, 138, 144, 165, 183, 194
Shrove Tuesday Greaze, 11
Simla, 124
Skilbeck, Clement O., 55, 87
Society of SS Peter and Paul, 3
Society of St Osmund, 79
Somerset House, Maida Vale, 5, 10, 12
Somerset House, Strand, 20
Songs of Praise, 138, 140–1, 144–5, 149, 153, 188, 195
Spencer, Albert, 59, 89
St Dunstan's Society, 72–3, 133
St Paul's Cathedral, 15, 24–5, 34, 64, 96, 169
St Paul's Ecclesiological Society, 50
St Stephen's College, Delhi, 124
Stobart, Mabel St Clair, 97–101, 106
Stone, Dr Darwell, 164–5
Stopes, Dr Marie, 179–80
Storr, Canon V. F., 144, 173–4
Streatham School, 10
Strong, Bishop Thomas Banks, 115–16
Strong, Sir Roy, 13
Studdart-Kennedy, Geoffrey, 194
Student Christian Movement (SCM), 23, 116, 121, 130, 135

Sulva Bay, 107–8
Sunday School, 160
Swanwick, 130
Sykes, Lady (see Dearmer, Nancy)
Symondson, Fr Anthony, SJ, 132, 133
Syrett, Netta, 33, 85

Tablet, 178
Talbot, Bishop E. S., 35, 79
Talbot, Rt. Hon. J. G., MP, 159
Tanner, Lawrence, 174–5
Tatlow, Canon Tissington, 121, 130, 183
Temple, Archbishop Frederick, 34, 58
Temple, Archbishop William, 113, 121, 137, 150, 165, 170–1, 183
Terry, Ellen, 69
Thaxted, 77, 195
Times, 97, 168, 174, 177, 189–93
Times Literary Supplement (TLS), 190–3
Timms, Ven. George, ix
Travers, Martin, 74
Tressell, Robert, 37
Truth about Fasting, 146–9
Tuckwell, Gertrude, 32–3
Turner, Archie, 121

Vasilijevic, Marina, 107
Vatican II, 78
Vaughan Williams, Dr Ralph, 63–7, 70, 139–40, 142, 170, 195, 197
Vaughan Williams, Ursula, 64
Vevey, Switzerland, 12, 90
Victoria and Albert Museum, 12–13, 23
Victoria Women's Settlement, Liverpool, 150
Voysey, Annesley, 72

Walker, Dr Jane, 127, 171
Ward, W. R., 39
Warham Guild, 73–4, 133
Wellington, Duke of, 11

Wells Cathedral, 36, 90
West Heath School, 84
Westcott, Bishop B. F., 24
Western (or Roman) Use, 35, 40, 44, 79, 161
Westminster Abbey:
  Abbey Library, 195
  Coronations, 55, 187
  Dean and Chapter, 7, 19, 25, 33, 171–4
  Dean of Westminster (see also Norris, Foxley), 7, 11
  Great Garth, 11, 188
  Little Cloister, 11, 33, 172, 183
Westminster Missal, 49
Westminster School, 7, 9–11, 64, 84, 175
White, Surgeon-Major William, 28
Whittier, John Greenleaf, 66
Wickham Legg, Dr John, 38, 48–51, 131–3
Widdrington, P. E. T., 30
Wiesbaden, 10
Wilde, Oscar, 1, 33
Wilkinson, Canon Alan, 4, 16
Williams, Bishop N. P., 165
Wilson, Bishop H. A., 139
Winnington-Ingram, Bishop Arthur, 96
Women's Sick and Wounded Convoy Corps., 97–8
Woods, Bishop Edward, 165, 182–3
Woodward, Bishop C. S., 173–4
Woodward, George Ratcliffe, 63, 68, 142
Woollcombe, Juliet, 154
Wordsworth, Christopher, 163
Wordsworth, William, 193
Working Men's College, 17
Wyatt, E. G. P., 164

Y.M.C.A., 110, 115–16, 118–19, 121, 123
Yeats, W. B., 33, 37, 86
Yellow Book, 33, 37, 73, 85

Printed in September 2021
by Rotomail Italia S.p.A., Vignate (MI) - Italy